Based on the Screenplay By

Neil Gaiman & Roger Avary

BEOWULF

IDW Publishing • San Diego, CA

BEOWULF

Based on the Screenplay By
Neil Gaiman & Roger Avary

Written by Chris Ryall
Art and Cover by Gabriel Rodriguez
Colors by Jay Fotos
Additional Covers by Mark A. Nelson
Letters by Robbie Robbins
Collection Edits by Justin Eisinger
Book Design by Neil Uyetake

IDW Publishing i
Ted Adams, Presiden
Robbie Robbins, EVP/Sr. Graphic Arti
Clifford Meth, EVP of Strategies/Editoria
Chris Ryall, Publisher/Editor-in-Chi
Alan Payne, VP of Sale
Neil Uyetake, Art Director
Dan Taylor, Edit
Justin Eisinger, Assistant Edit
Tom Waltz, Assistant Edit
Chris Mowry, Graphic Arti
Amauri Osorio, Graphic Arti
Matthew Ruzicka, CPA, Controll
Alonzo Simon, Shipping Manag
Kris Oprisko, Editor/Foreign Lic. Re

ISBN: 978-1-60010-128-1
10 09 08 07   1 2 3 4

Special thanks to Steve Starkey, Doug Chiang,
and Risa Kessler for their invaluable assistance.

www.IDWPUBLISHING.com

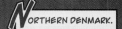 ORTHERN DENMARK.

518 A.D.

THE AGE OF HEROES.

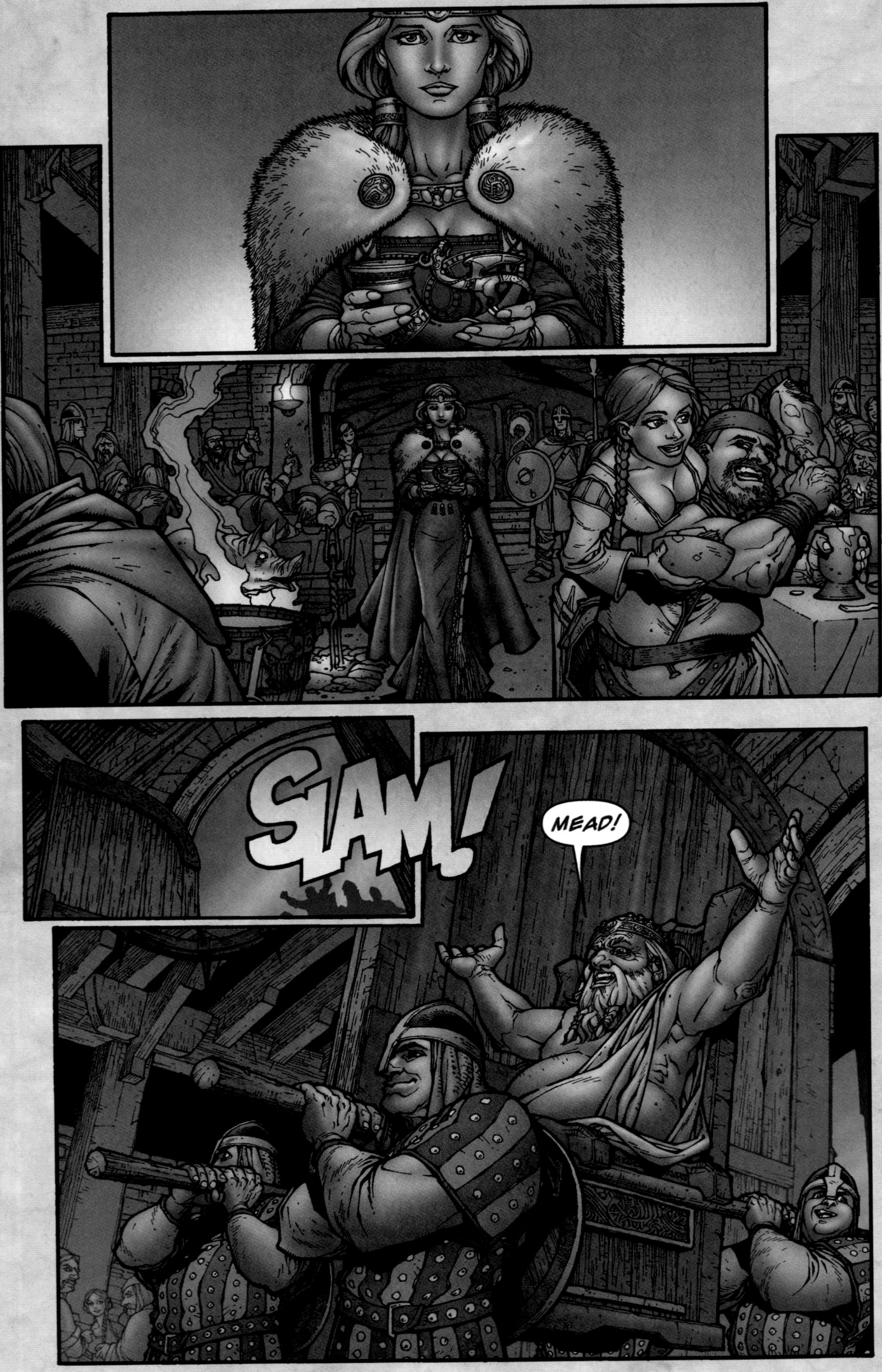
SLAM!
MEAD!

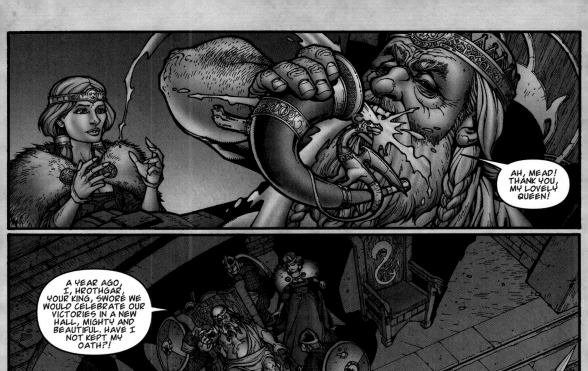

AH, MEAD! THANK YOU, MY LOVELY QUEEN!

A YEAR AGO, I, HROTHGAR, YOUR KING, SWORE WE WOULD CELEBRATE OUR VICTORIES IN A NEW HALL, MIGHTY AND BEAUTIFUL. HAVE I NOT KEPT MY OATH?!

IN THIS HALL, WE SHALL FEAST AND TELL OF VICTORIES! THE SCOPS SHALL SING THEIR SAGAS! I NAME THIS HALL... HEROT!

UNFERTH, MY WISEST ADVISOR, VIOLATOR OF VIRGINS, WHERE THE HELL ARE YOU? UNFERTH, YOU WEASEL-FACED BASTARD—

...WE HAVE TO TAKE THIS SERIOUSLY, AESHER. I'M TOLD THE BELIEVERS NOW EXTEND FROM ROME ALL THE WAY NORTH TO THE LAND OF THE FRANKS.

WELL, ANSWER THIS, UNFERTH... WHO D'YOU THINK'D WIN A KNIFE FIGHT, ODIN OR THIS CHRIST JESUS?

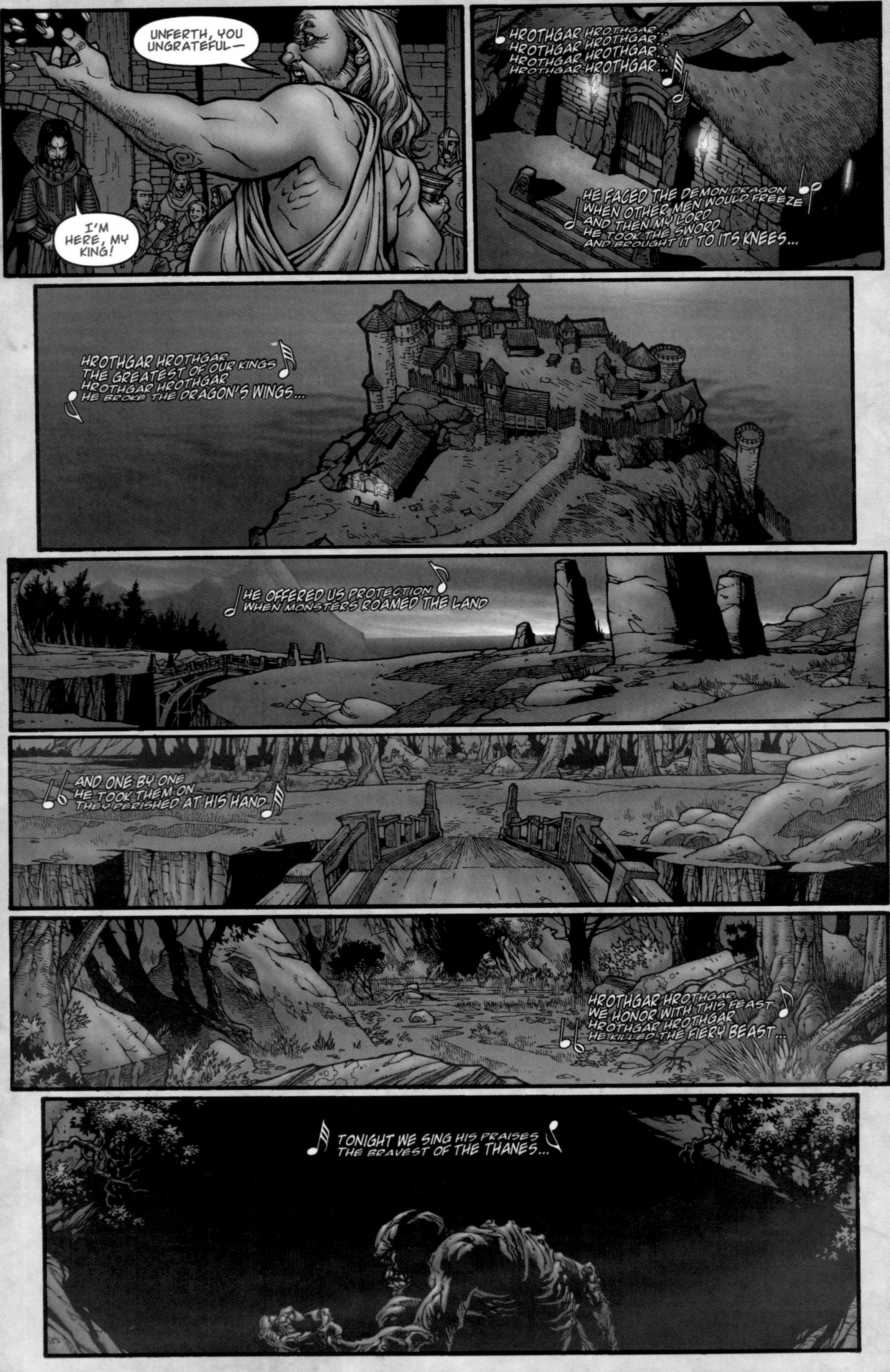

UNFERTH, YOU UNGRATEFUL—
I'M HERE, MY KING!
HROTHGAR HROTHGAR... HROTHGAR HROTHGAR... HROTHGAR HROTHGAR... HROTHGAR HROTHGAR...
HE FACED THE DEMON DRAGON WHEN OTHER MEN WOULD FREEZE AND THEN MY LORD HE TOOK THE SWORD AND BROUGHT IT TO ITS KNEES...
HROTHGAR HROTHGAR THE GREATEST OF OUR KINGS HROTHGAR HROTHGAR HE BROKE THE DRAGON'S WINGS...
HE OFFERED US PROTECTION WHEN MONSTERS ROAMED THE LAND
AND ONE BY ONE HE TOOK THEM ON THEY PERISHED AT HIS HAND
HROTHGAR HROTHGAR WE HONOR WITH THIS FEAST HROTHGAR HROTHGAR HE KILLED THE FIERY BEAST...
TONIGHT WE SING HIS PRAISES THE BRAVEST OF THE THANES...

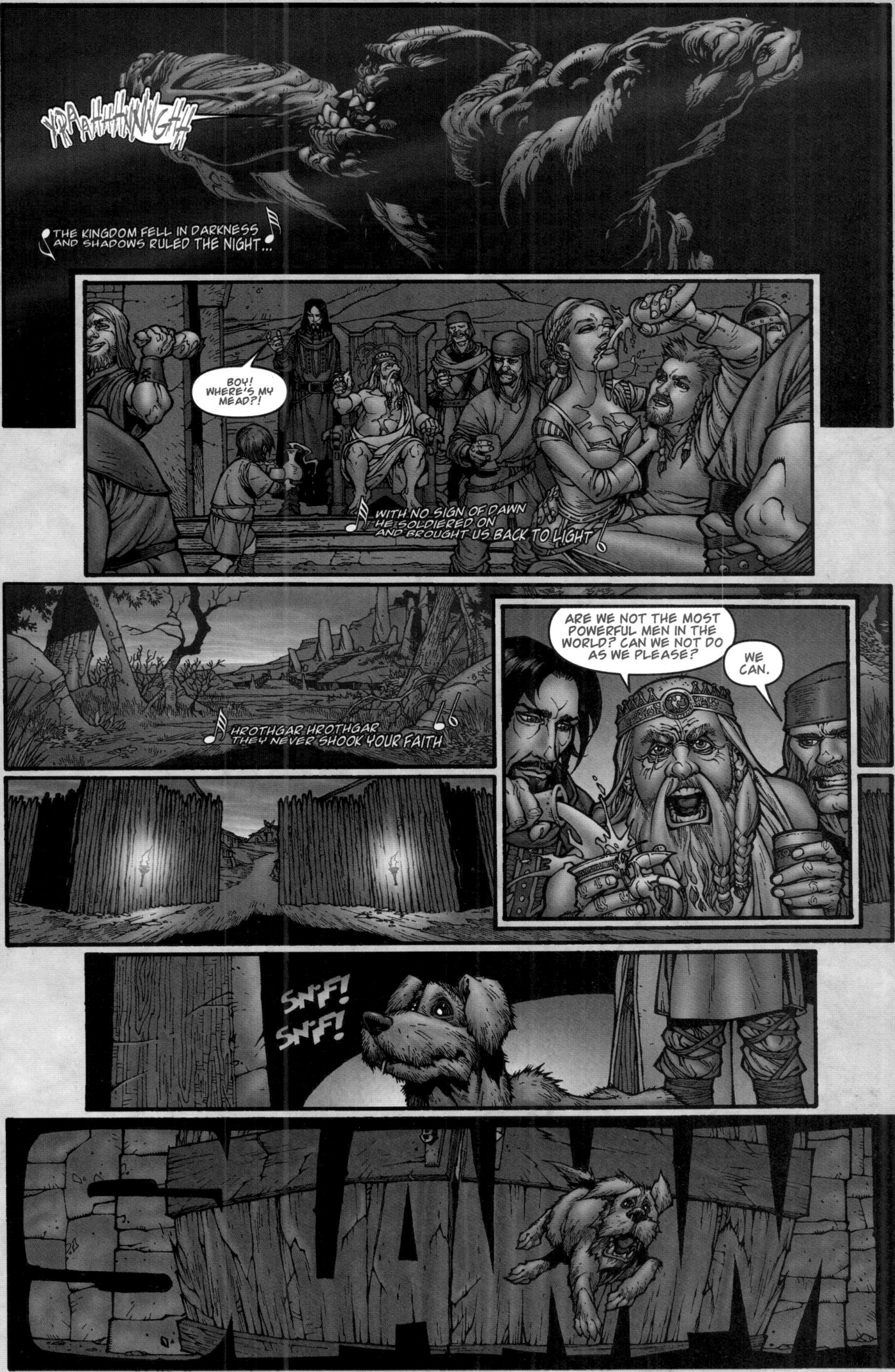
YRAAHHHNNGHH
THE KINGDOM FELL IN DARKNESS
AND SHADOWS RULED THE NIGHT...
BOY! WHERE'S MY MEAD?!
WITH NO SIGN OF DAWN
HE SOLDIERED ON
AND BROUGHT US BACK TO LIGHT
HROTHGAR HROTHGAR
THEY NEVER SHOOK YOUR FAITH
ARE WE NOT THE MOST POWERFUL MEN IN THE WORLD? CAN WE NOT DO AS WE PLEASE?
WE CAN.
SNIFF! SNIFF!
SMANN

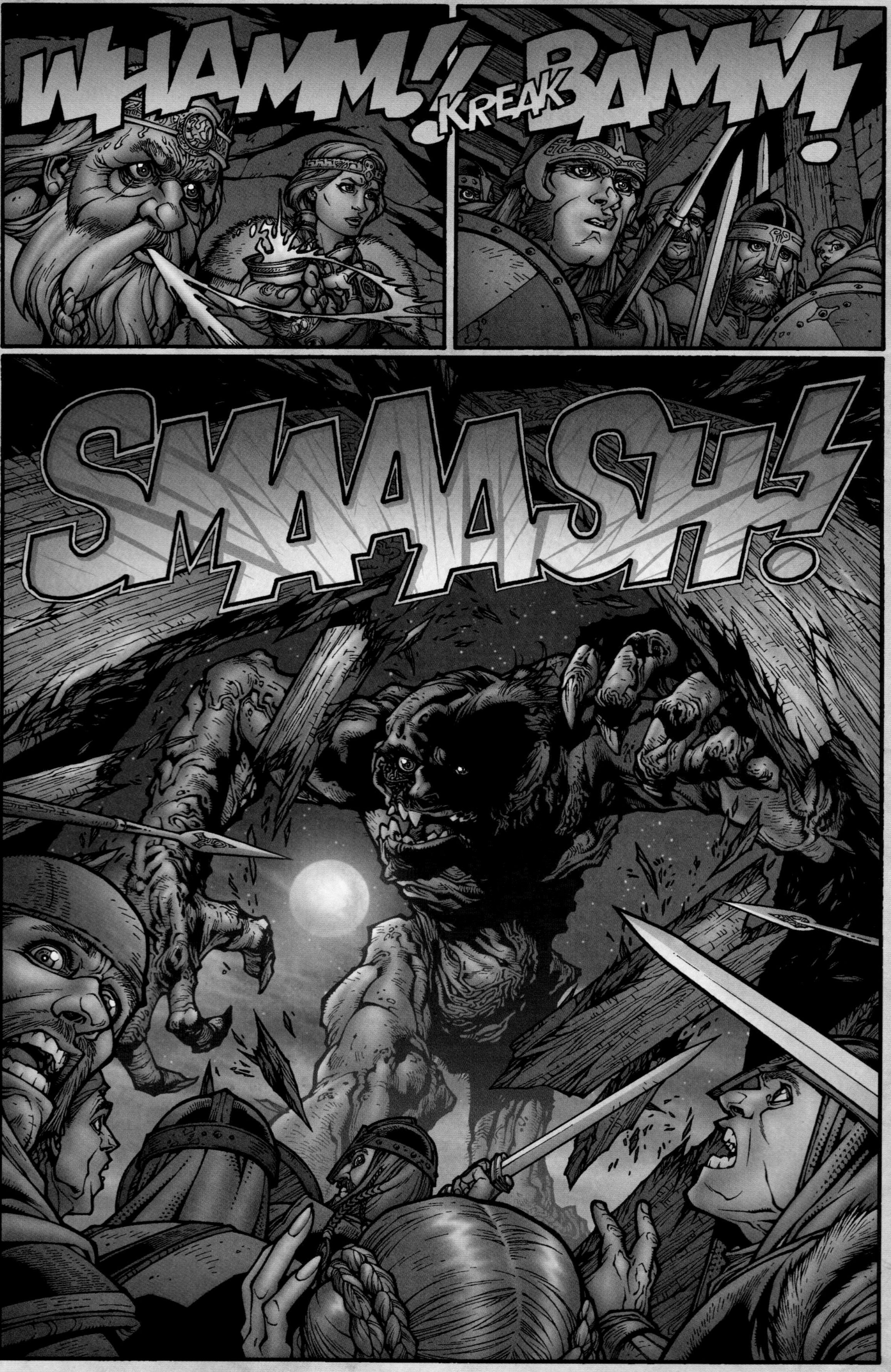
WHAMM!
KREAK
BAMM!
SMAASH!

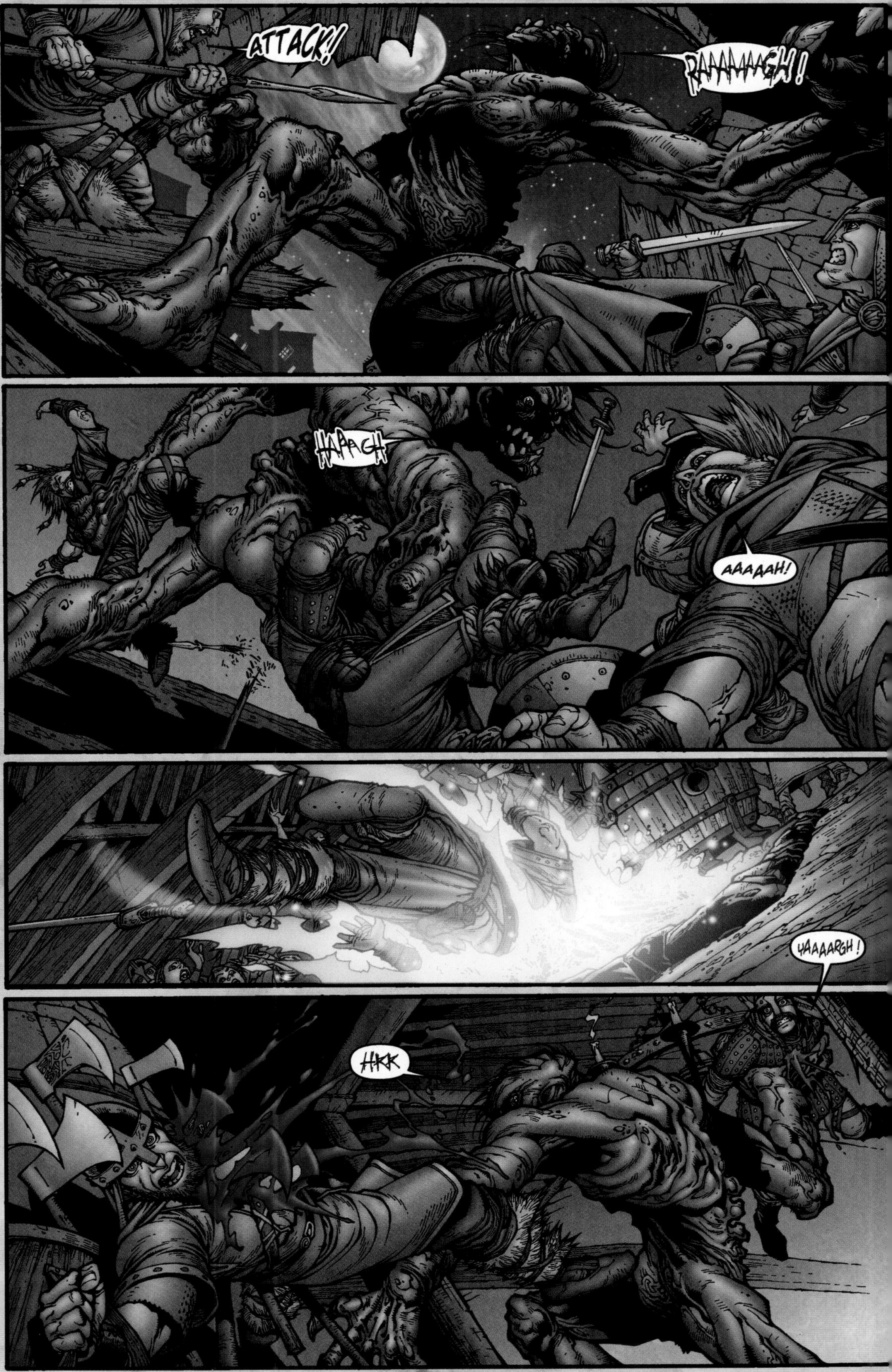
ATTACK!
RAAAAAAAGH!
HARAGH
AAAAAH!
YAAAARGH!
HKK

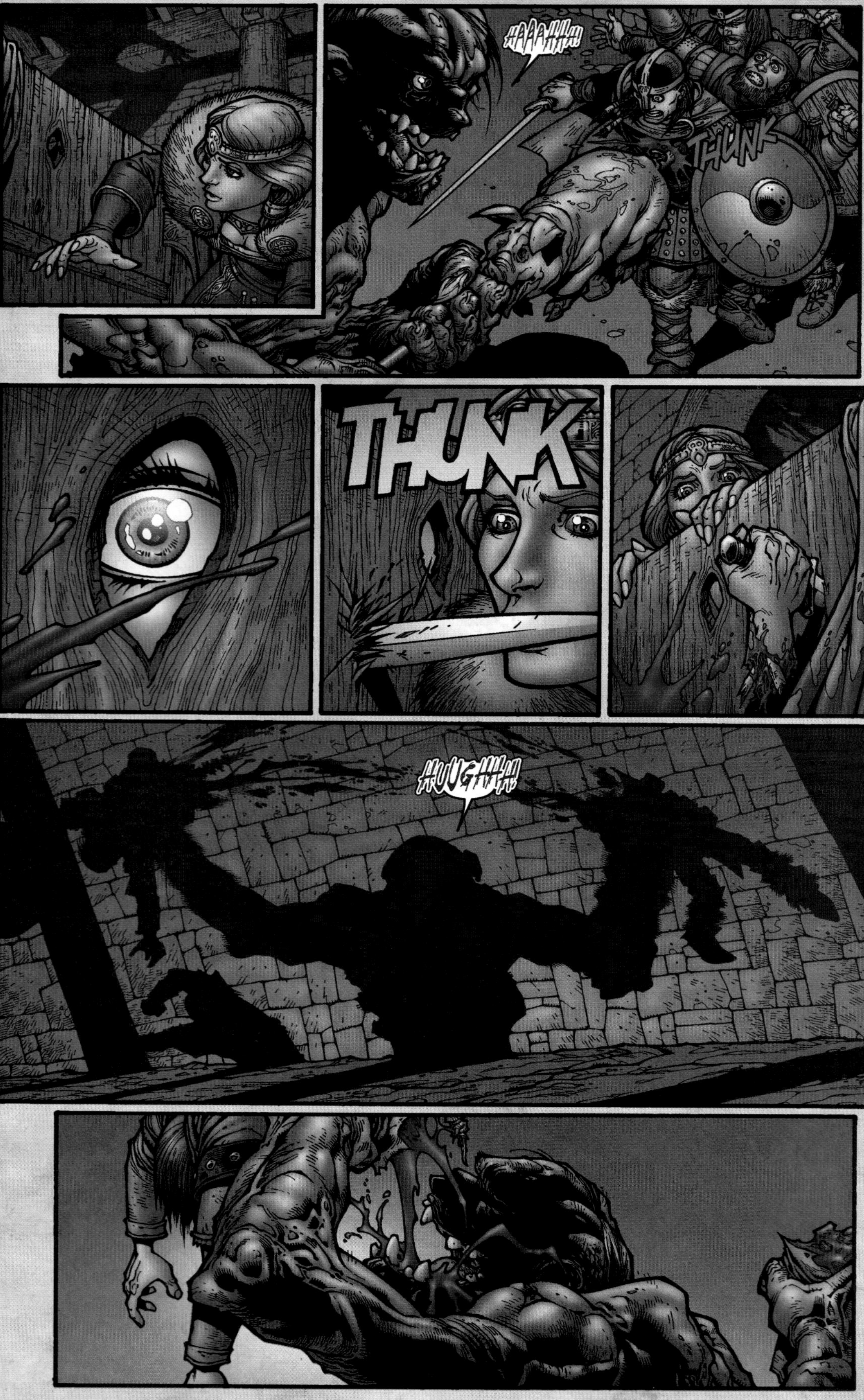
HAAAHH!!
THUNK
THUNK
HUUGHHA!

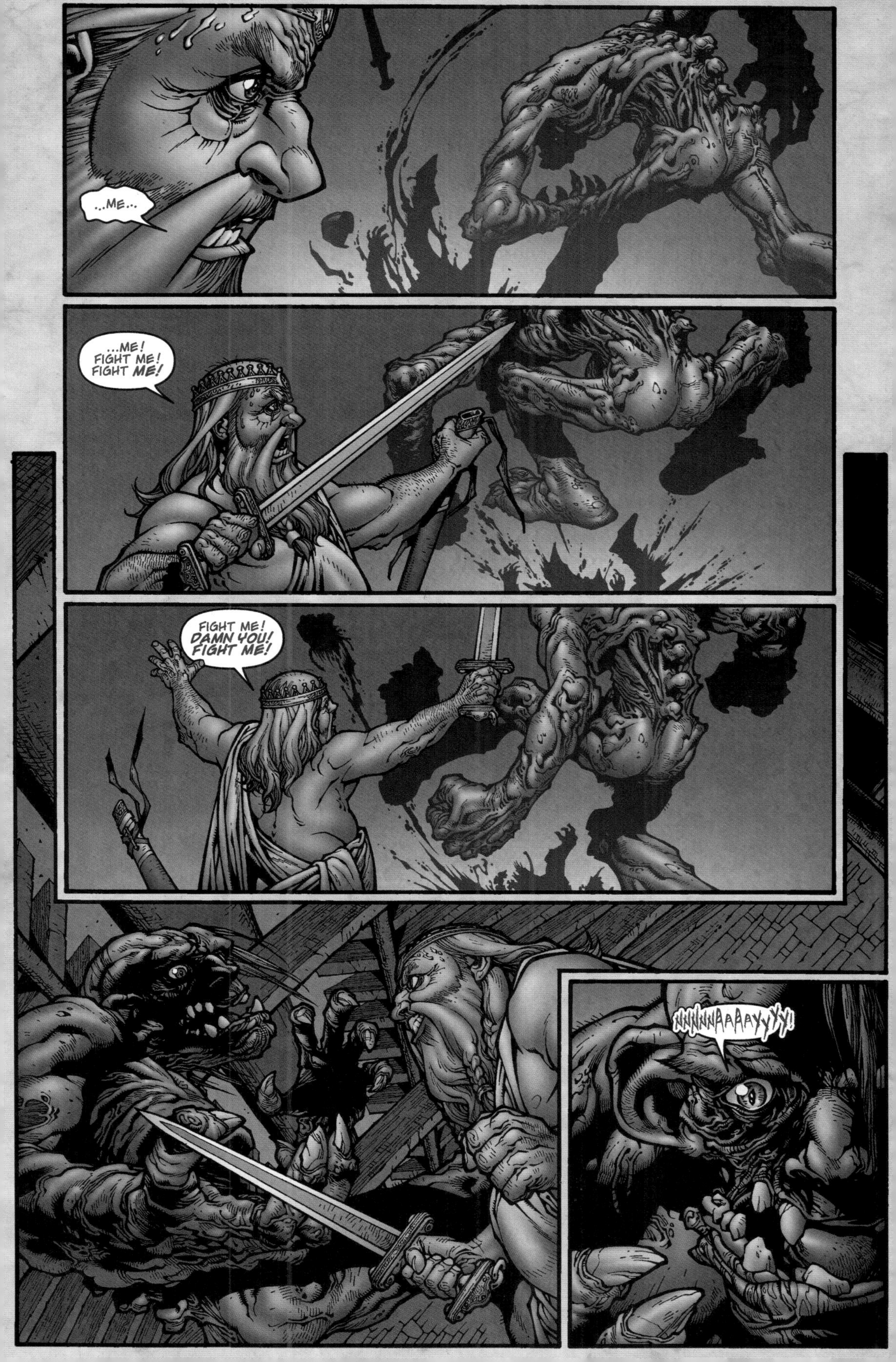
...ME...
...ME! FIGHT ME! FIGHT ME!
FIGHT ME! DAMN YOU! FIGHT ME!
NNNNNAAAAAYYYY!

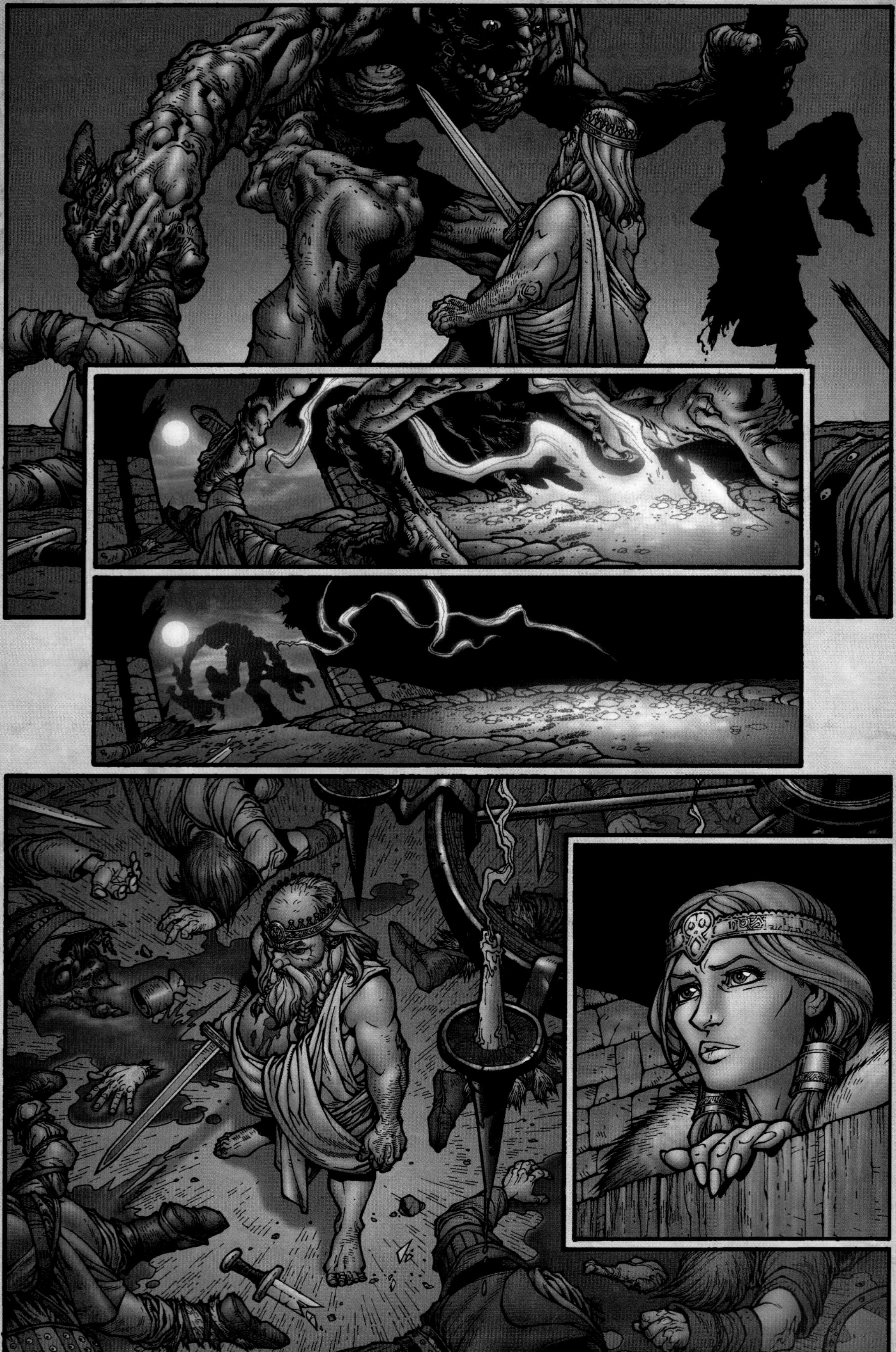

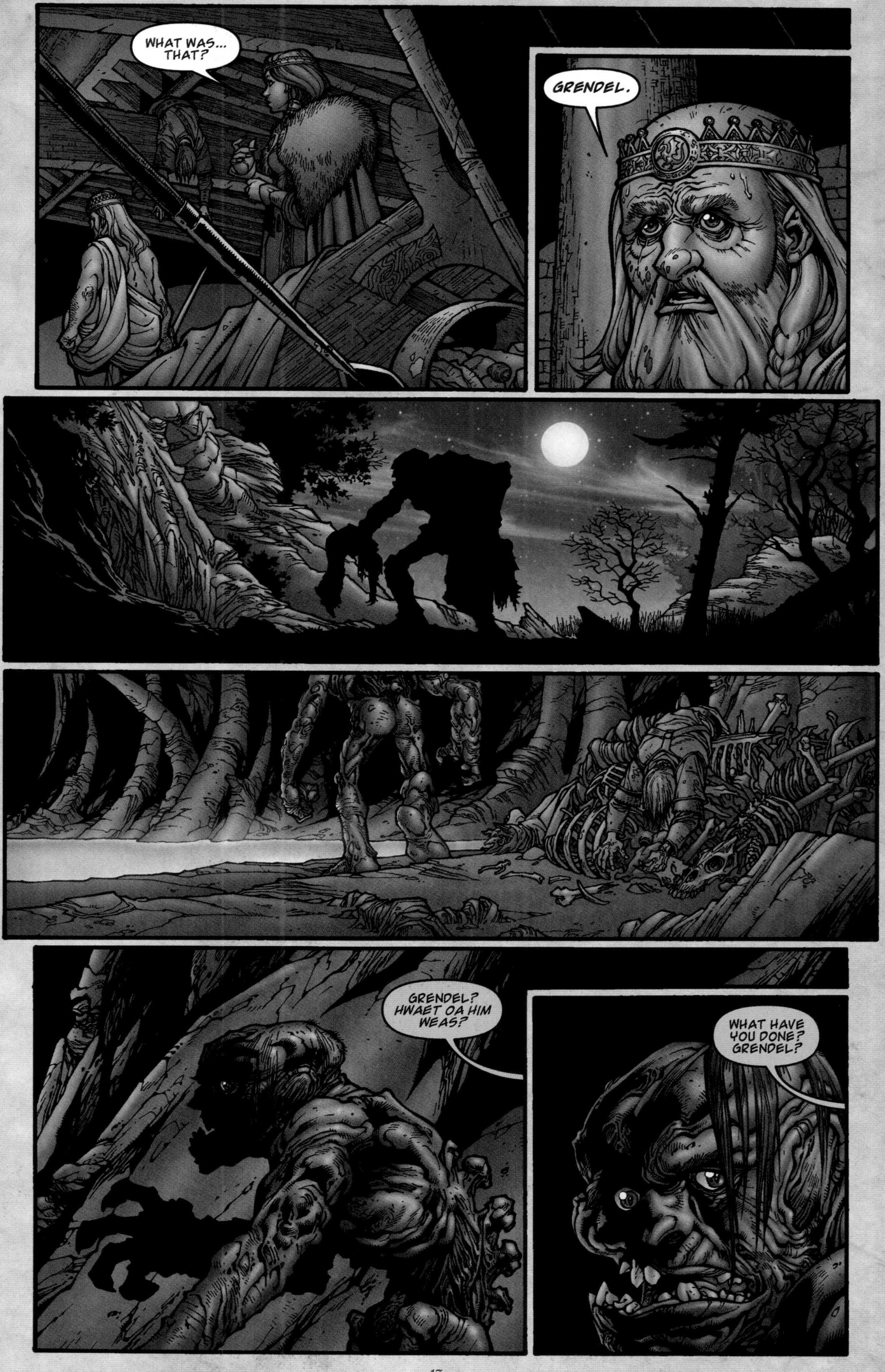
WHAT WAS... THAT?
GRENDEL.
GRENDEL? HWAET OA HIM WEAS?
WHAT HAVE YOU DONE? GRENDEL?

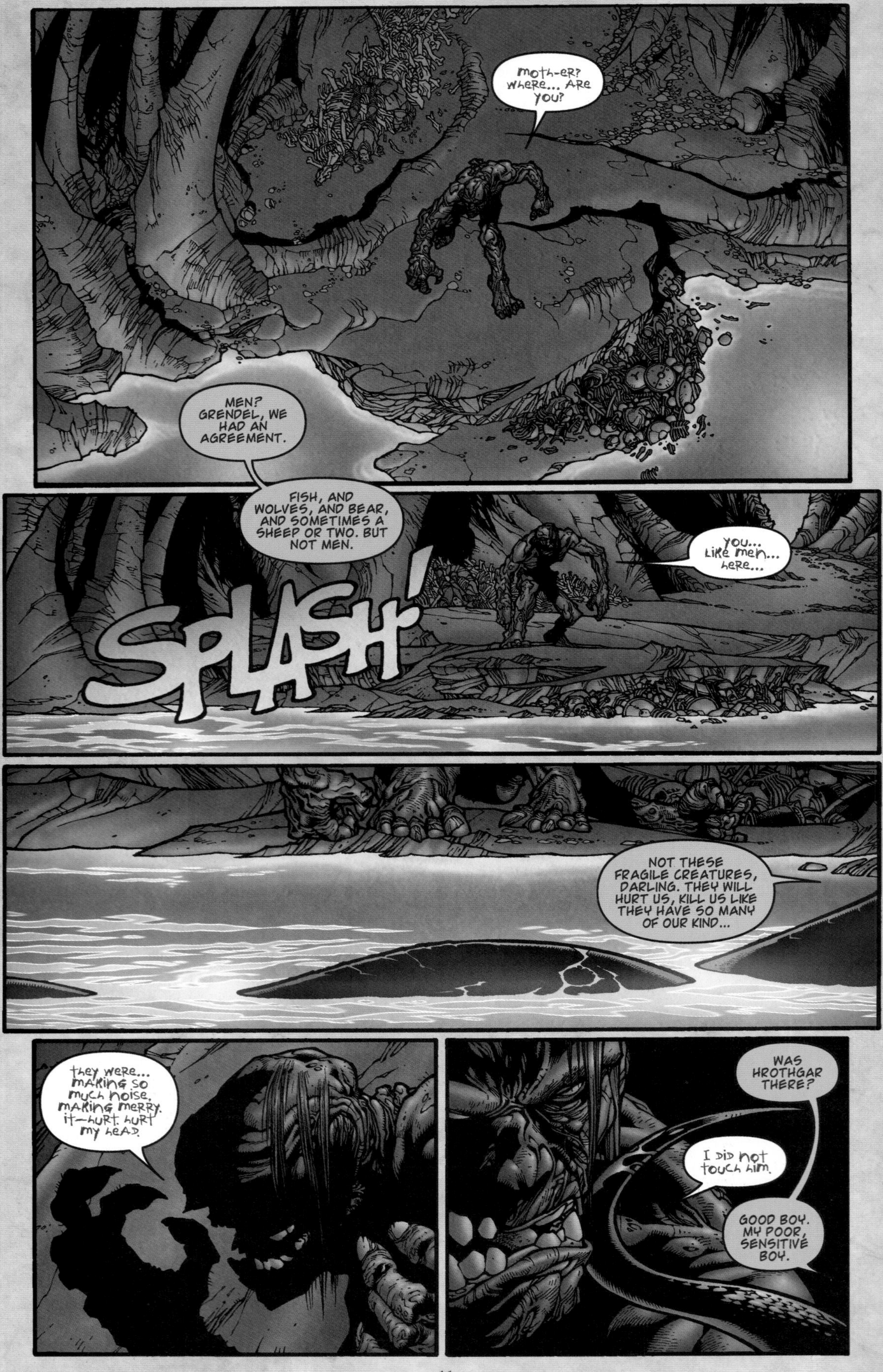
moth-er? where... are you?
MEN? GRENDEL, WE HAD AN AGREEMENT.
FISH, AND WOLVES, AND BEAR, AND SOMETIMES A SHEEP OR TWO. BUT NOT MEN.
you... like men... here...
SPLASH!
NOT THESE FRAGILE CREATURES, DARLING. THEY WILL HURT US, KILL US LIKE THEY HAVE SO MANY OF OUR KIND...
they were... making so much noise, making merry. it--hurt. hurt my head.
WAS HROTHGAR THERE?
I did not touch him.
GOOD BOY. MY POOR, SENSITIVE BOY.

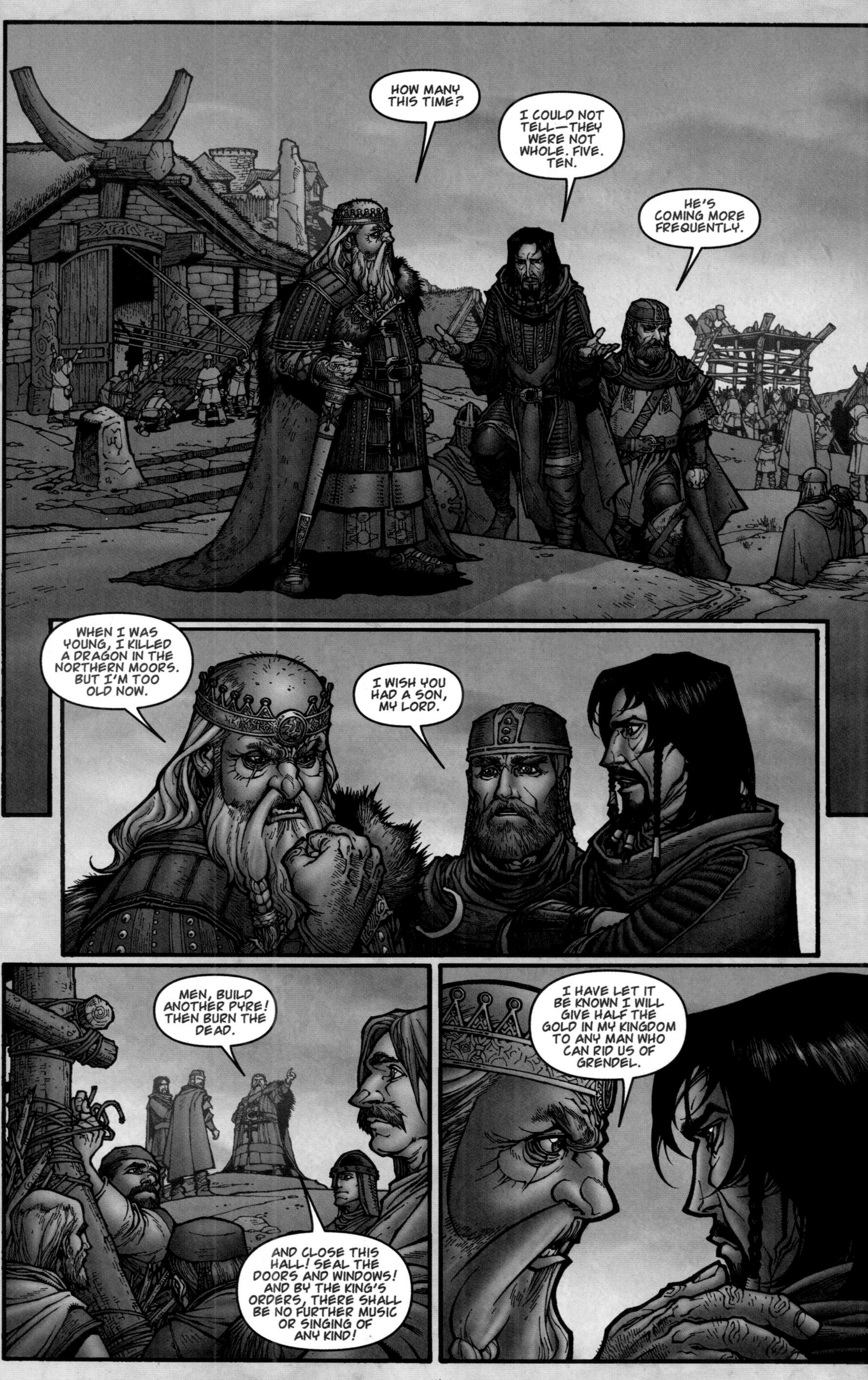
HOW MANY THIS TIME?
I COULD NOT TELL—THEY WERE NOT WHOLE. FIVE. TEN.
HE'S COMING MORE FREQUENTLY.
WHEN I WAS YOUNG, I KILLED A DRAGON IN THE NORTHERN MOORS. BUT I'M TOO OLD NOW.
I WISH YOU HAD A SON, MY LORD.
MEN, BUILD ANOTHER PYRE! THEN BURN THE DEAD.
AND CLOSE THIS HALL! SEAL THE DOORS AND WINDOWS! AND BY THE KING'S ORDERS, THERE SHALL BE NO FURTHER MUSIC OR SINGING OF ANY KIND!
I HAVE LET IT BE KNOWN I WILL GIVE HALF THE GOLD IN MY KINGDOM TO ANY MAN WHO CAN RID US OF GRENDEL.

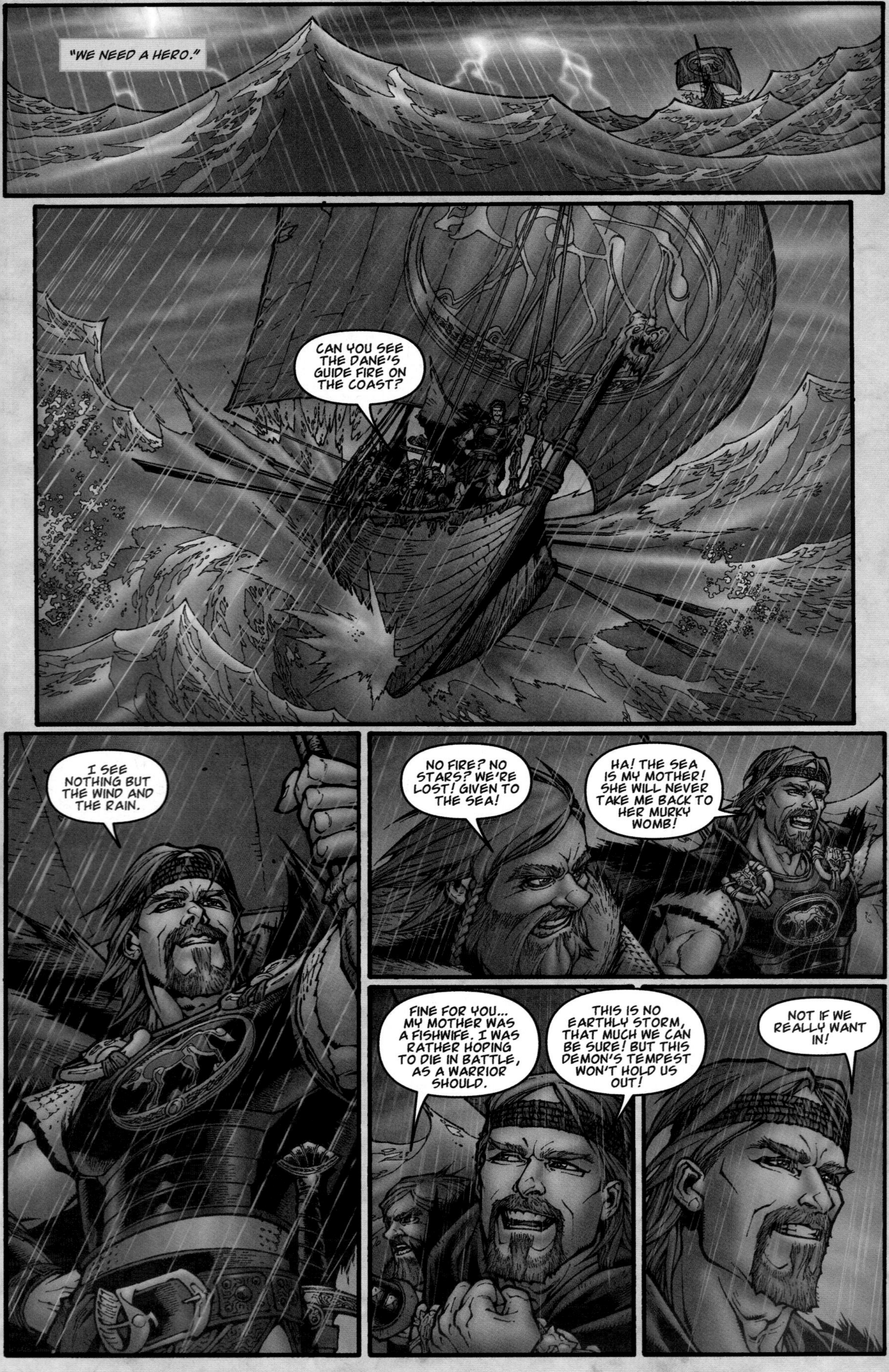
"WE NEED A HERO."
CAN YOU SEE THE DANE'S GUIDE FIRE ON THE COAST?
I SEE NOTHING BUT THE WIND AND THE RAIN.
NO FIRE? NO STARS? WE'RE LOST! GIVEN TO THE SEA!
HA! THE SEA IS MY MOTHER! SHE WILL NEVER TAKE ME BACK TO HER MURKY WOMB!
FINE FOR YOU... MY MOTHER WAS A FISHWIFE. I WAS RATHER HOPING TO DIE IN BATTLE, AS A WARRIOR SHOULD.
THIS IS NO EARTHLY STORM, THAT MUCH WE CAN BE SURE! BUT THIS DEMON'S TEMPEST WON'T HOLD US OUT!
NOT IF WE REALLY WANT IN!

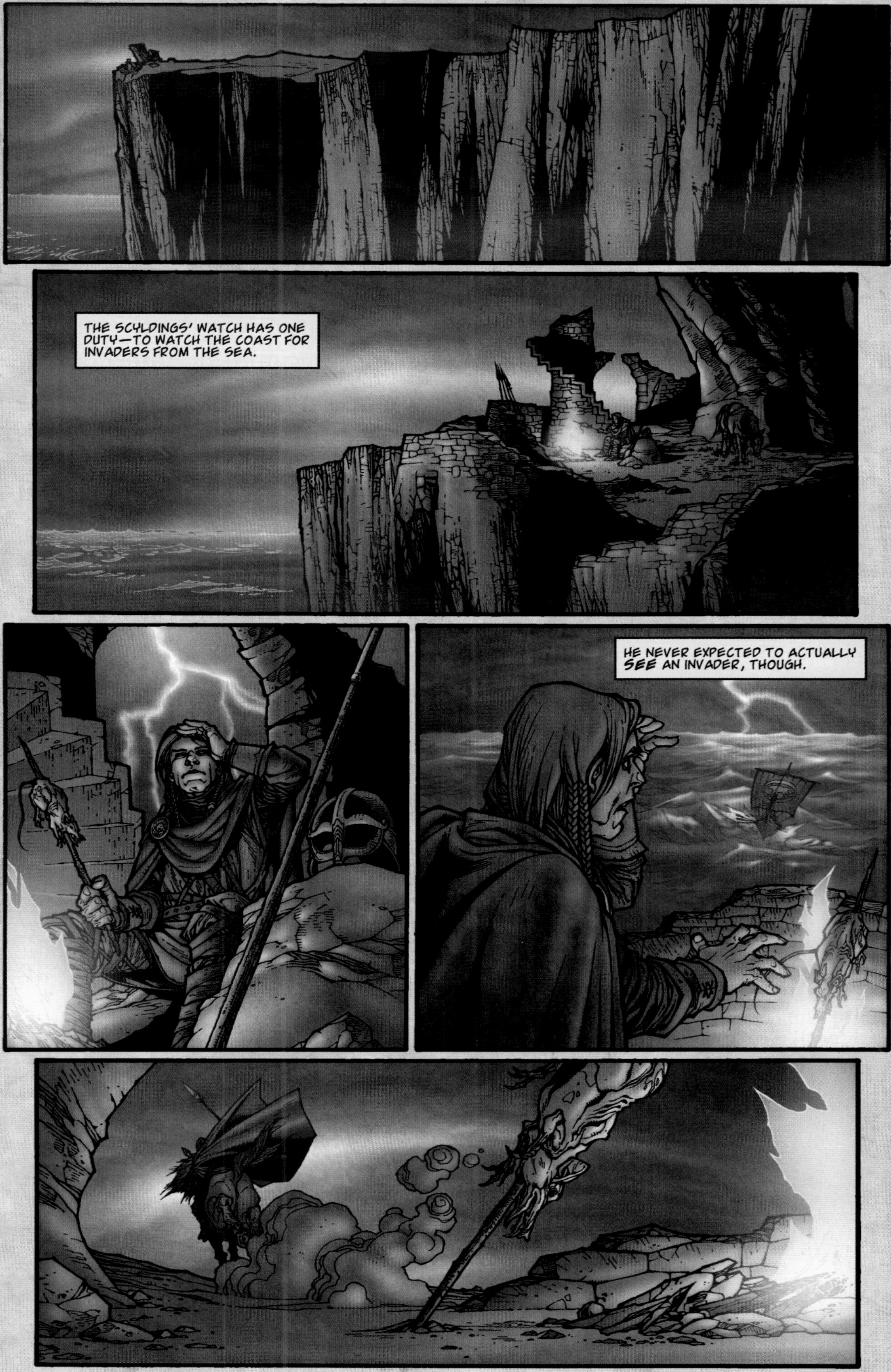
THE SCYLDINGS' WATCH HAS ONE DUTY—TO WATCH THE COAST FOR INVADERS FROM THE SEA.
HE NEVER EXPECTED TO ACTUALLY SEE AN INVADER, THOUGH.

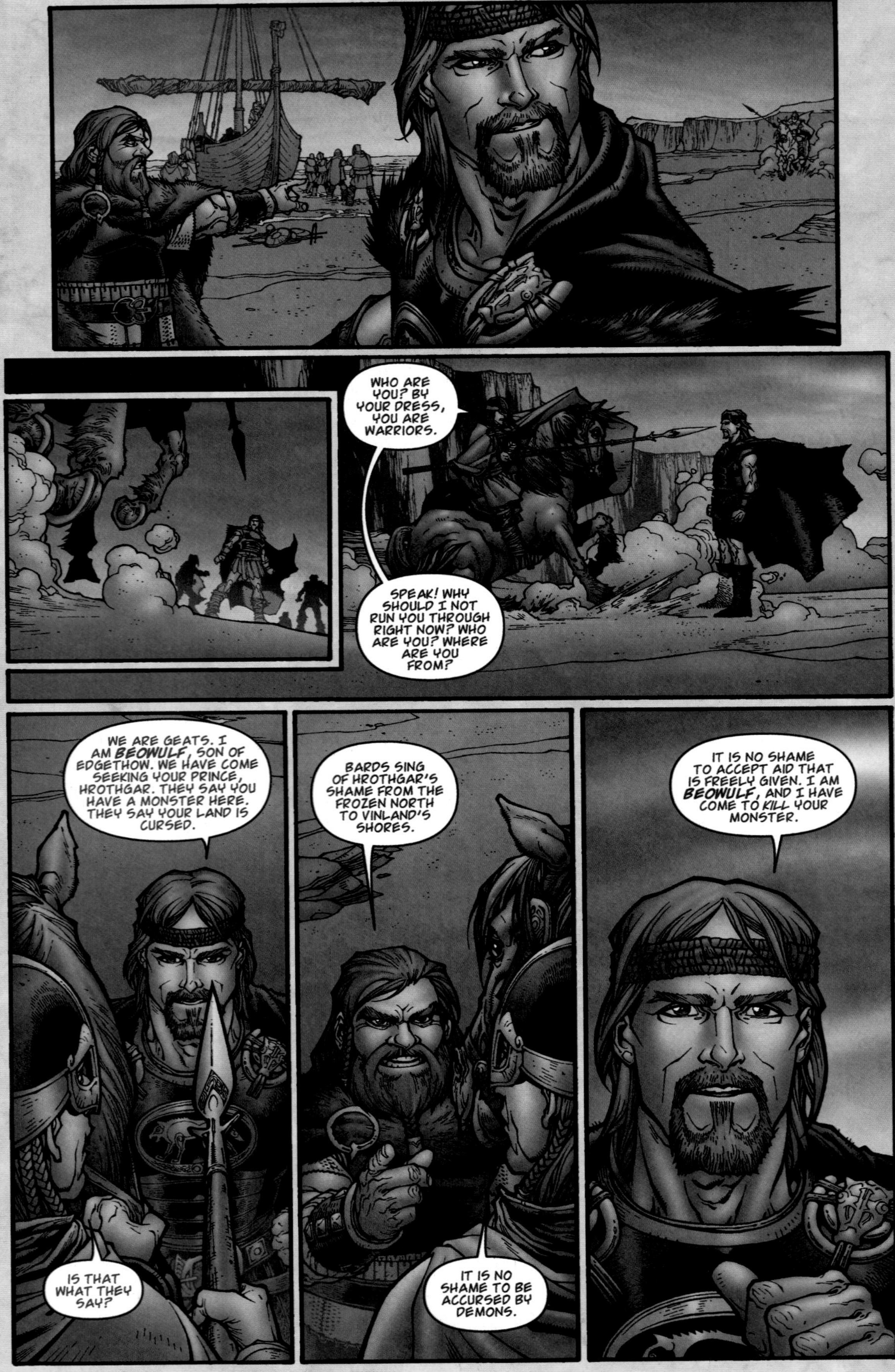
WHO ARE YOU? BY YOUR DRESS, YOU ARE WARRIORS.
SPEAK! WHY SHOULD I NOT RUN YOU THROUGH RIGHT NOW? WHO ARE YOU? WHERE ARE YOU FROM?
WE ARE GEATS. I AM ***BEOWULF***, SON OF EDGETHOW. WE HAVE COME SEEKING YOUR PRINCE, HROTHGAR. THEY SAY YOU HAVE A MONSTER HERE. THEY SAY YOUR LAND IS CURSED.
IS THAT WHAT THEY SAY?
BARDS SING OF HROTHGAR'S SHAME FROM THE FROZEN NORTH TO VINLAND'S SHORES.
IT IS NO SHAME TO BE ACCURSED BY DEMONS.
IT IS NO SHAME TO ACCEPT AID THAT IS FREELY GIVEN. I AM ***BEOWULF***, AND I HAVE COME TO *KILL* YOUR MONSTER.

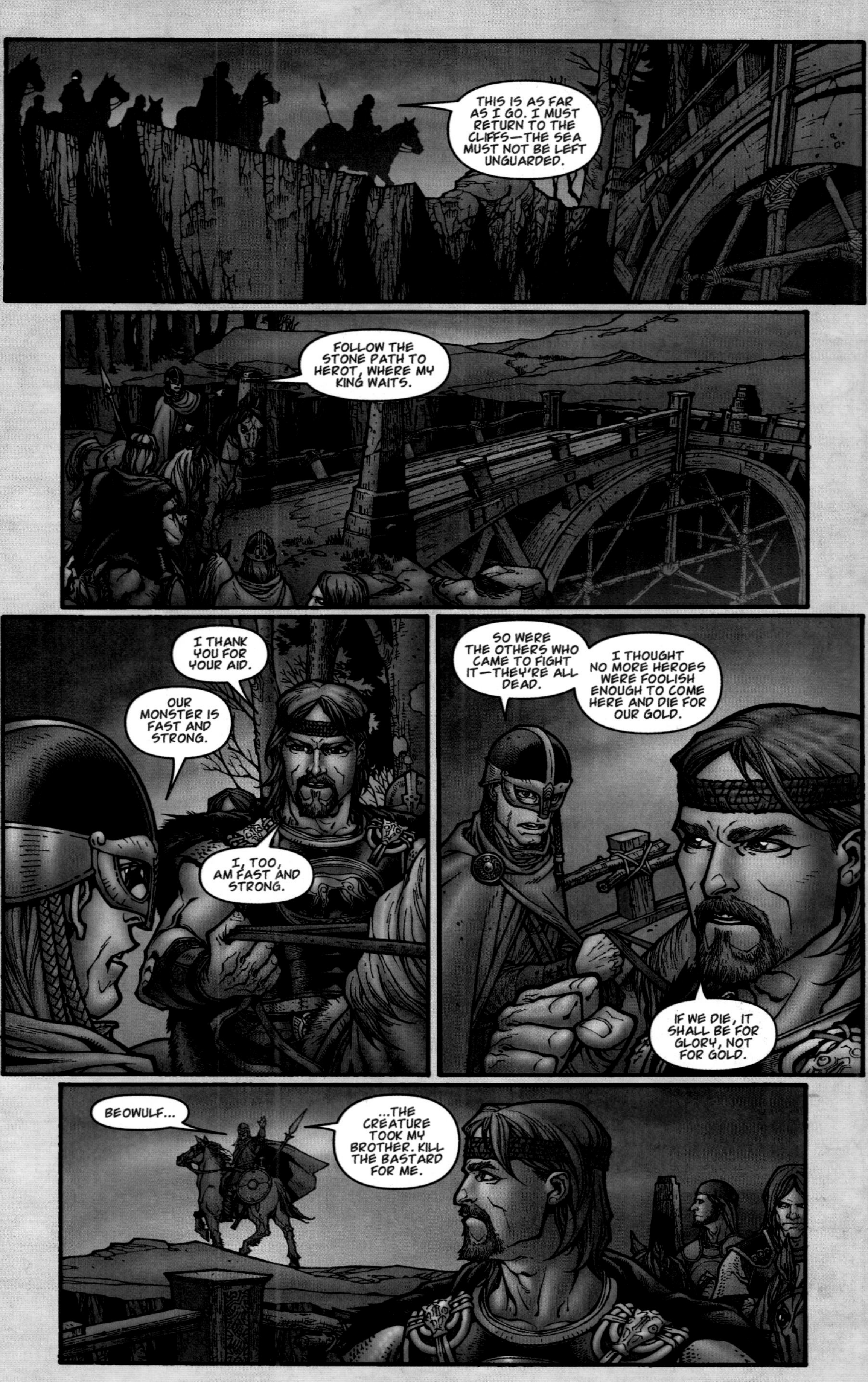
THIS IS AS FAR AS I GO. I MUST RETURN TO THE CLIFFS—THE SEA MUST NOT BE LEFT UNGUARDED.
FOLLOW THE STONE PATH TO HEROT, WHERE MY KING WAITS.
I THANK YOU FOR YOUR AID.
OUR MONSTER IS FAST AND STRONG.
I, TOO, AM FAST AND STRONG.
SO WERE THE OTHERS WHO CAME TO FIGHT IT—THEY'RE ALL DEAD.
I THOUGHT NO MORE HEROES WERE FOOLISH ENOUGH TO COME HERE AND DIE FOR OUR GOLD.
IF WE DIE, IT SHALL BE FOR GLORY, NOT FOR GOLD.
BEOWULF...
...THE CREATURE TOOK MY BROTHER. KILL THE BASTARD FOR ME.

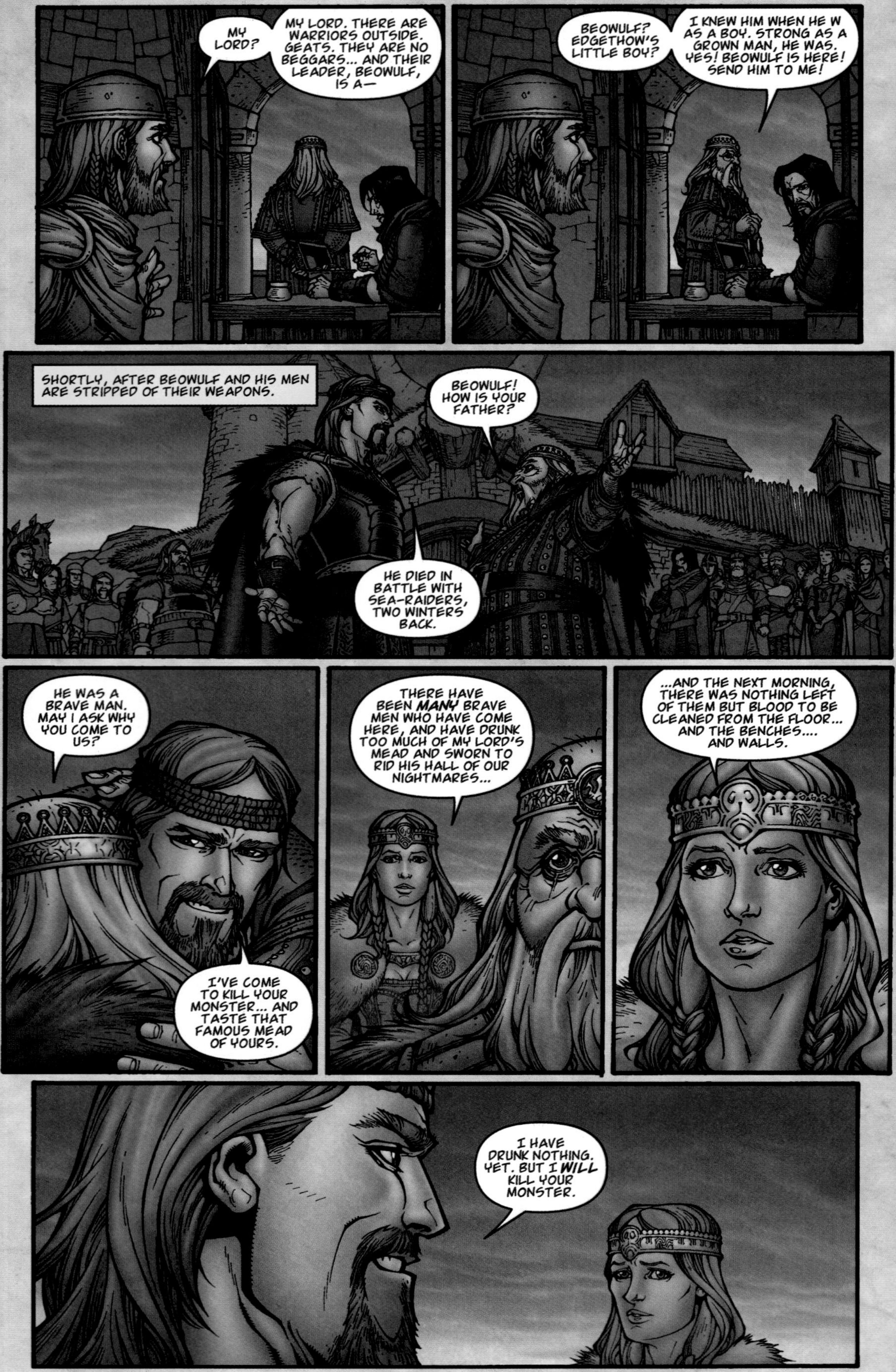
MY LORD?
MY LORD. THERE ARE WARRIORS OUTSIDE. GEATS. THEY ARE NO BEGGARS... AND THEIR LEADER, BEOWULF, IS A—
BEOWULF? EDGETHOW'S LITTLE BOY?
I KNEW HIM WHEN HE W AS A BOY. STRONG AS A GROWN MAN, HE WAS. YES! BEOWULF IS HERE! SEND HIM TO ME!
SHORTLY, AFTER BEOWULF AND HIS MEN ARE STRIPPED OF THEIR WEAPONS.
BEOWULF! HOW IS YOUR FATHER?
HE DIED IN BATTLE WITH SEA-RAIDERS, TWO WINTERS BACK.
HE WAS A BRAVE MAN. MAY I ASK WHY YOU COME TO US?
I'VE COME TO KILL YOUR MONSTER... AND TASTE THAT FAMOUS MEAD OF YOURS.
THERE HAVE BEEN MANY BRAVE MEN WHO HAVE COME HERE, AND HAVE DRUNK TOO MUCH OF MY LORD'S MEAD AND SWORN TO RID HIS HALL OF OUR NIGHTMARES...
...AND THE NEXT MORNING, THERE WAS NOTHING LEFT OF THEM BUT BLOOD TO BE CLEANED FROM THE FLOOR... AND THE BENCHES.... AND WALLS.
I HAVE DRUNK NOTHING. YET. BUT I WILL KILL YOUR MONSTER.

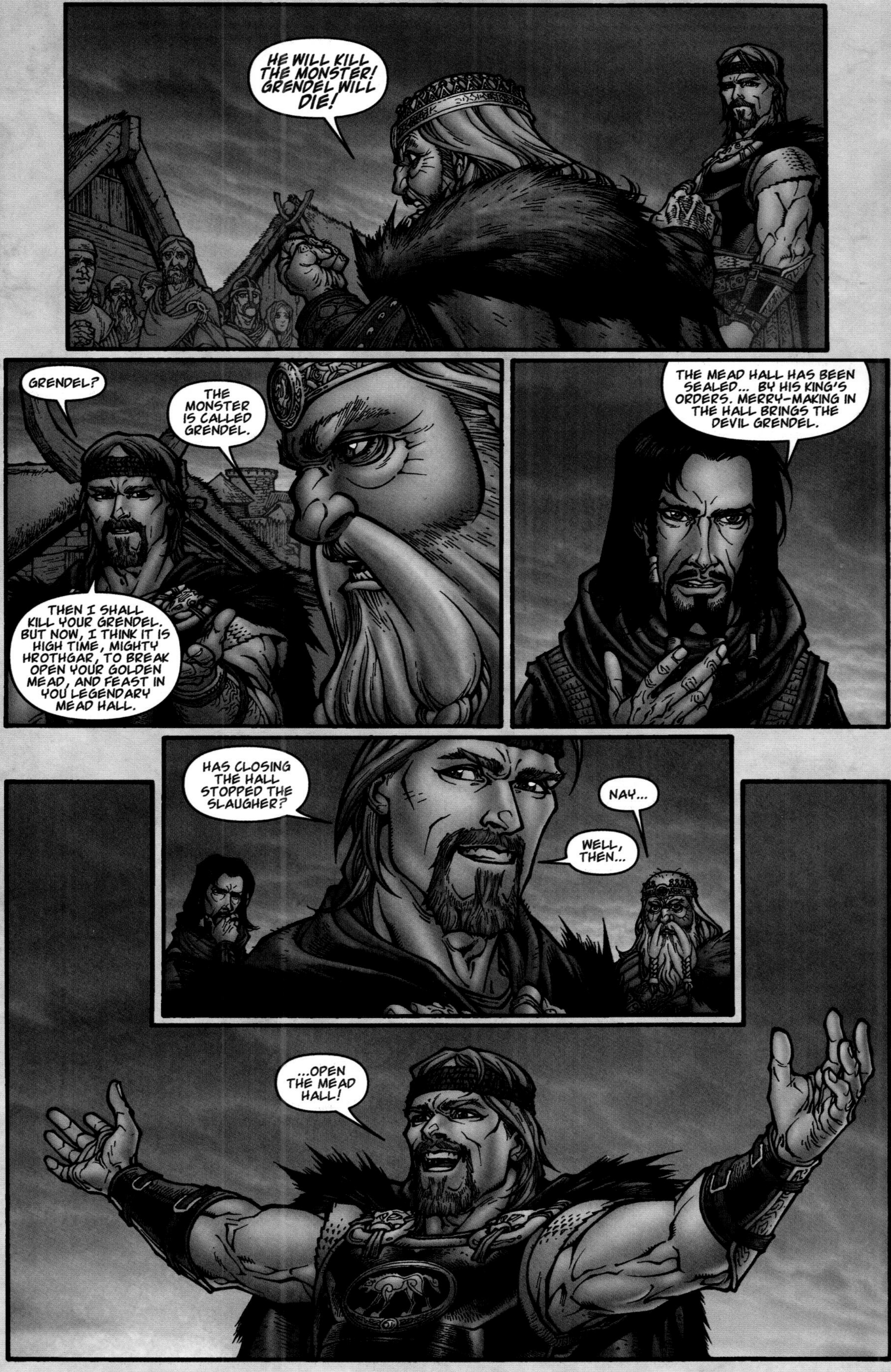
HE WILL KILL THE MONSTER! GRENDEL WILL DIE!
GRENDEL?
THE MONSTER IS CALLED GRENDEL.
THEN I SHALL KILL YOUR GRENDEL. BUT NOW, I THINK IT IS HIGH TIME, MIGHTY HROTHGAR, TO BREAK OPEN YOUR GOLDEN MEAD, AND FEAST IN YOU LEGENDARY MEAD HALL.
THE MEAD HALL HAS BEEN SEALED... BY HIS KING'S ORDERS. MERRY-MAKING IN THE HALL BRINGS THE DEVIL GRENDEL.
HAS CLOSING THE HALL STOPPED THE SLAUGHER?
NAY...
WELL, THEN...
...OPEN THE MEAD HALL!

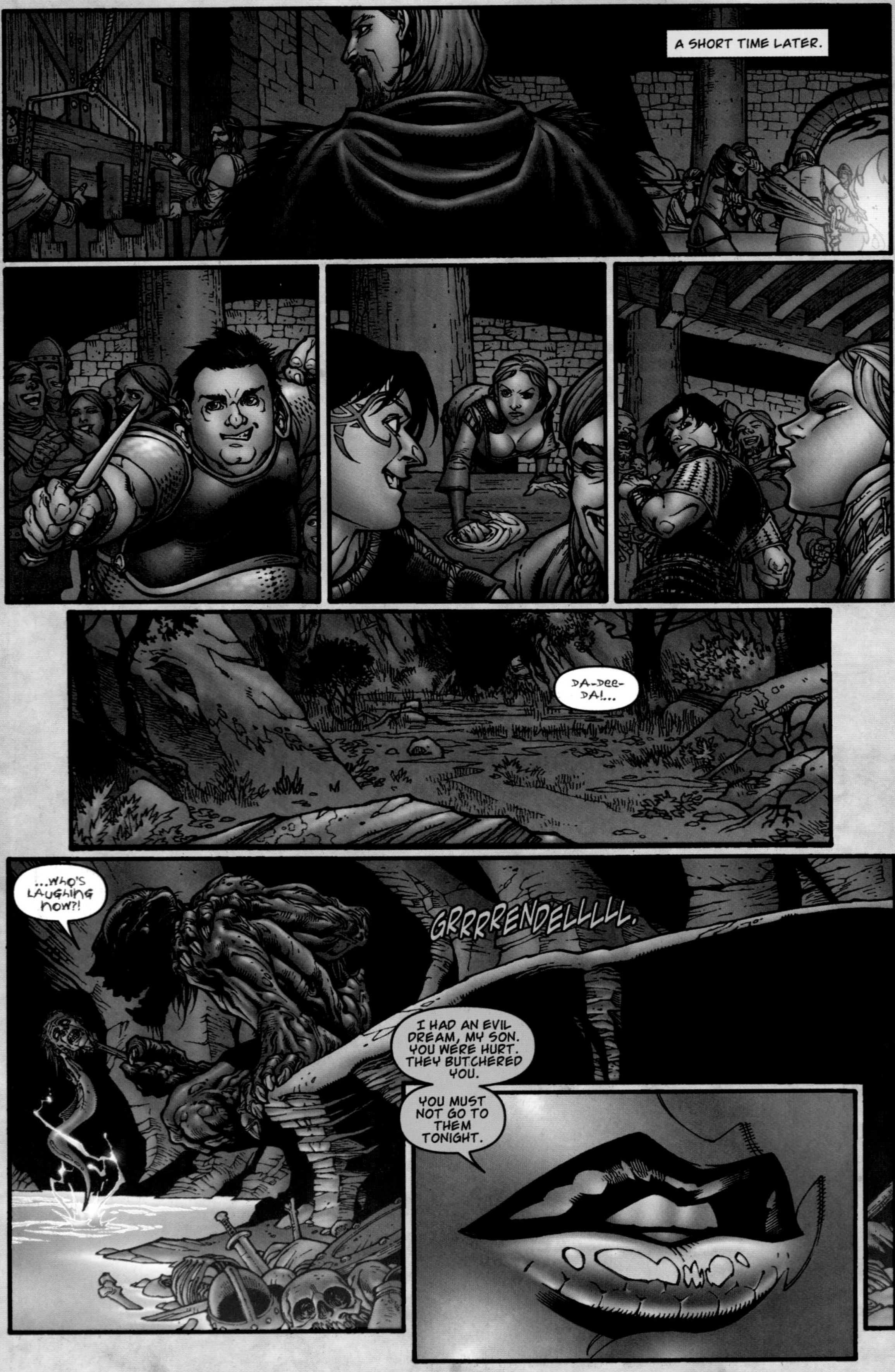
A SHORT TIME LATER.
DA-DEE-DA!...
...WHO'S LAUGHING NOW?!
GRRRRENDELLLLL.
I HAD AN EVIL DREAM, MY SON. YOU WERE HURT. THEY BUTCHERED YOU.
YOU MUST NOT GO TO THEM TONIGHT.

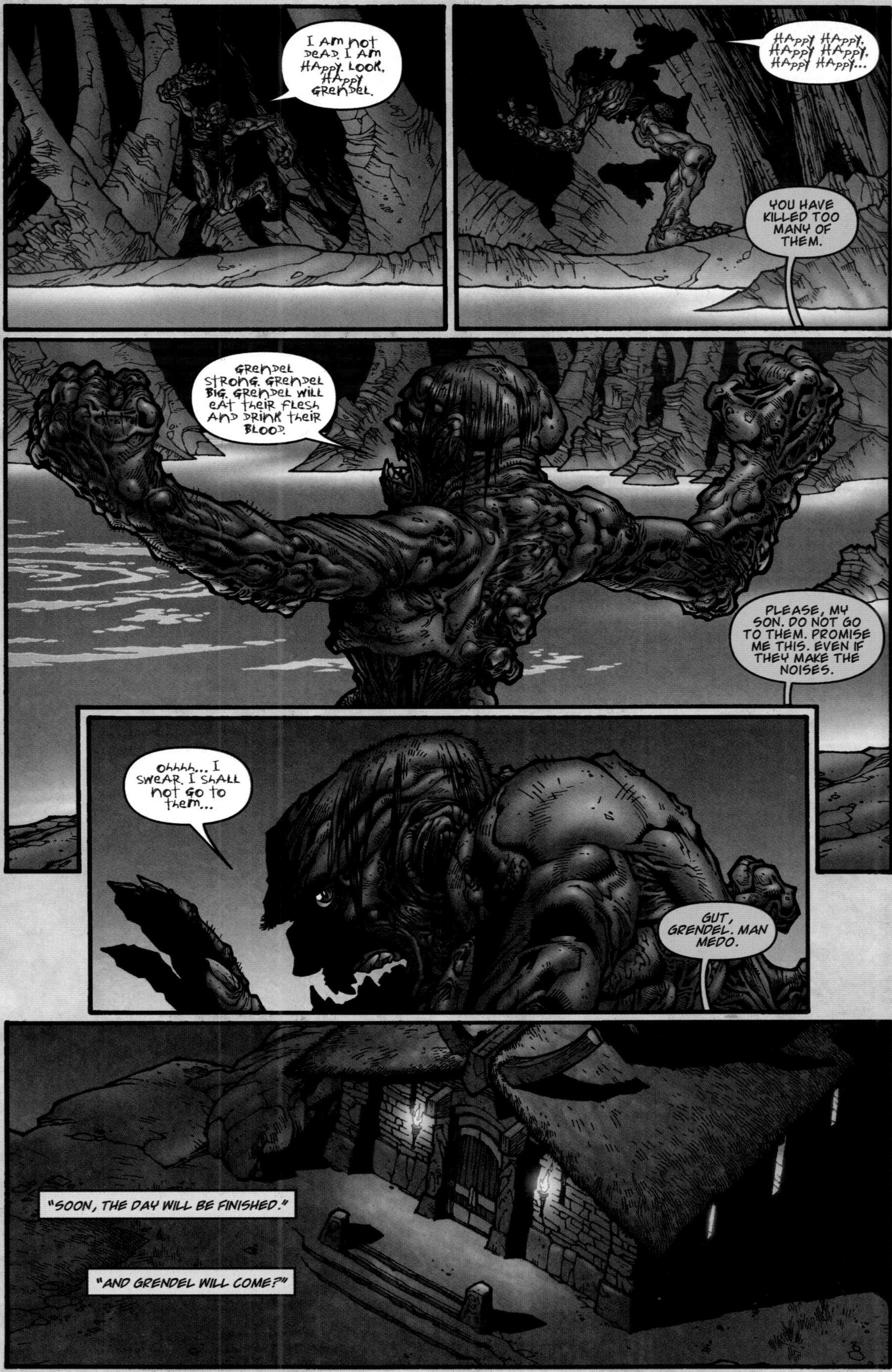
I AM NOT DEAD. I AM HAPPY. LOOK. HAPPY GRENDEL.
HAPPY HAPPY, HAPPY HAPPY, HAPPY HAPPY...
YOU HAVE KILLED TOO MANY OF THEM.
GRENDEL STRONG. GRENDEL BIG. GRENDEL WILL EAT THEIR FLESH AND DRINK THEIR BLOOD.
PLEASE, MY SON. DO NOT GO TO THEM. PROMISE ME THIS. EVEN IF THEY MAKE THE NOISES.
OHHHH... I SWEAR. I SHALL NOT GO TO THEM...
GUT, GRENDEL. MAN MEDO.
"SOON, THE DAY WILL BE FINISHED."
"AND GRENDEL WILL COME?"

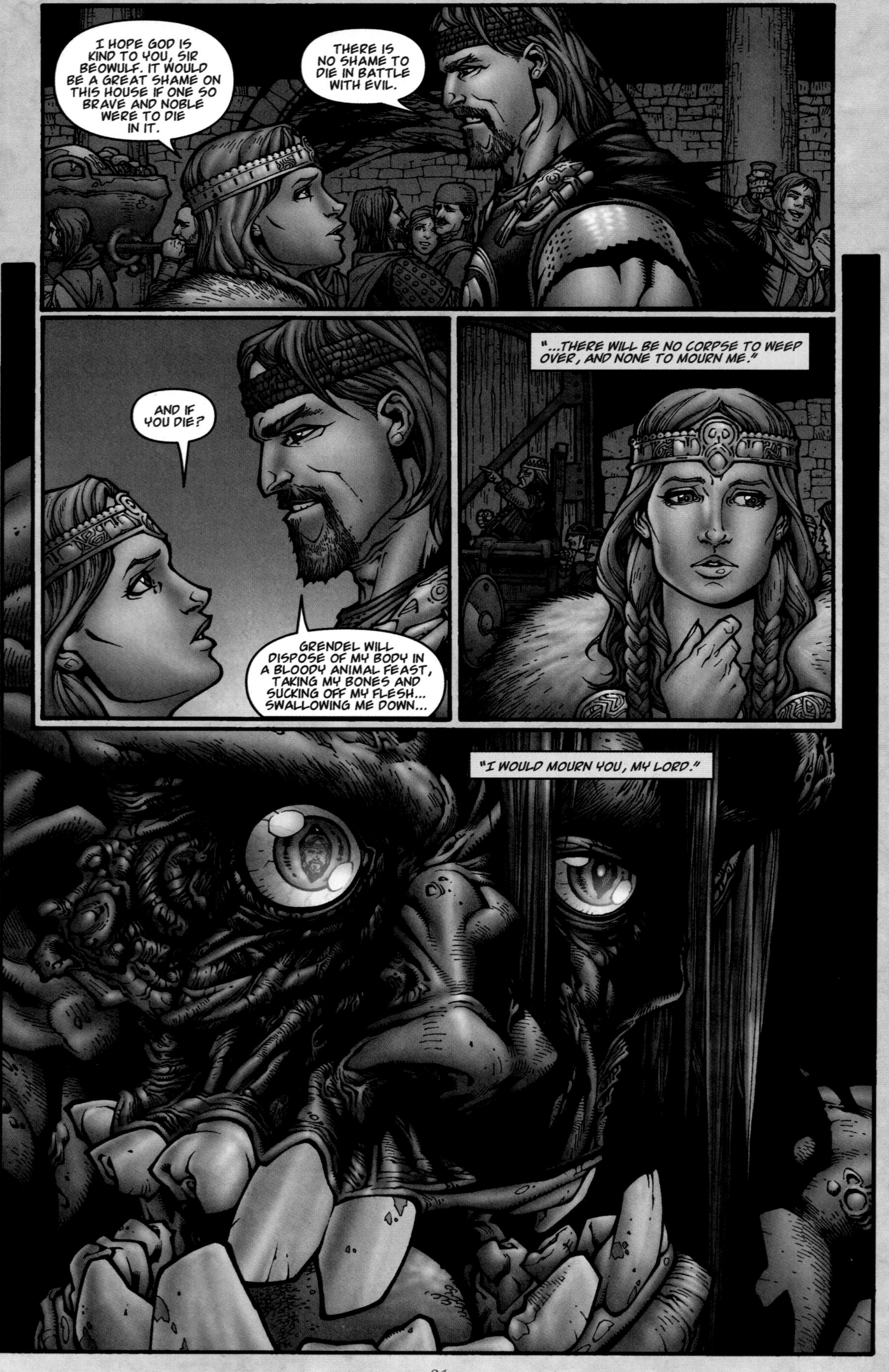
I HOPE GOD IS KIND TO YOU, SIR BEOWULF. IT WOULD BE A GREAT SHAME ON THIS HOUSE IF ONE SO BRAVE AND NOBLE WERE TO DIE IN IT.
THERE IS NO SHAME TO DIE IN BATTLE WITH EVIL.
AND IF YOU DIE?
GRENDEL WILL DISPOSE OF MY BODY IN A BLOODY ANIMAL FEAST, TAKING MY BONES AND SUCKING OFF MY FLESH... SWALLOWING ME DOWN...
"...THERE WILL BE NO CORPSE TO WEEP OVER, AND NONE TO MOURN ME."
"I WOULD MOURN YOU, MY LORD."

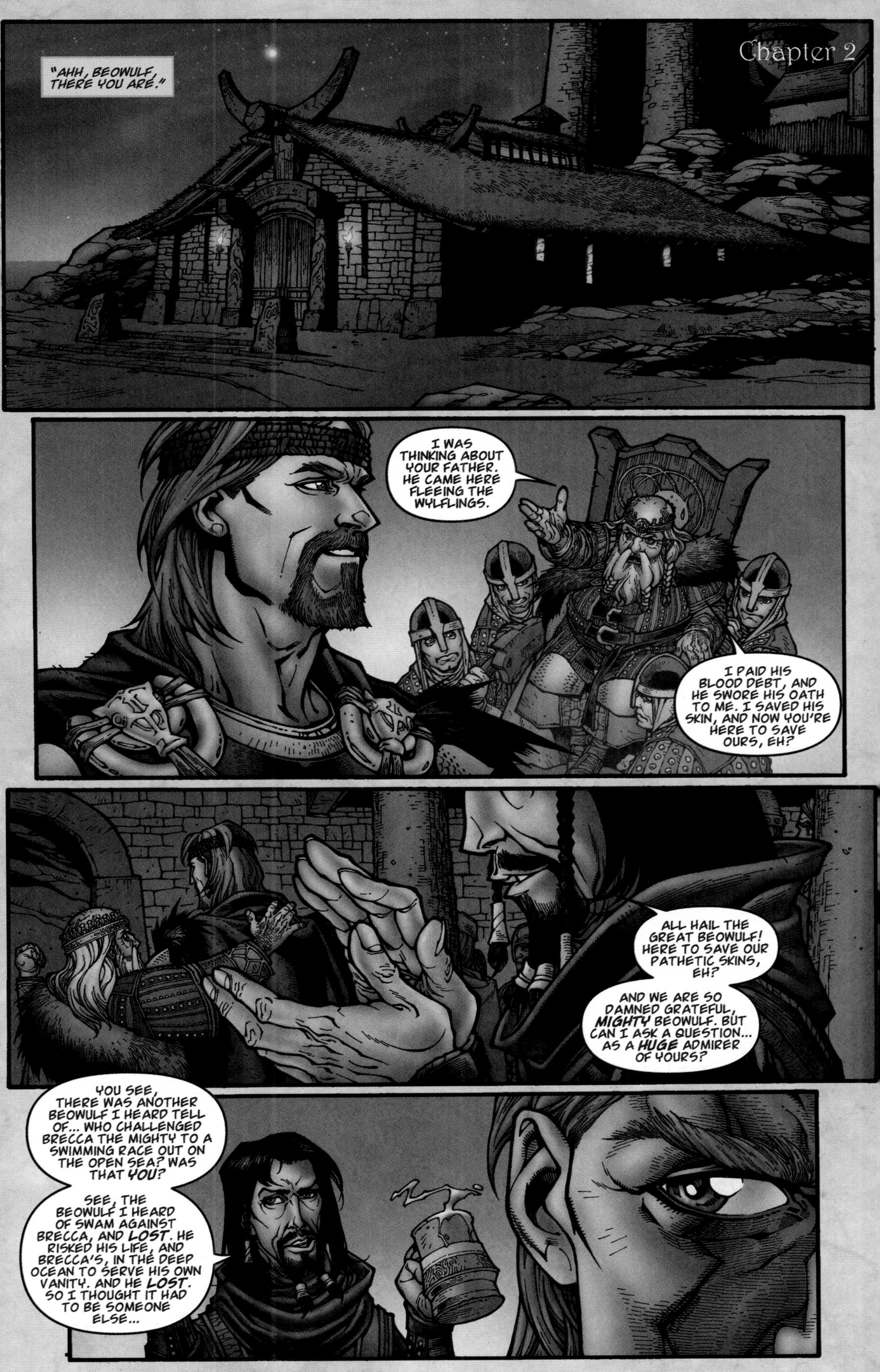
Chapter 2
"AHH, BEOWULF, THERE YOU ARE."
I WAS THINKING ABOUT YOUR FATHER. HE CAME HERE FLEEING THE WYLFINGS.
I PAID HIS BLOOD DEBT, AND HE SWORE HIS OATH TO ME. I SAVED HIS SKIN, AND NOW YOU'RE HERE TO SAVE OURS, EH?
ALL HAIL THE GREAT BEOWULF! HERE TO SAVE OUR PATHETIC SKINS, EH?
AND WE ARE SO DAMNED GRATEFUL, MIGHTY BEOWULF. BUT CAN I ASK A QUESTION... AS A HUGE ADMIRER OF YOURS?
YOU SEE, THERE WAS ANOTHER BEOWULF I HEARD TELL OF... WHO CHALLENGED BRECCA THE MIGHTY TO A SWIMMING RACE OUT ON THE OPEN SEA? WAS THAT YOU?
SEE, THE BEOWULF I HEARD OF SWAM AGAINST BRECCA, AND LOST. HE RISKED HIS LIFE, AND BRECCA'S, IN THE DEEP OCEAN TO SERVE HIS OWN VANITY. AND HE LOST. SO I THOUGHT IT HAD TO BE SOMEONE ELSE...

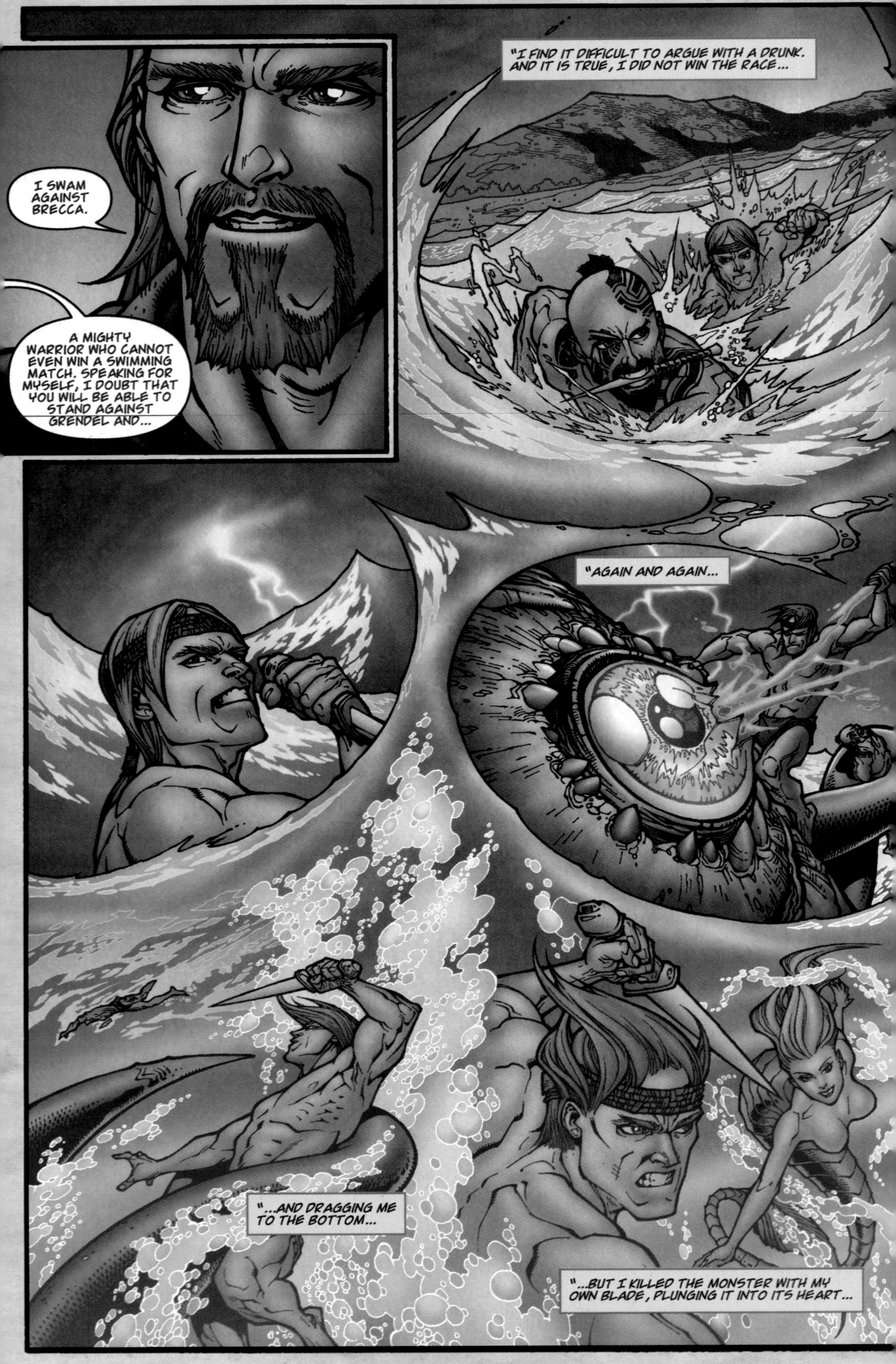
I SWAM AGAINST BRECCA.
"I FIND IT DIFFICULT TO ARGUE WITH A DRUNK. AND IT IS TRUE, I DID NOT WIN THE RACE...
A MIGHTY WARRIOR WHO CANNOT EVEN WIN A SWIMMING MATCH. SPEAKING FOR MYSELF, I DOUBT THAT YOU WILL BE ABLE TO STAND AGAINST GRENDEL AND...
"AGAIN AND AGAIN...
"...AND DRAGGING ME TO THE BOTTOM...
"...BUT I KILLED THE MONSTER WITH MY OWN BLADE, PLUNGING IT INTO ITS HEART...

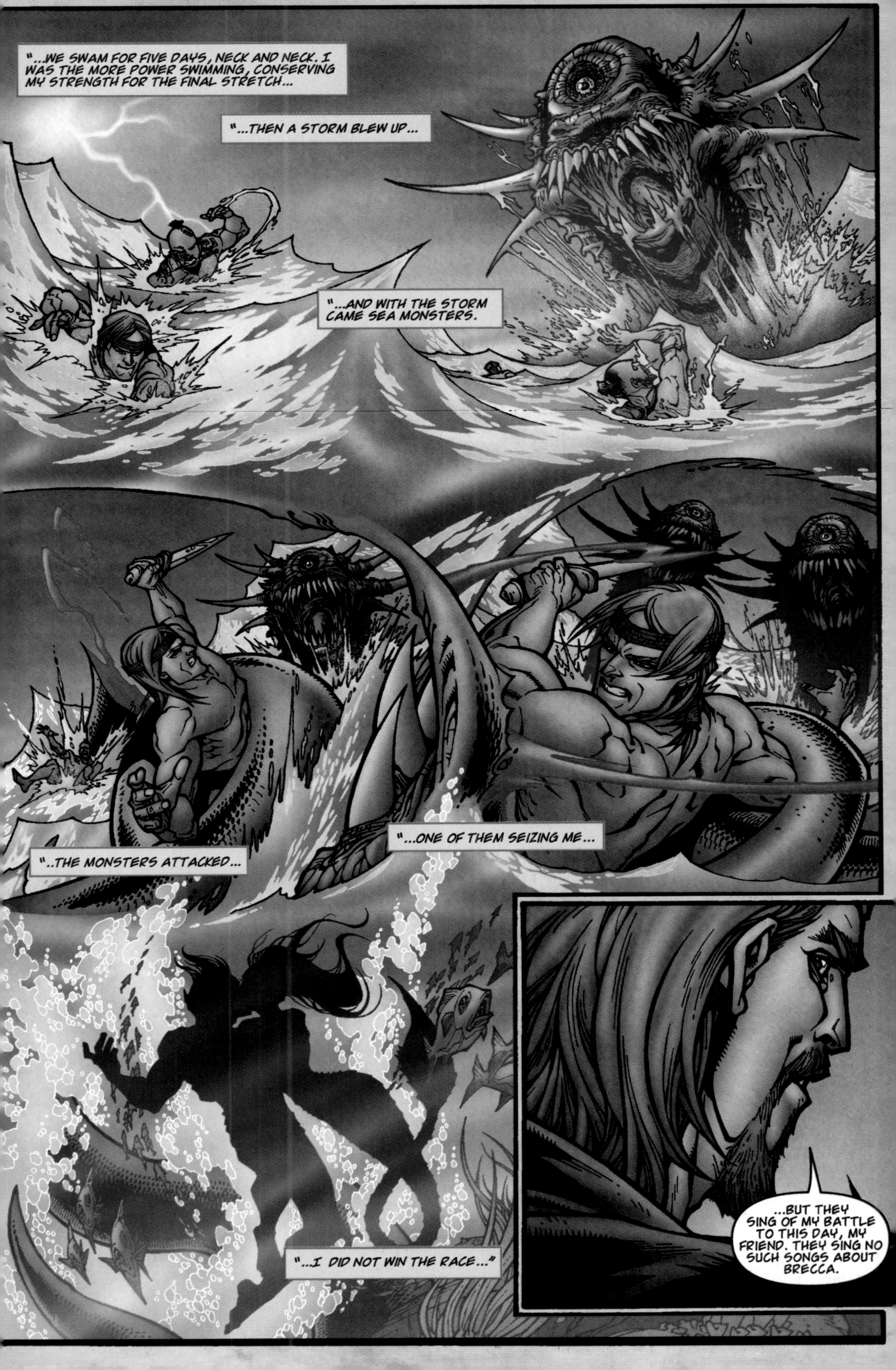
"...WE SWAM FOR FIVE DAYS, NECK AND NECK. I WAS THE MORE POWER SWIMMING, CONSERVING MY STRENGTH FOR THE FINAL STRETCH...
"...THEN A STORM BLEW UP...
"...AND WITH THE STORM CAME SEA MONSTERS.
"..THE MONSTERS ATTACKED...
"...ONE OF THEM SEIZING ME...
"...I DID NOT WIN THE RACE..."
...BUT THEY SING OF MY BATTLE TO THIS DAY, MY FRIEND. THEY SING NO SUCH SONGS ABOUT BRECCA.

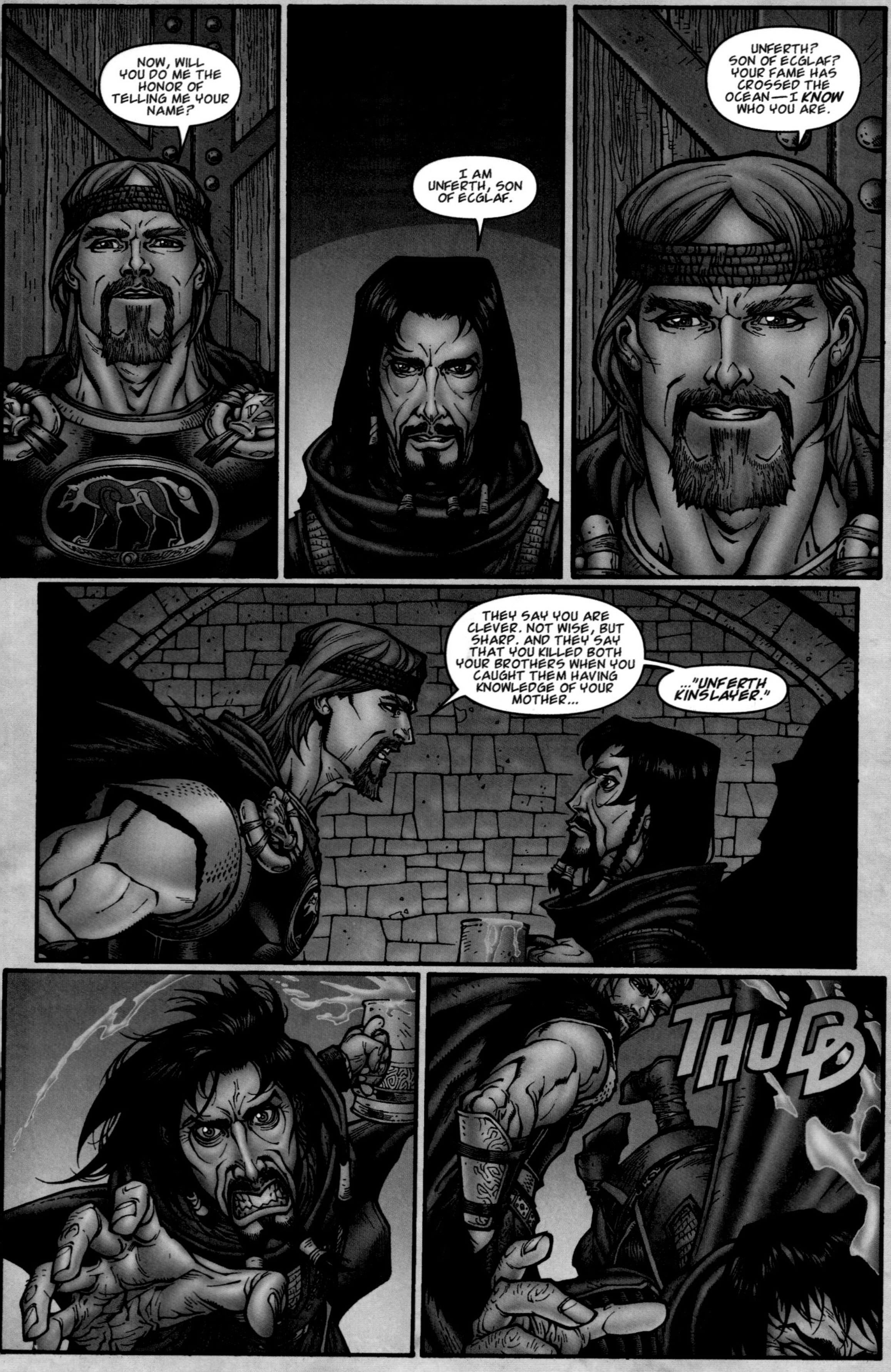
NOW, WILL YOU DO ME THE HONOR OF TELLING ME YOUR NAME?
I AM UNFERTH, SON OF ECGLAF.
UNFERTH? SON OF ECGLAF? YOUR FAME HAS CROSSED THE OCEAN—I *KNOW* WHO YOU ARE.
THEY SAY YOU ARE CLEVER. NOT WISE, BUT SHARP. AND THEY SAY THAT YOU KILLED BOTH YOUR BROTHERS WHEN YOU CAUGHT THEM HAVING KNOWLEDGE OF YOUR MOTHER...
..."UNFERTH KINSLAYER."
THUDD

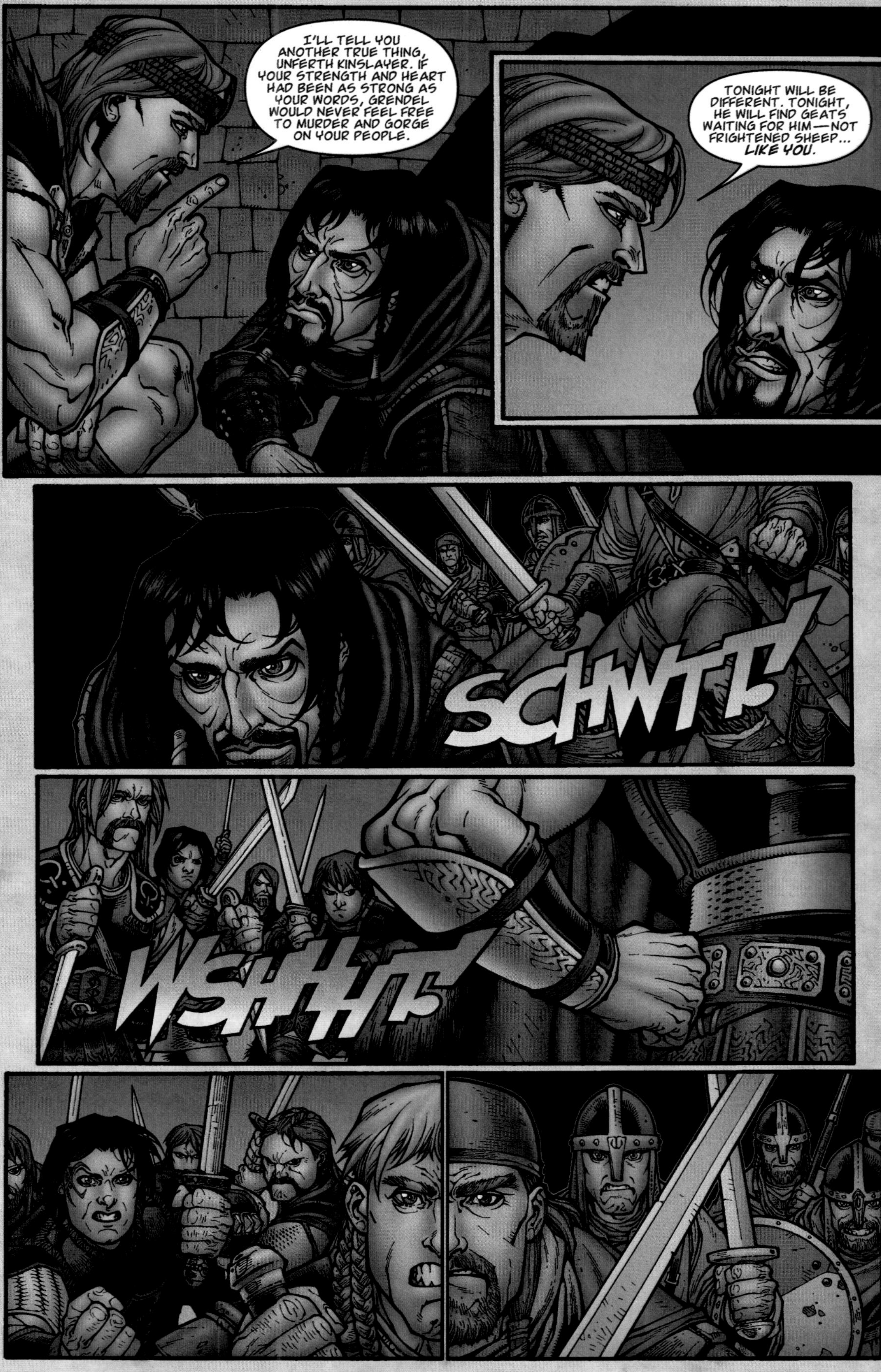
I'LL TELL YOU ANOTHER TRUE THING, UNFERTH KINSLAYER. IF YOUR STRENGTH AND HEART HAD BEEN AS STRONG AS YOUR WORDS, GRENDEL WOULD NEVER FEEL FREE TO MURDER AND GORGE ON YOUR PEOPLE.
TONIGHT WILL BE DIFFERENT. TONIGHT, HE WILL FIND GEATS WAITING FOR HIM—NOT FRIGHTENED SHEEP... LIKE YOU.
SCHWTT!
WSHHT!

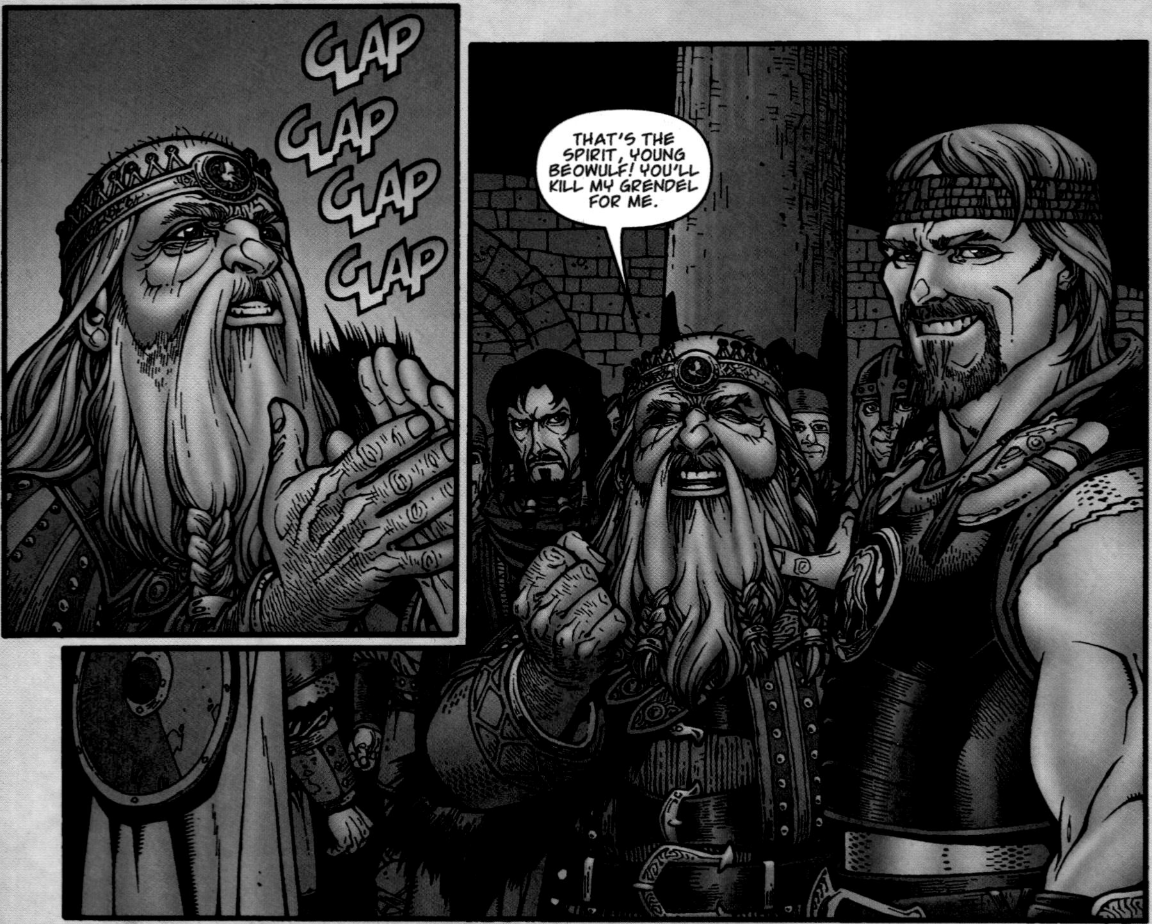
CLAP CLAP CLAP CLAP
THAT'S THE SPIRIT, YOUNG BEOWULF! YOU'LL KILL MY GRENDEL FOR ME.

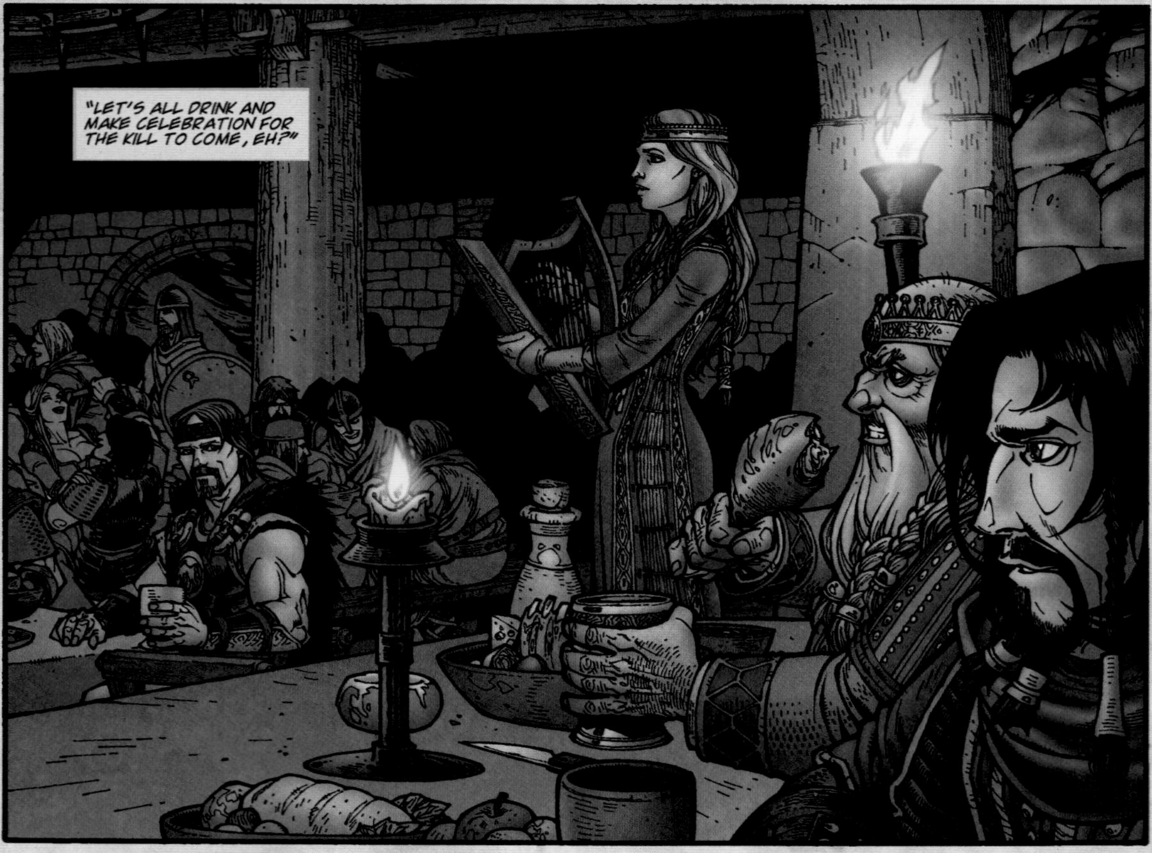
"LET'S ALL DRINK AND MAKE CELEBRATION FOR THE KILL TO COME, EH?"

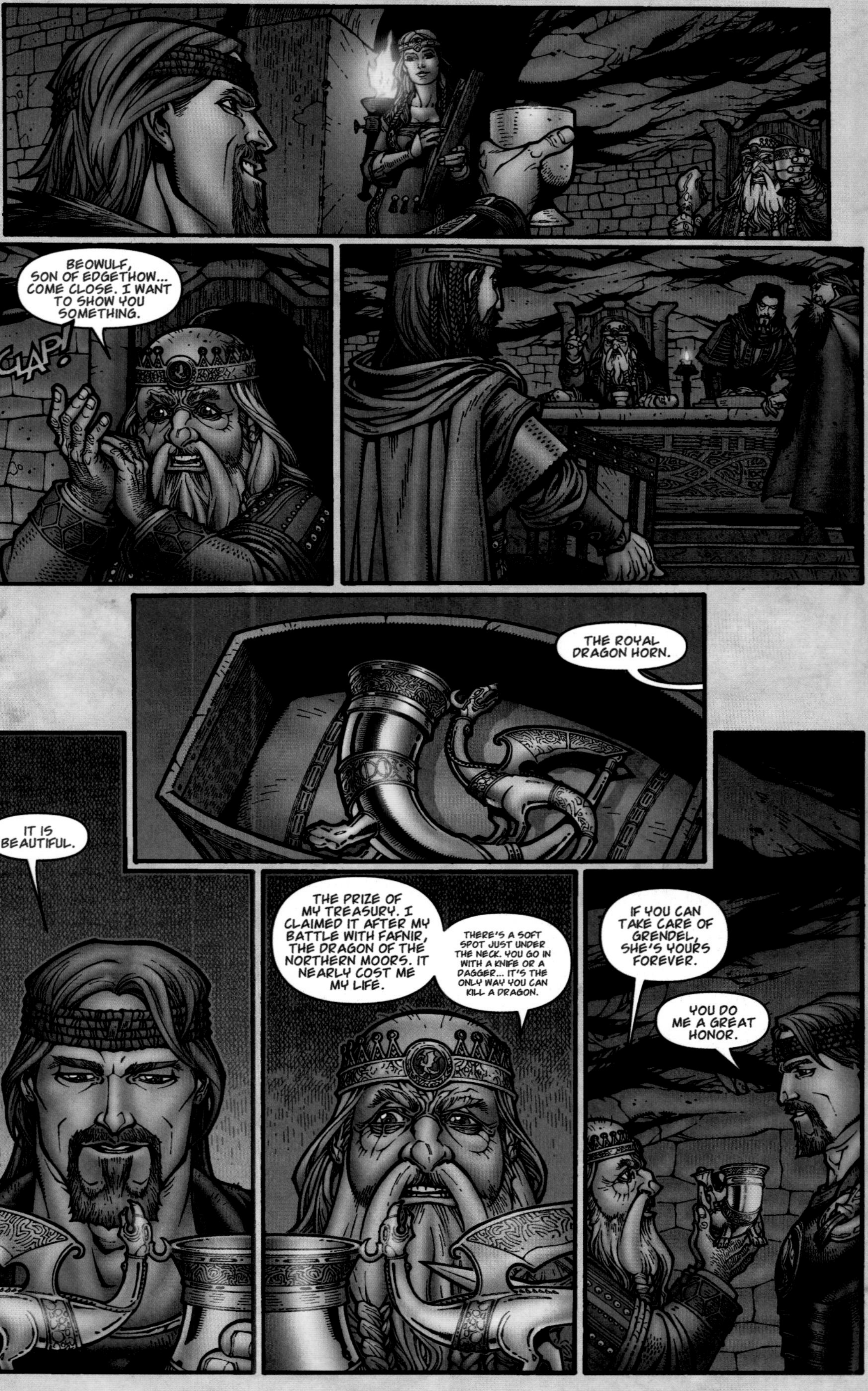
BEOWULF, SON OF EDGETHOW... COME CLOSE. I WANT TO SHOW YOU SOMETHING.
CLAP!
THE ROYAL DRAGON HORN.
IT IS BEAUTIFUL.
THE PRIZE OF MY TREASURY. I CLAIMED IT AFTER MY BATTLE WITH FAFNIR, THE DRAGON OF THE NORTHERN MOORS. IT NEARLY COST ME MY LIFE.
THERE'S A SOFT SPOT JUST UNDER THE NECK. YOU GO IN WITH A KNIFE OR A DAGGER... IT'S THE ONLY WAY YOU CAN KILL A DRAGON.
IF YOU CAN TAKE CARE OF GRENDEL, SHE'S YOURS FOREVER.
YOU DO ME A GREAT HONOR.

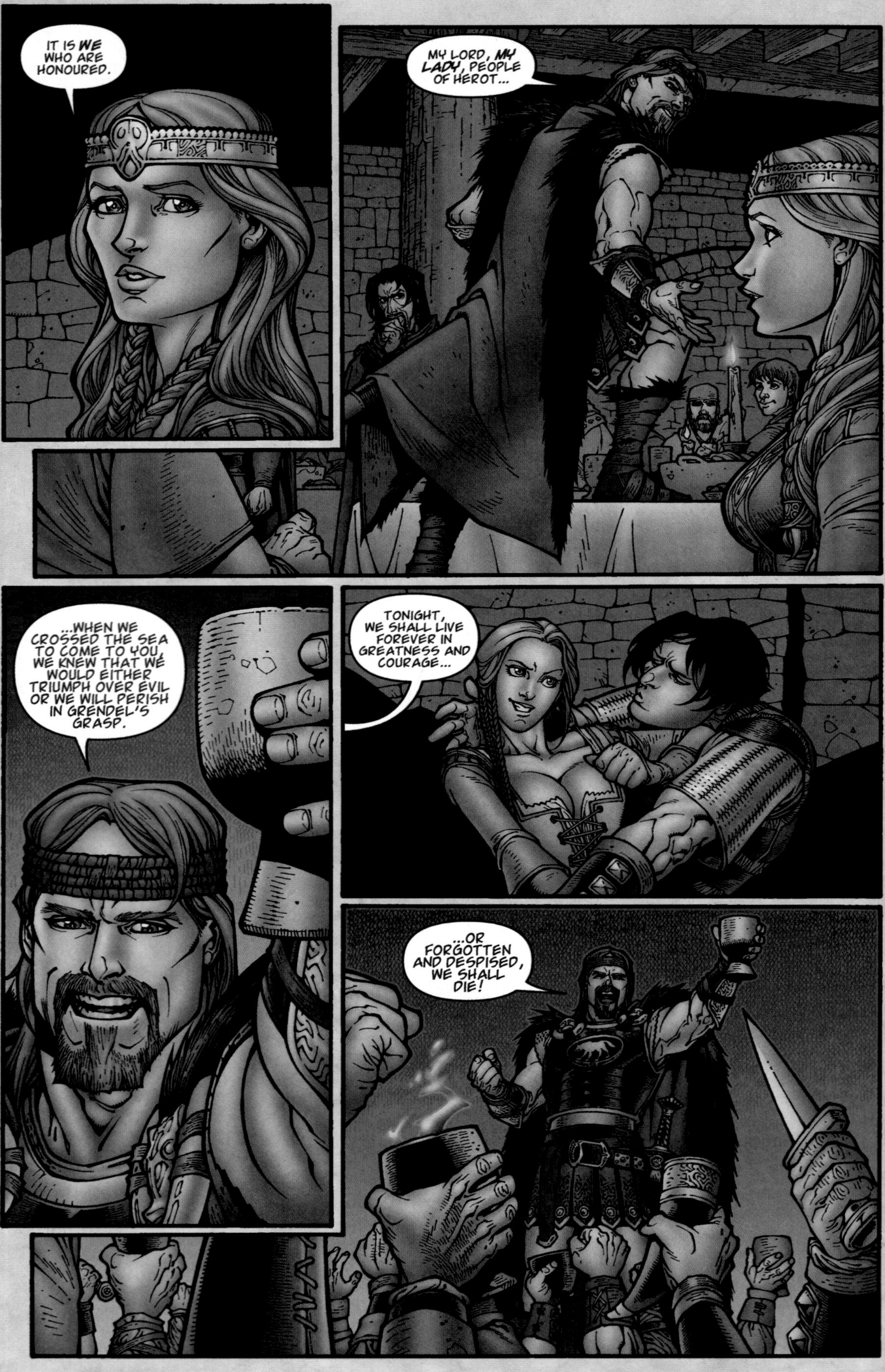
IT IS WE WHO ARE HONOURED.
MY LORD, MY LADY, PEOPLE OF HEROT...
...WHEN WE CROSSED THE SEA TO COME TO YOU, WE KNEW THAT WE WOULD EITHER TRIUMPH OVER EVIL OR WE WILL PERISH IN GRENDEL'S GRASP.
TONIGHT, WE SHALL LIVE FOREVER IN GREATNESS AND COURAGE...
...OR FORGOTTEN AND DESPISED, WE SHALL DIE!

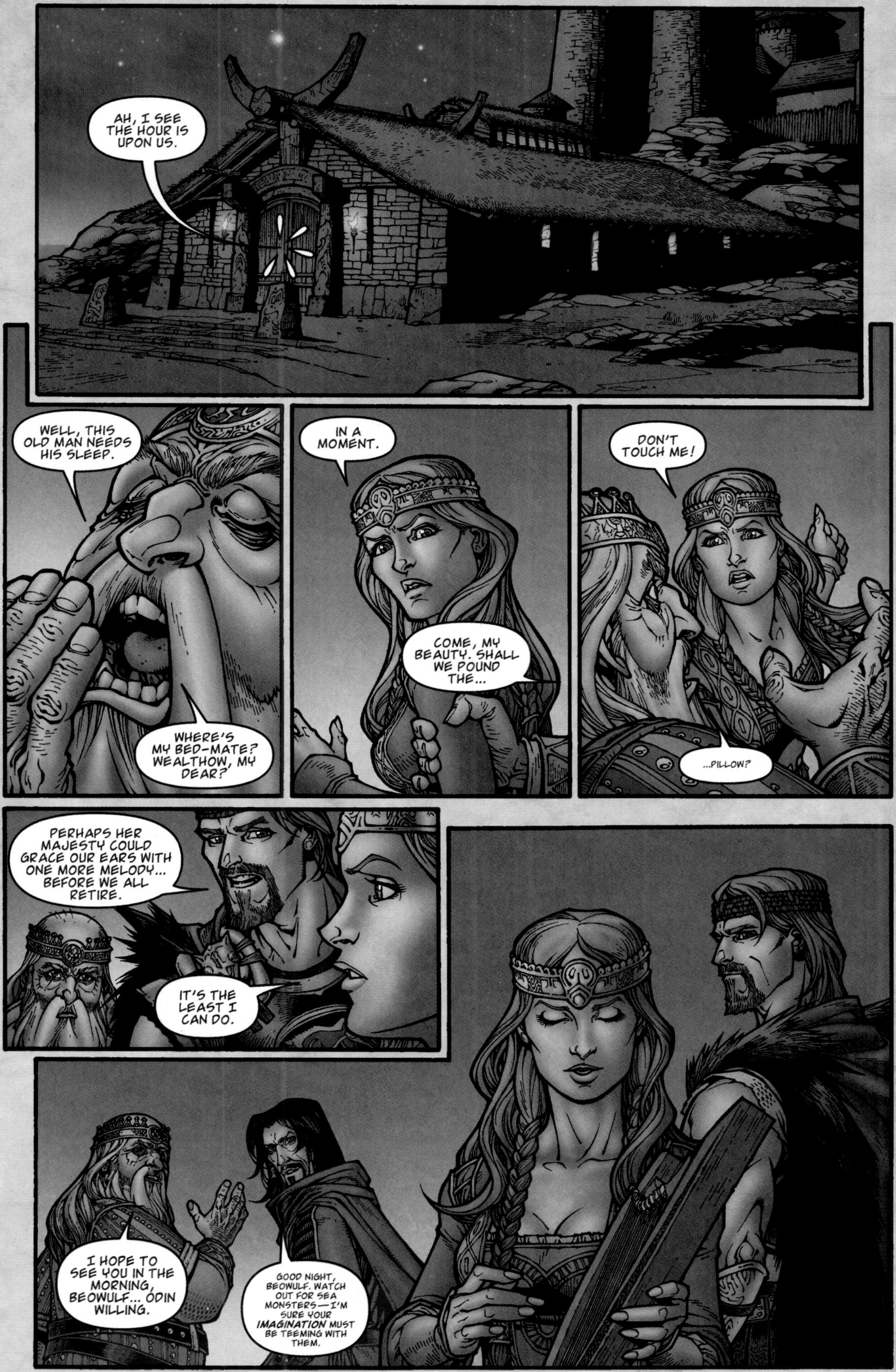
AH, I SEE THE HOUR IS UPON US.
WELL, THIS OLD MAN NEEDS HIS SLEEP.
WHERE'S MY BED-MATE? WEALTHOW, MY DEAR?
IN A MOMENT.
COME, MY BEAUTY. SHALL WE POUND THE...
DON'T TOUCH ME!
...PILLOW?
PERHAPS HER MAJESTY COULD GRACE OUR EARS WITH ONE MORE MELODY... BEFORE WE ALL RETIRE.
IT'S THE LEAST I CAN DO.
I HOPE TO SEE YOU IN THE MORNING, BEOWULF... ODIN WILLING.
GOOD NIGHT, BEOWULF. WATCH OUT FOR SEA MONSTERS—I'M SURE YOUR *IMAGINATION* MUST BE TEEMING WITH THEM.

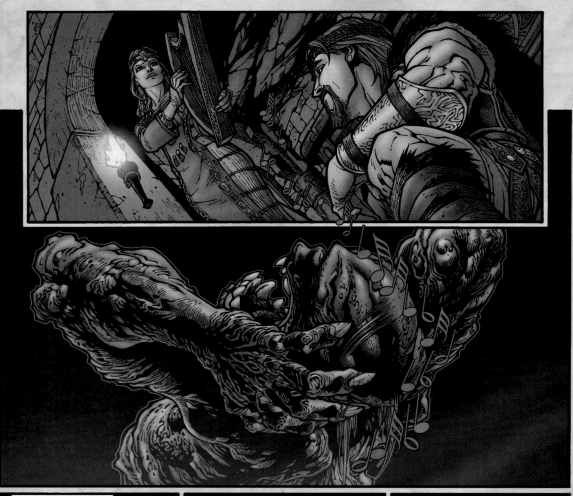

THAT WAS BEAUTIFUL. BUT YOU NEED TO GO NOW, YOUR MAJESTY.

OF COURSE, GRENDEL.

THE DEMON... IS MY HUSBAND'S CURSE. NO, SHAME. HE HAS NO OTHER... NO SONS. AND HE WILL HAVE NO MORE, FOR ALL HIS TALK.

YOU... REALLY NEED TO GO NOW, YOUR MAJESTY.

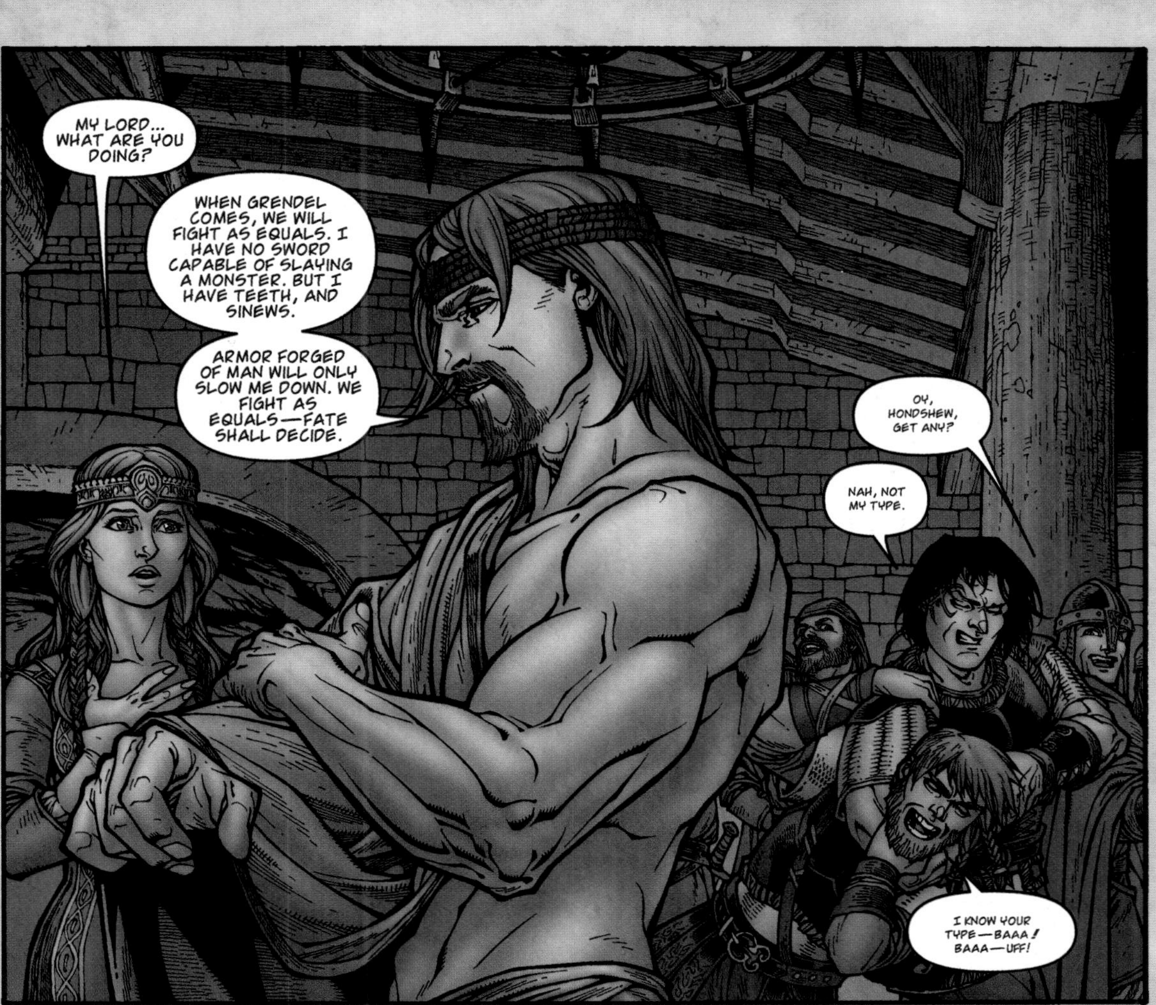
MY LORD... WHAT ARE YOU DOING?
WHEN GRENDEL COMES, WE WILL FIGHT AS EQUALS. I HAVE NO SWORD CAPABLE OF SLAYING A MONSTER. BUT I HAVE TEETH, AND SINEWS.
ARMOR FORGED OF MAN WILL ONLY SLOW ME DOWN. WE FIGHT AS EQUALS—FATE SHALL DECIDE.
OY, HONDSHEW, GET ANY?
NAH, NOT MY TYPE.
I KNOW YOUR TYPE—BAAA! BAAA—UFF!

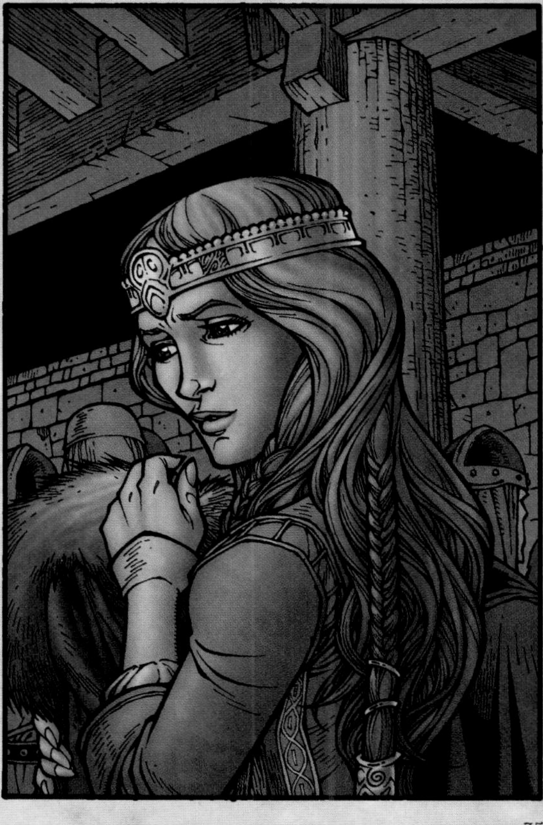

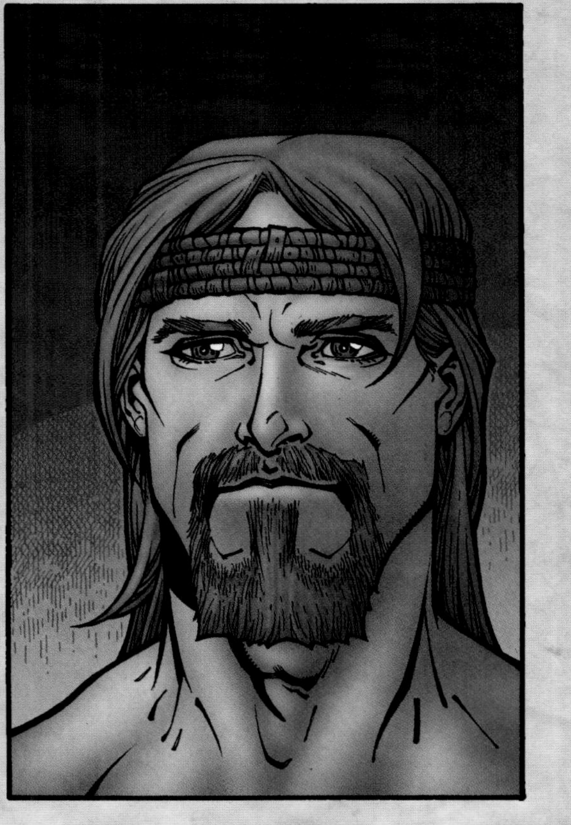

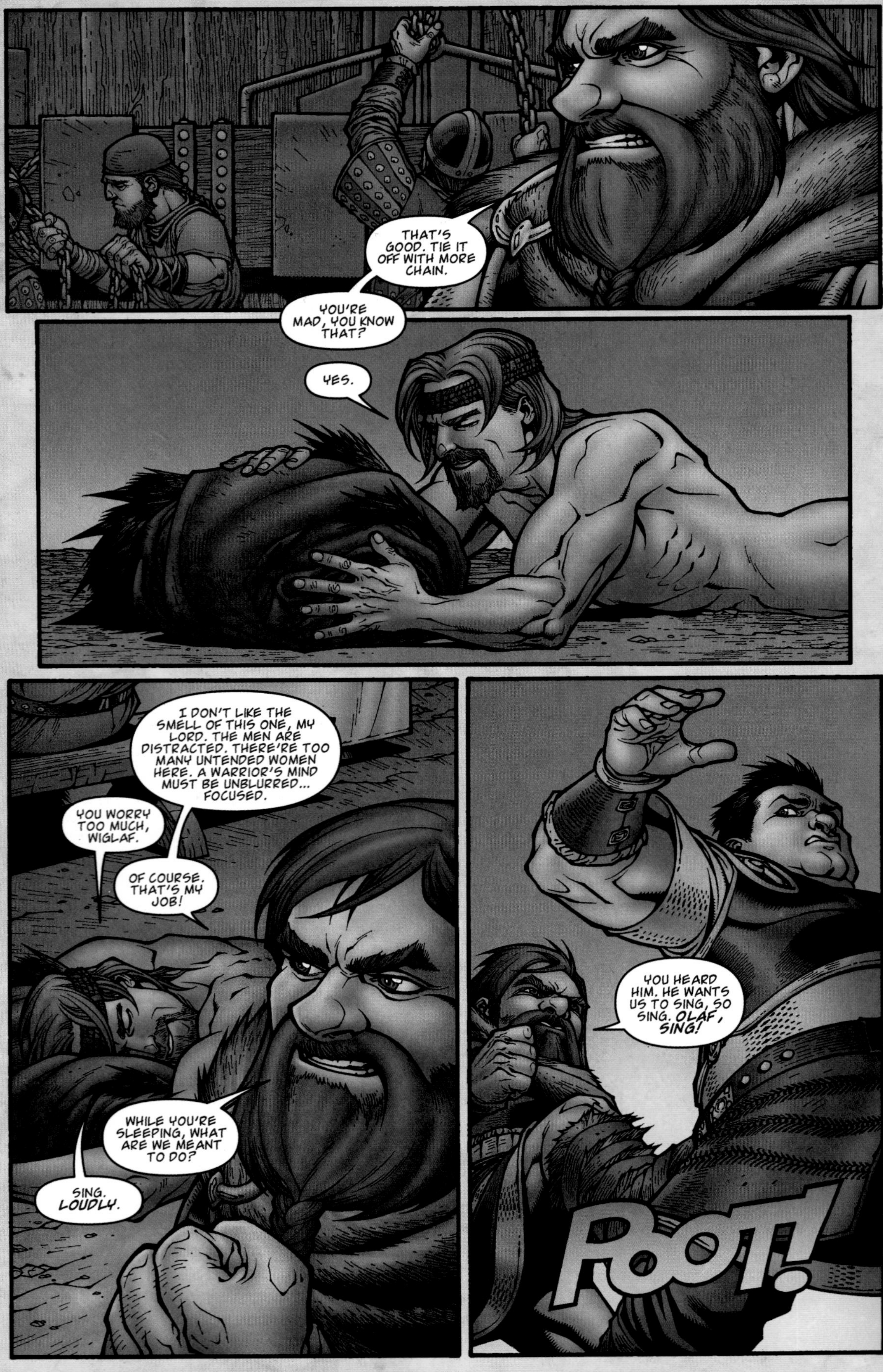
THAT'S GOOD. TIE IT OFF WITH MORE CHAIN.
YOU'RE MAD, YOU KNOW THAT?
YES.
I DON'T LIKE THE SMELL OF THIS ONE, MY LORD. THE MEN ARE DISTRACTED. THERE'RE TOO MANY UNTENDED WOMEN HERE. A WARRIOR'S MIND MUST BE UNBLURRED... FOCUSED.
YOU WORRY TOO MUCH, WIGLAF.
OF COURSE. THAT'S MY JOB!
WHILE YOU'RE SLEEPING, WHAT ARE WE MEANT TO DO?
SING. LOUDLY.
YOU HEARD HIM. HE WANTS US TO SING, SO SING. OLAF, SING!
POOT!

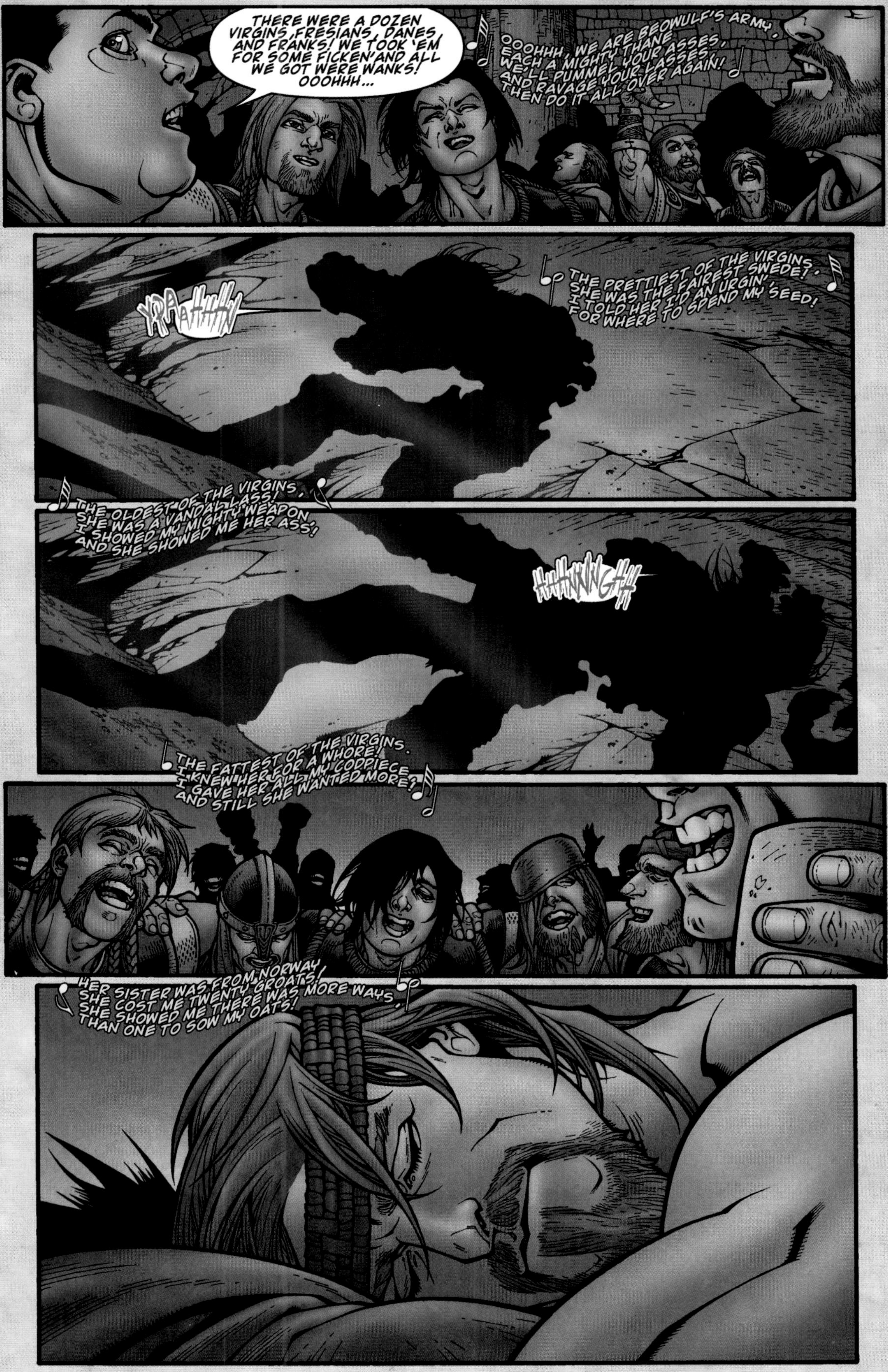
THERE WERE A DOZEN VIRGINS, FRESIANS, DANES AND FRANKS! WE TOOK 'EM FOR SOME FICKEN' AND ALL WE GOT WERE WANKS! OOOHHH...
OOOHHH, WE ARE BEOWULF'S ARMY, EACH A MIGHTY THANE. WE'LL PUMMEL YOUR ASSES, AND RAVAGE YOUR LASSES, THEN DO IT ALL OVER AGAIN!
YRAAHHH
THE PRETTIEST OF THE VIRGINS, SHE WAS THE FAIREST SWEDE! I TOLD HER I'D AN URGIN', FOR WHERE TO SPEND MY SEED!
THE OLDEST OF THE VIRGINS, SHE WAS A VANDAL LASS! I SHOWED MY MIGHTY WEAPON AND SHE SHOWED ME HER ASS!
HHHNNNGHH
THE FATTEST OF THE VIRGINS. I KNEW HER FOR A WHORE! I GAVE HER ALL MY CODPIECE AND STILL SHE WANTED MORE!
HER SISTER WAS FROM NORWAY SHE COST ME TWENTY GROATS! SHE SHOWED ME THERE WAS MORE WAYS THAN ONE TO SOW MY OATS!

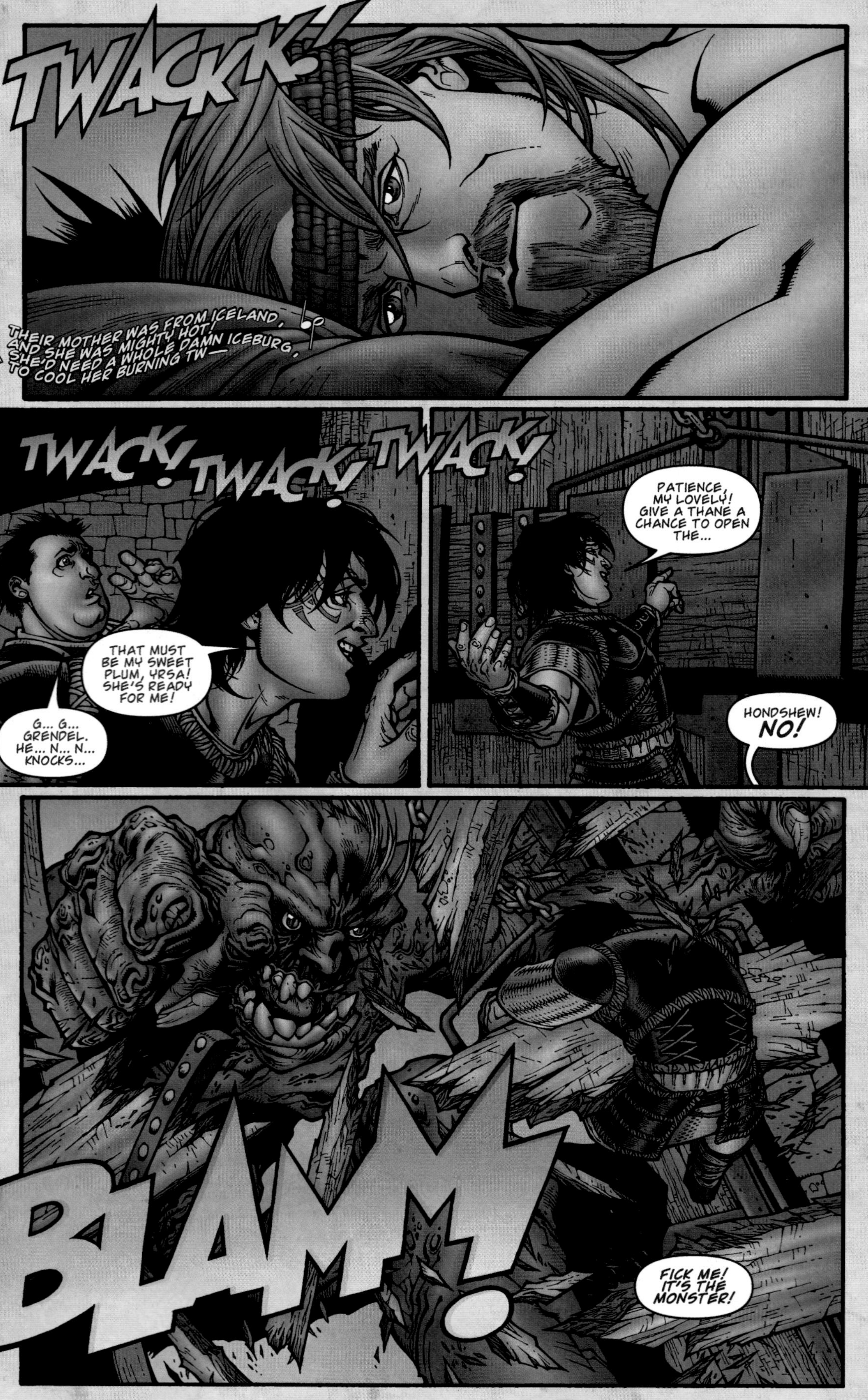
TWACKK!
THEIR MOTHER WAS FROM ICELAND, AND SHE WAS MIGHTY HOT! SHE'D NEED A WHOLE DAMN ICEBURG, TO COOL HER BURNING TW—
TWACK! TWACK! TWACK!
THAT MUST BE MY SWEET PLUM, YRSA! SHE'S READY FOR ME!
G... G... GRENDEL. HE... N... N... KNOCKS...
PATIENCE, MY LOVELY! GIVE A THANE A CHANCE TO OPEN THE...
HONDSHEW! NO!
BLAM!
FICK ME! IT'S THE MONSTER!

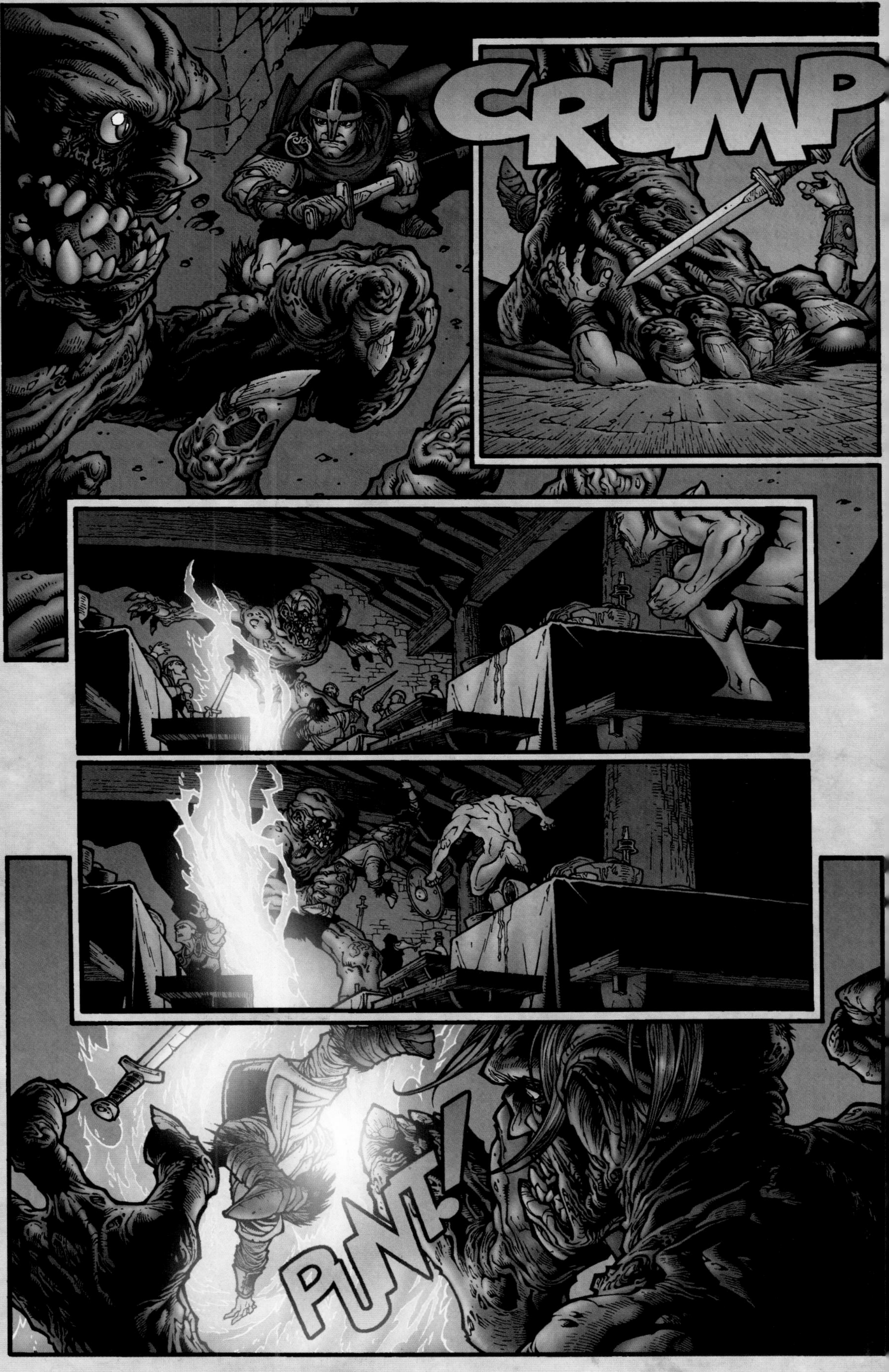
CRUMP
PUNT!

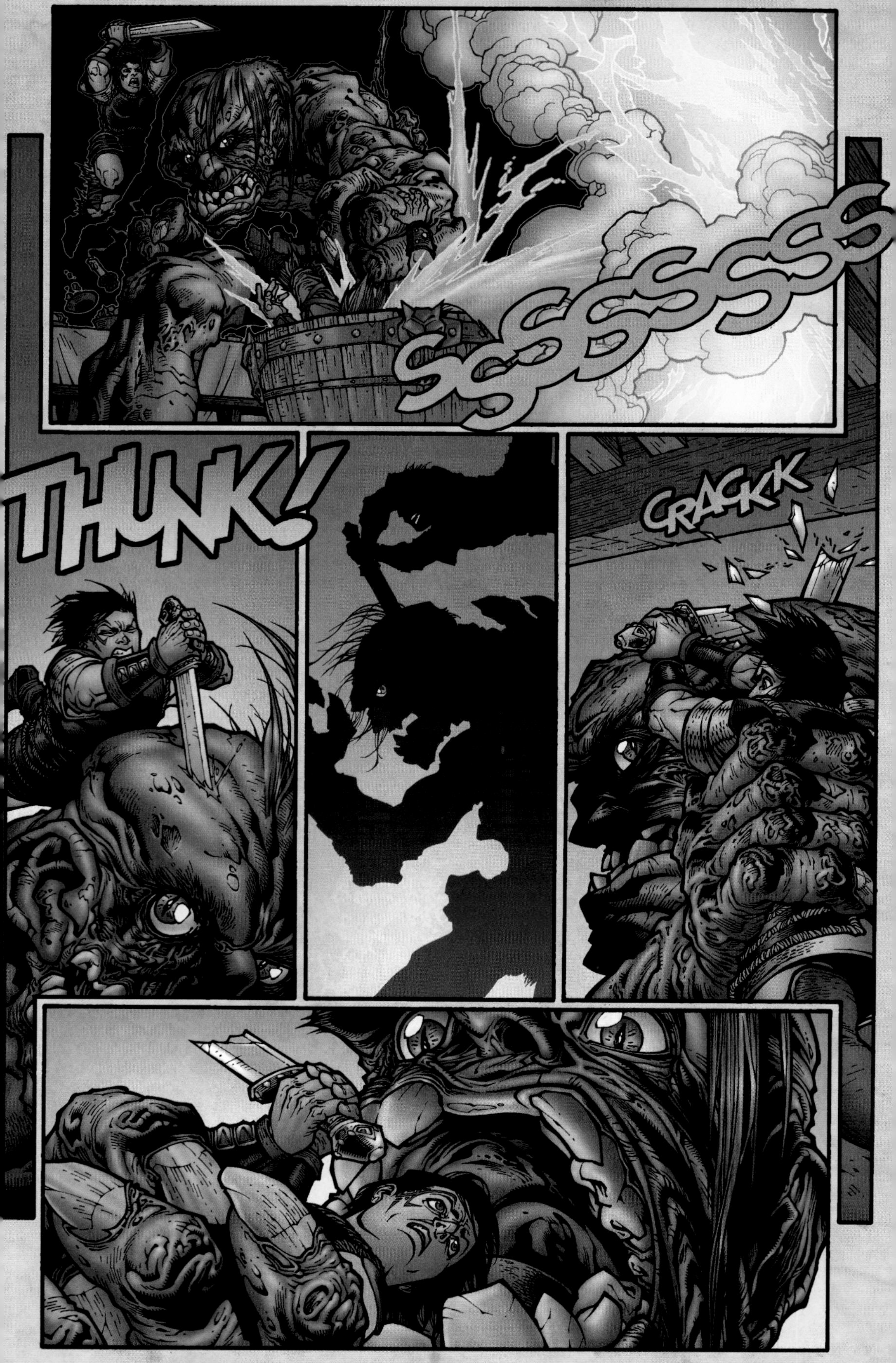
SSSSSSSSS
THUNK!
CRACKK

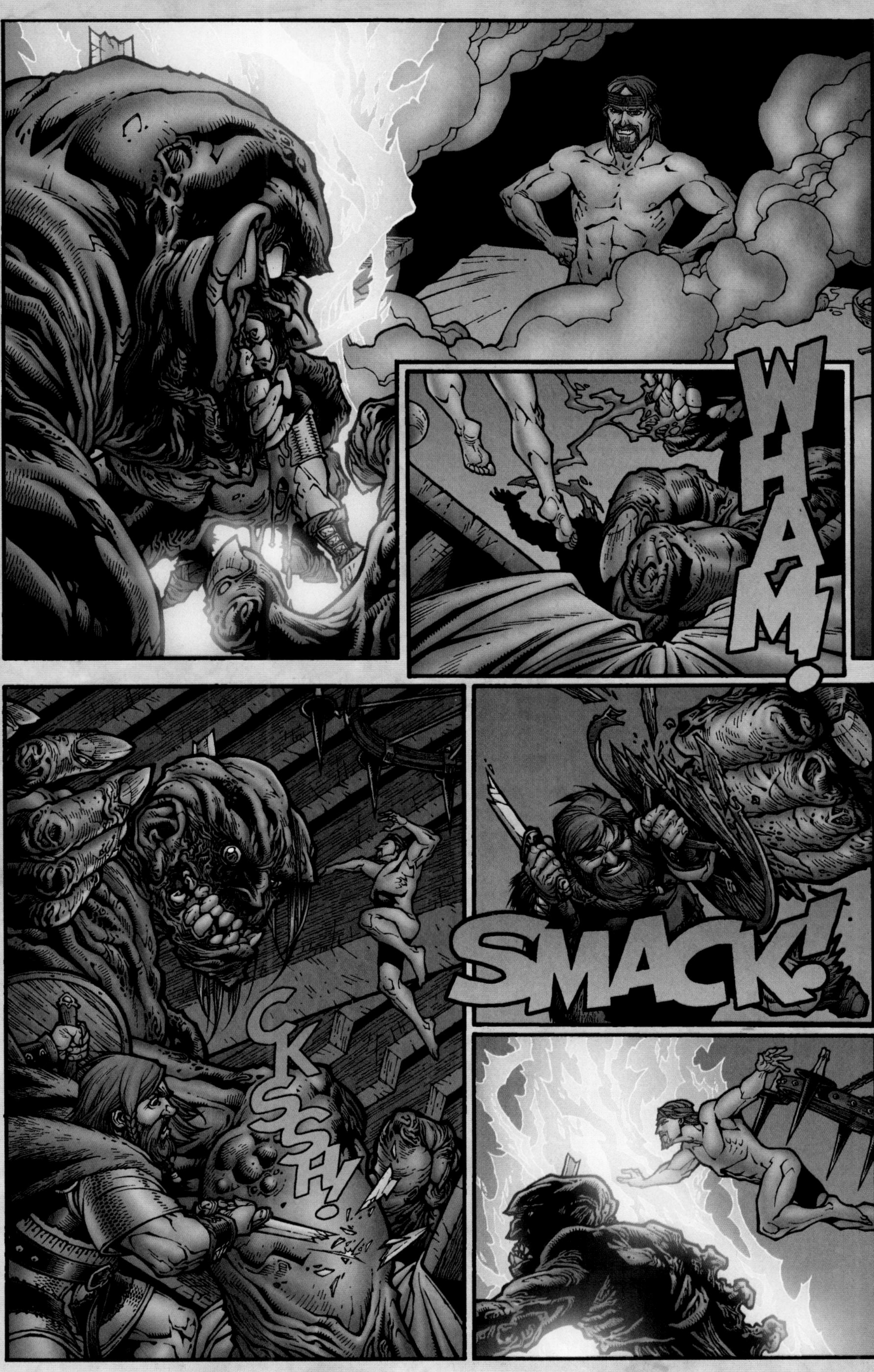
WHAM!
SMACK!
CKSSH!

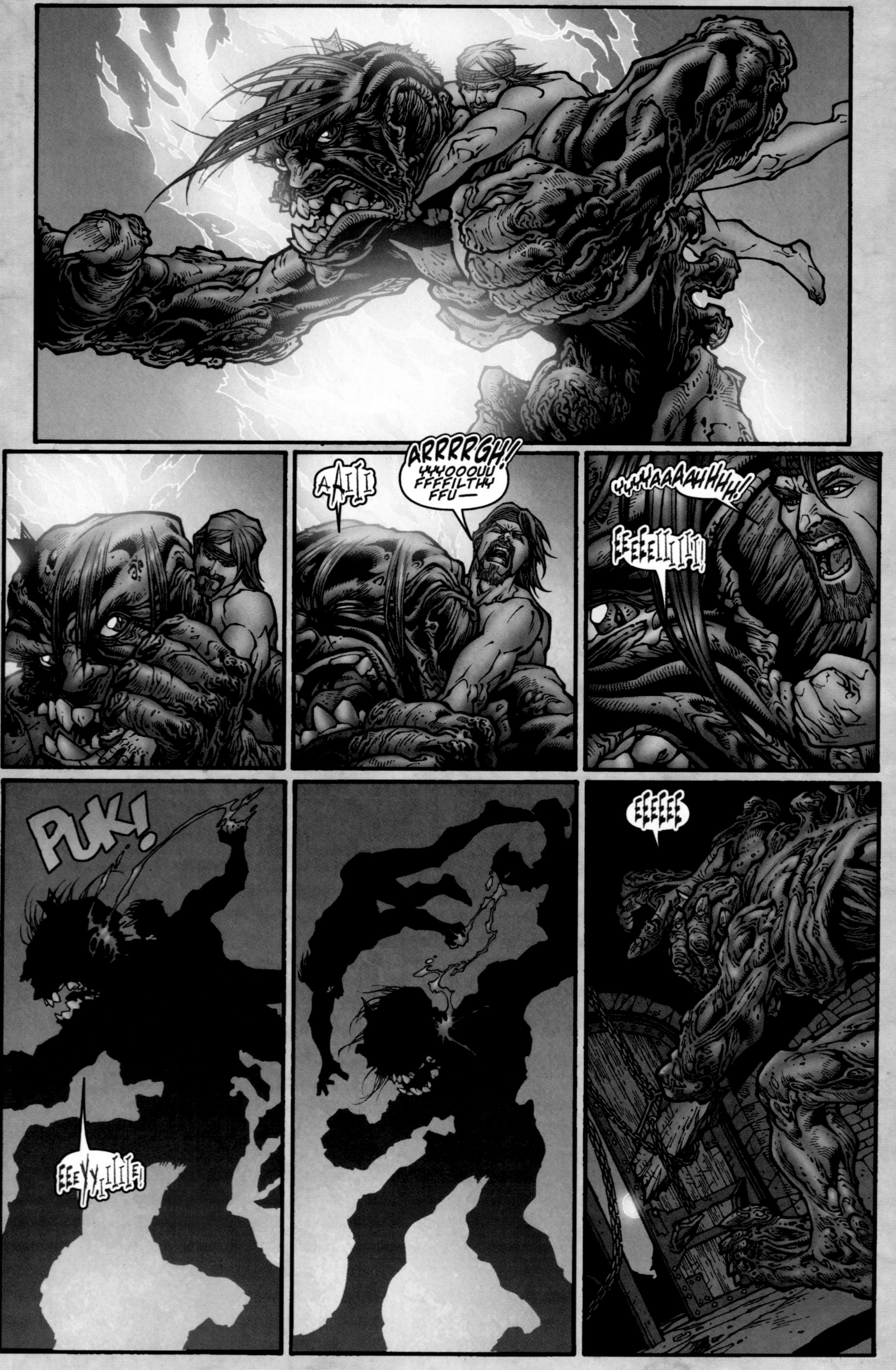
AAIII
ARRRRGH! YYYOOOUU FFFFILTHY FFU—
YYHAAAAAHHHH!
EEEEEIIIIH!
PUK!
EEEYYIIIIIE!
EEEEE

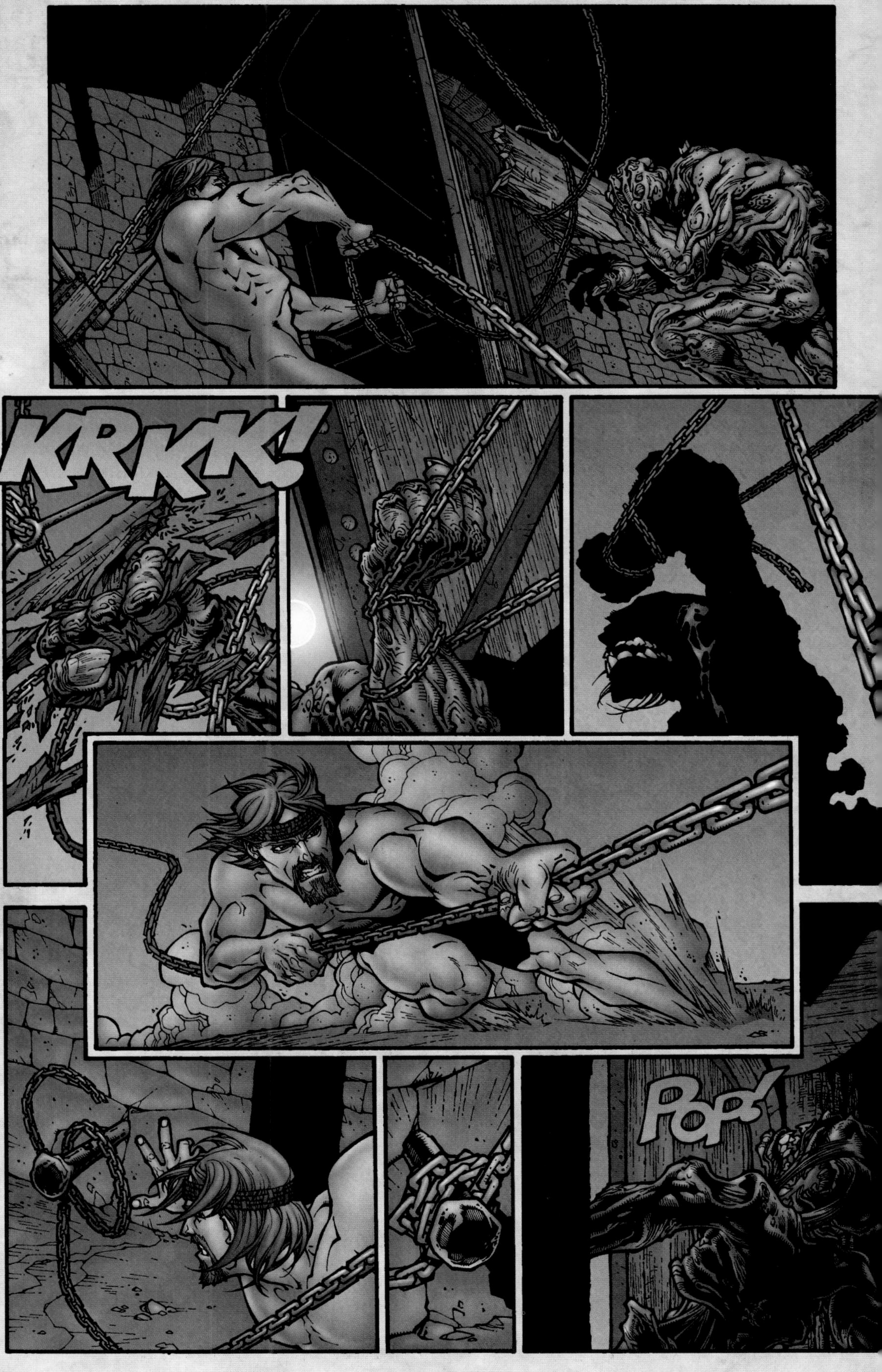
KRKK!
POP!

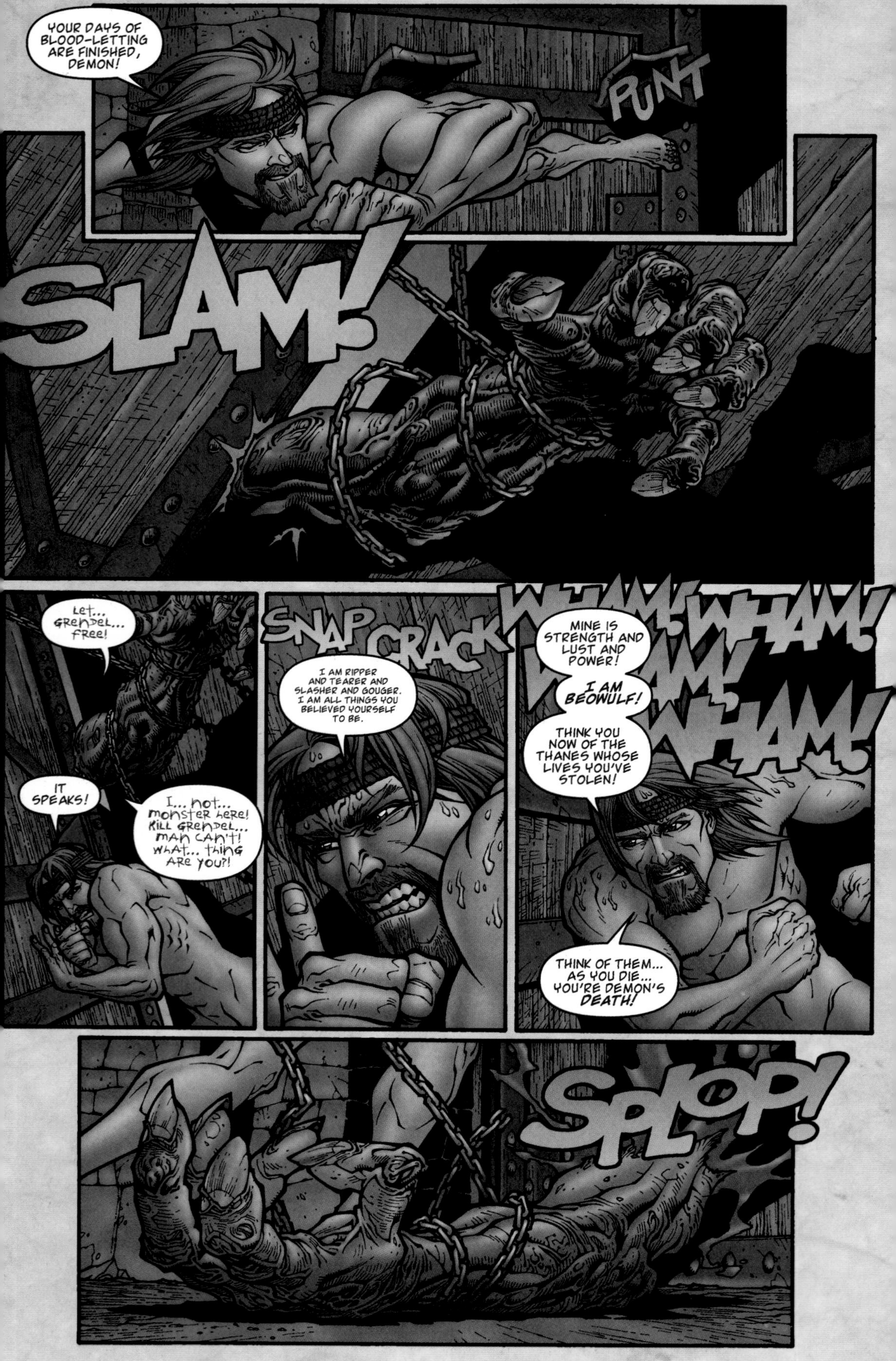
YOUR DAYS OF BLOOD-LETTING ARE FINISHED, DEMON!
PUNT
SLAM!
Let... Grendel... free!
IT SPEAKS!
I... not... monster here! Kill Grendel... man can't! What... thing are you?!
SNAP
CRACK
I AM RIPPER AND TEARER AND SLASHER AND GOUGER. I AM ALL THINGS YOU BELIEVED YOURSELF TO BE.
WHAM! WHAM!
WHAM!
WHAM!
MINE IS STRENGTH AND LUST AND POWER!
I AM BEOWULF!
THINK YOU NOW OF THE THANES WHOSE LIVES YOU'VE STOLEN!
THINK OF THEM... AS YOU DIE... YOU'RE DEMON'S DEATH!
SPLOP!

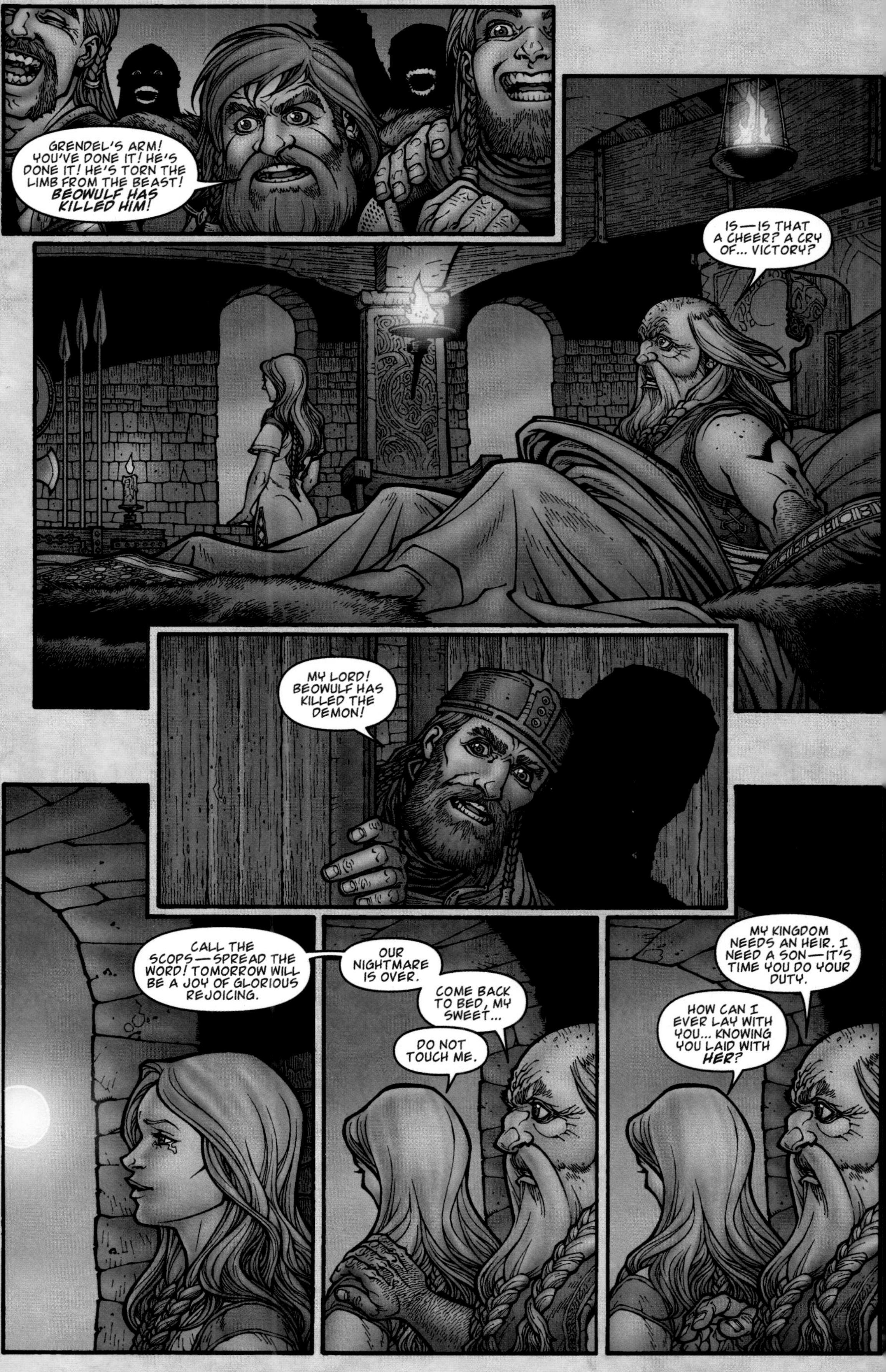
GRENDEL'S ARM! YOU'VE DONE IT! HE'S DONE IT! HE'S TORN THE LIMB FROM THE BEAST! BEOWULF HAS KILLED HIM!
IS—IS THAT A CHEER? A CRY OF... VICTORY?
MY LORD! BEOWULF HAS KILLED THE DEMON!
CALL THE SCOPS—SPREAD THE WORD! TOMORROW WILL BE A JOY OF GLORIOUS REJOICING.
OUR NIGHTMARE IS OVER.
COME BACK TO BED, MY SWEET...
DO NOT TOUCH ME.
MY KINGDOM NEEDS AN HEIR. I NEED A SON—IT'S TIME YOU DO YOUR DUTY.
HOW CAN I EVER LAY WITH YOU... KNOWING YOU LAID WITH HER?

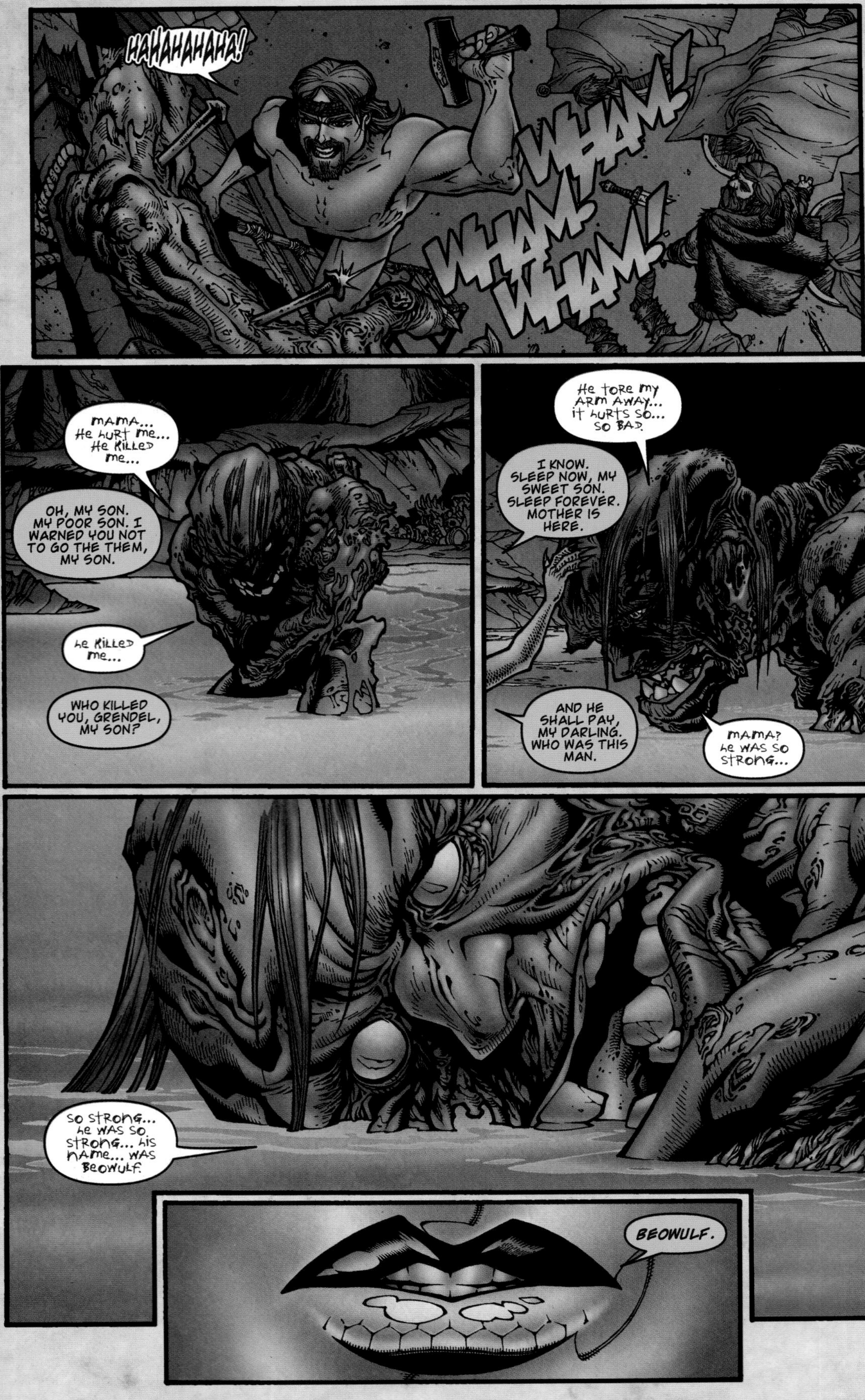
HAHAHAHAHA!
WHAM! WHAM! WHAM!
MAMA... HE HURT ME... HE KILLED ME...
OH, MY SON. MY POOR SON. I WARNED YOU NOT TO GO THE THEM, MY SON.
HE KILLED ME...
WHO KILLED YOU, GRENDEL, MY SON?
HE TORE MY ARM AWAY... IT HURTS SO... SO BAD.
I KNOW. SLEEP NOW, MY SWEET SON. SLEEP FOREVER. MOTHER IS HERE.
AND HE SHALL PAY, MY DARLING. WHO WAS THIS MAN.
MAMA? HE WAS SO STRONG...
SO STRONG... HE WAS SO STRONG... HIS NAME... WAS BEOWULF.
BEOWULF.

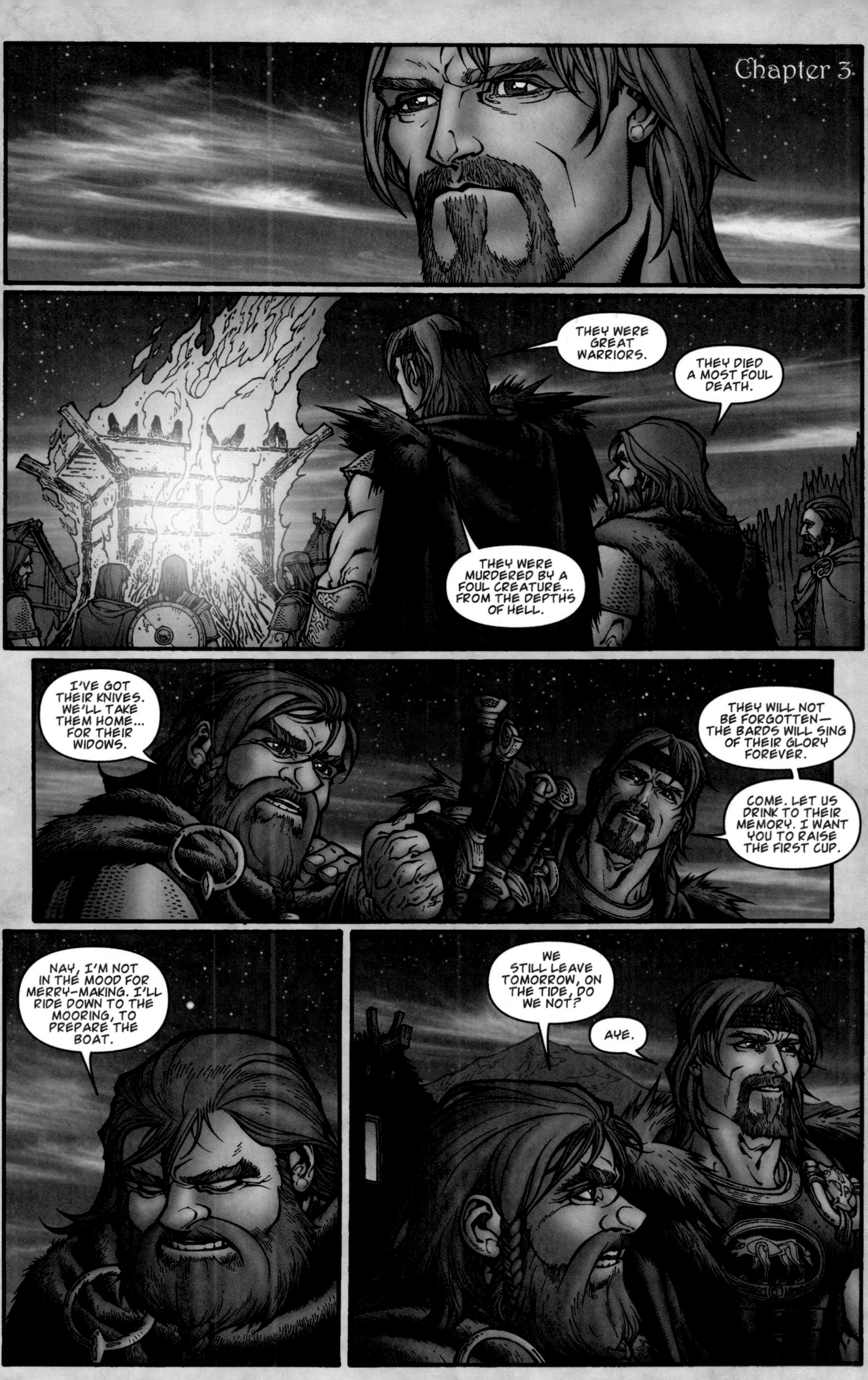
Chapter 3
THEY WERE GREAT WARRIORS.
THEY DIED A MOST FOUL DEATH.
THEY WERE MURDERED BY A FOUL CREATURE... FROM THE DEPTHS OF HELL.
I'VE GOT THEIR KNIVES. WE'LL TAKE THEM HOME... FOR THEIR WIDOWS.
THEY WILL NOT BE FORGOTTEN— THE BARDS WILL SING OF THEIR GLORY FOREVER.
COME. LET US DRINK TO THEIR MEMORY. I WANT YOU TO RAISE THE FIRST CUP.
NAY, I'M NOT IN THE MOOD FOR MERRY-MAKING. I'LL RIDE DOWN TO THE MOORING, TO PREPARE THE BOAT.
WE STILL LEAVE TOMORROW, ON THE TIDE, DO WE NOT?
AYE.

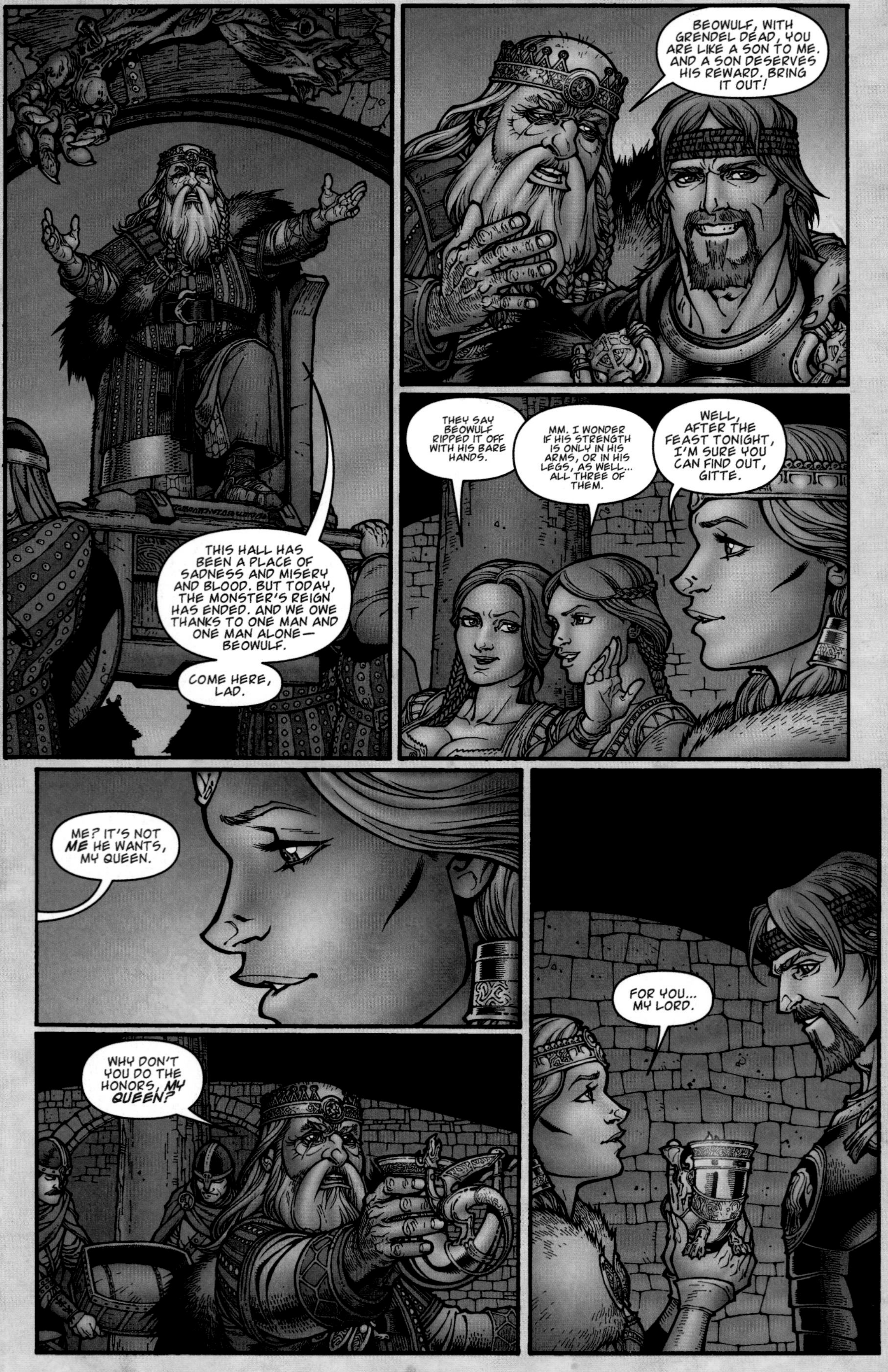
THIS HALL HAS BEEN A PLACE OF SADNESS AND MISERY AND BLOOD. BUT TODAY, THE MONSTER'S REIGN HAS ENDED. AND WE OWE THANKS TO ONE MAN AND ONE MAN ALONE— BEOWULF.
COME HERE, LAD.
BEOWULF, WITH GRENDEL DEAD, YOU ARE LIKE A SON TO ME. AND A SON DESERVES HIS REWARD. BRING IT OUT!
THEY SAY BEOWULF RIPPED IT OFF WITH HIS BARE HANDS.
MM. I WONDER IF HIS STRENGTH IS ONLY IN HIS ARMS, OR IN HIS LEGS, AS WELL... ALL THREE OF THEM.
WELL, AFTER THE FEAST TONIGHT, I'M SURE YOU CAN FIND OUT, GITTE.
ME? IT'S NOT ME HE WANTS, MY QUEEN.
WHY DON'T YOU DO THE HONORS, MY QUEEN?
FOR YOU... MY LORD.

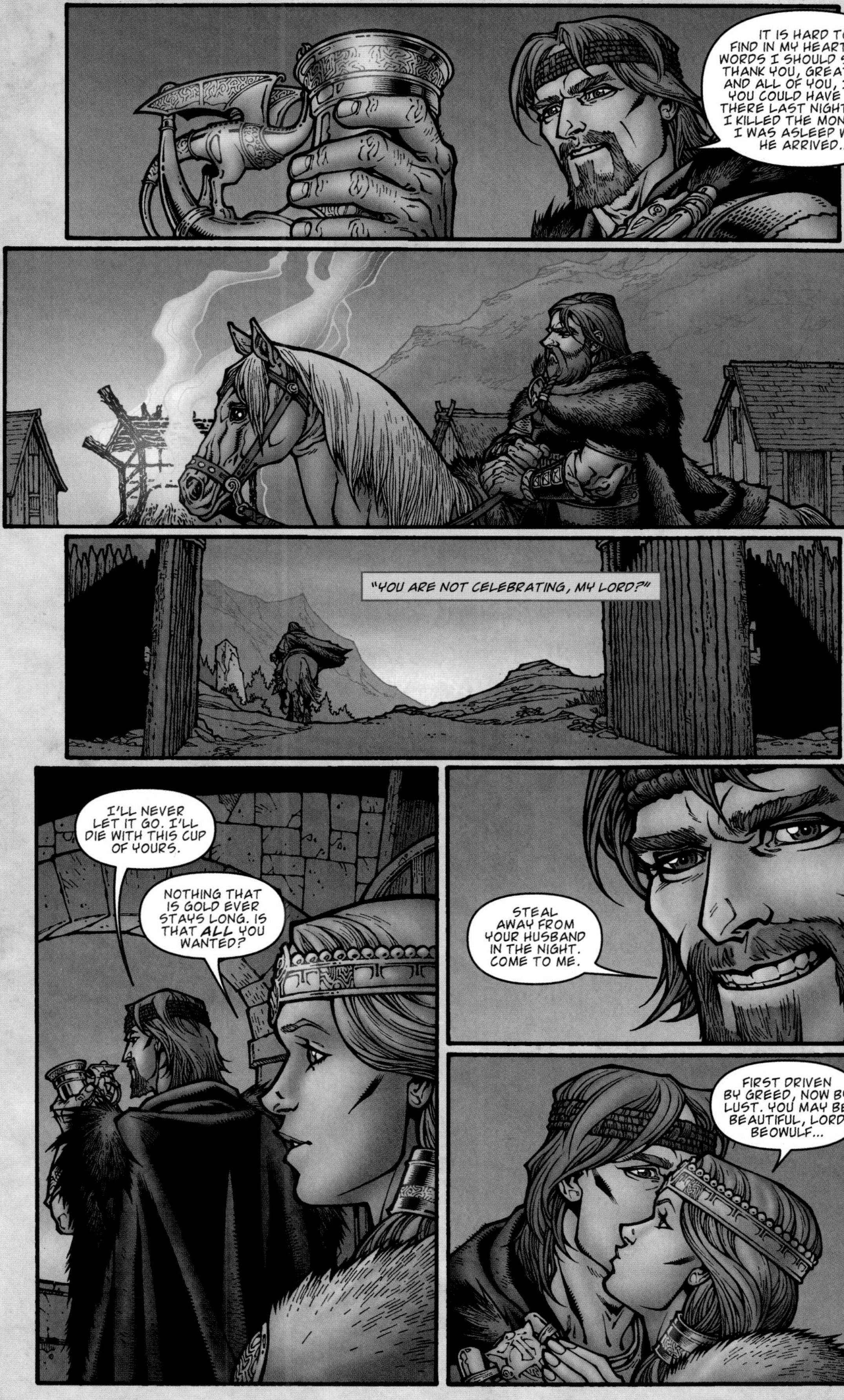
IT IS HARD TO FIND IN MY HEART THE WORDS I SHOULD SAY TO THANK YOU, GREAT KING. AND ALL OF YOU, I WISH YOU COULD HAVE BEEN THERE LAST NIGHT WHEN I KILLED THE MONSTER. I WAS ASLEEP WHEN HE ARRIVED...
"YOU ARE NOT CELEBRATING, MY LORD?"
I'LL NEVER LET IT GO. I'LL DIE WITH THIS CUP OF YOURS.
NOTHING THAT IS GOLD EVER STAYS LONG. IS THAT ALL YOU WANTED?
STEAL AWAY FROM YOUR HUSBAND IN THE NIGHT. COME TO ME.
FIRST DRIVEN BY GREED, NOW BY LUST. YOU MAY BE BEAUTIFUL, LORD BEOWULF...

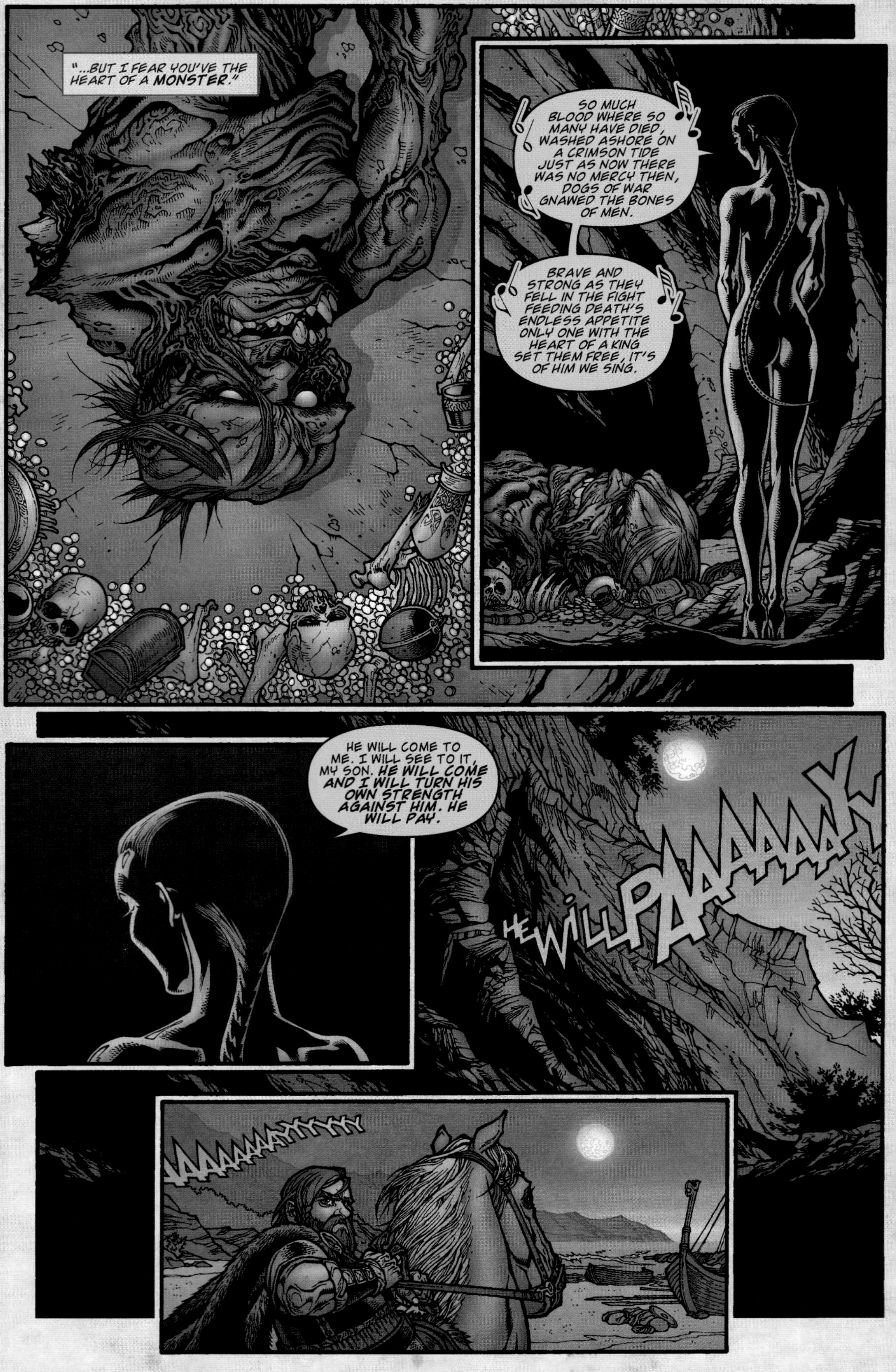

"...BUT I FEAR YOU'VE THE HEART OF A MONSTER."
SO MUCH BLOOD WHERE SO MANY HAVE DIED, WASHED ASHORE ON A CRIMSON TIDE JUST AS NOW THERE WAS NO MERCY THEN, DOGS OF WAR GNAWED THE BONES OF MEN.
BRAVE AND STRONG AS THEY FELL IN THE FIGHT FEEDING DEATH'S ENDLESS APPETITE ONLY ONE WITH THE HEART OF A KING SET THEM FREE, IT'S OF HIM WE SING.
HE WILL COME TO ME. I WILL SEE TO IT, MY SON. HE WILL COME AND I WILL TURN HIS OWN STRENGTH AGAINST HIM. HE WILL PAY.
HE WILL PAAAAAY
AAAAAAAYYYYYY

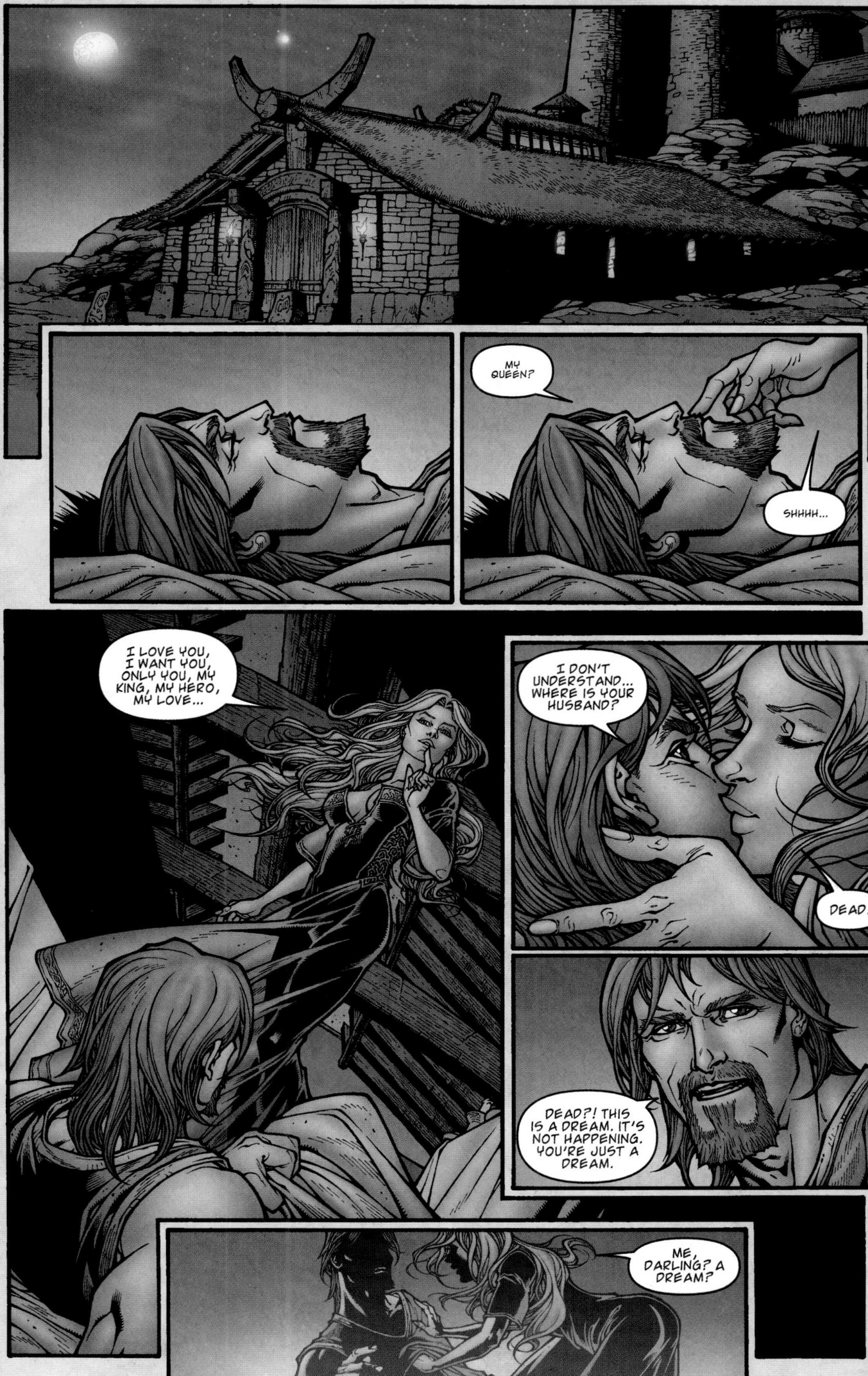
MY QUEEN?
SHHHH...
I LOVE YOU, I WANT YOU, ONLY YOU, MY KING, MY HERO, MY LOVE...
I DON'T UNDERSTAND... WHERE IS YOUR HUSBAND?
DEAD.
DEAD?! THIS IS A DREAM. IT'S NOT HAPPENING. YOU'RE JUST A DREAM.
ME, DARLING? A DREAM?

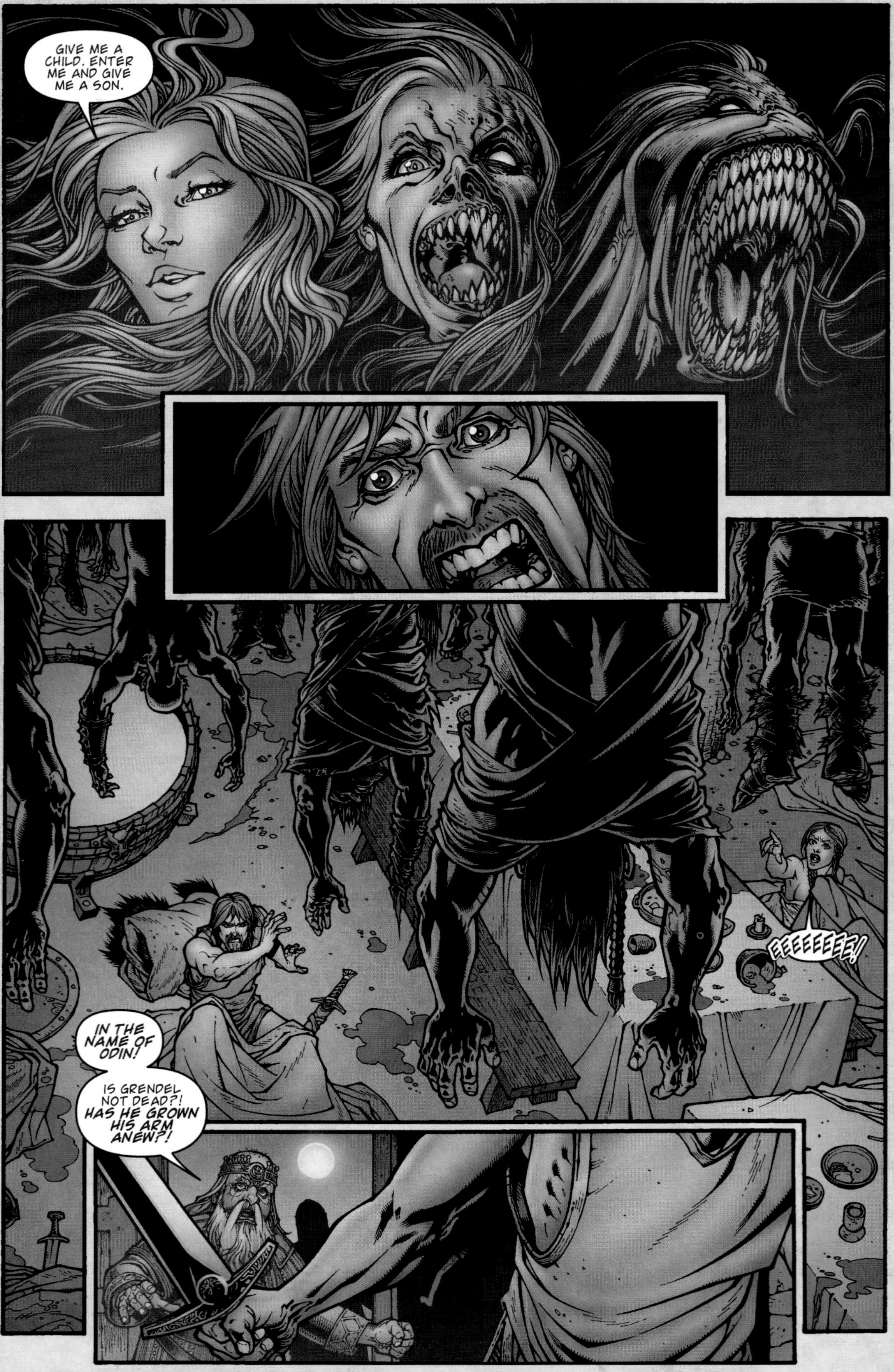
GIVE ME A CHILD. ENTER ME AND GIVE ME A SON.
EEEEEEEE!
IN THE NAME OF ODIN!
IS GRENDEL NOT DEAD?! HAS HE GROWN HIS ARM ANEW?!

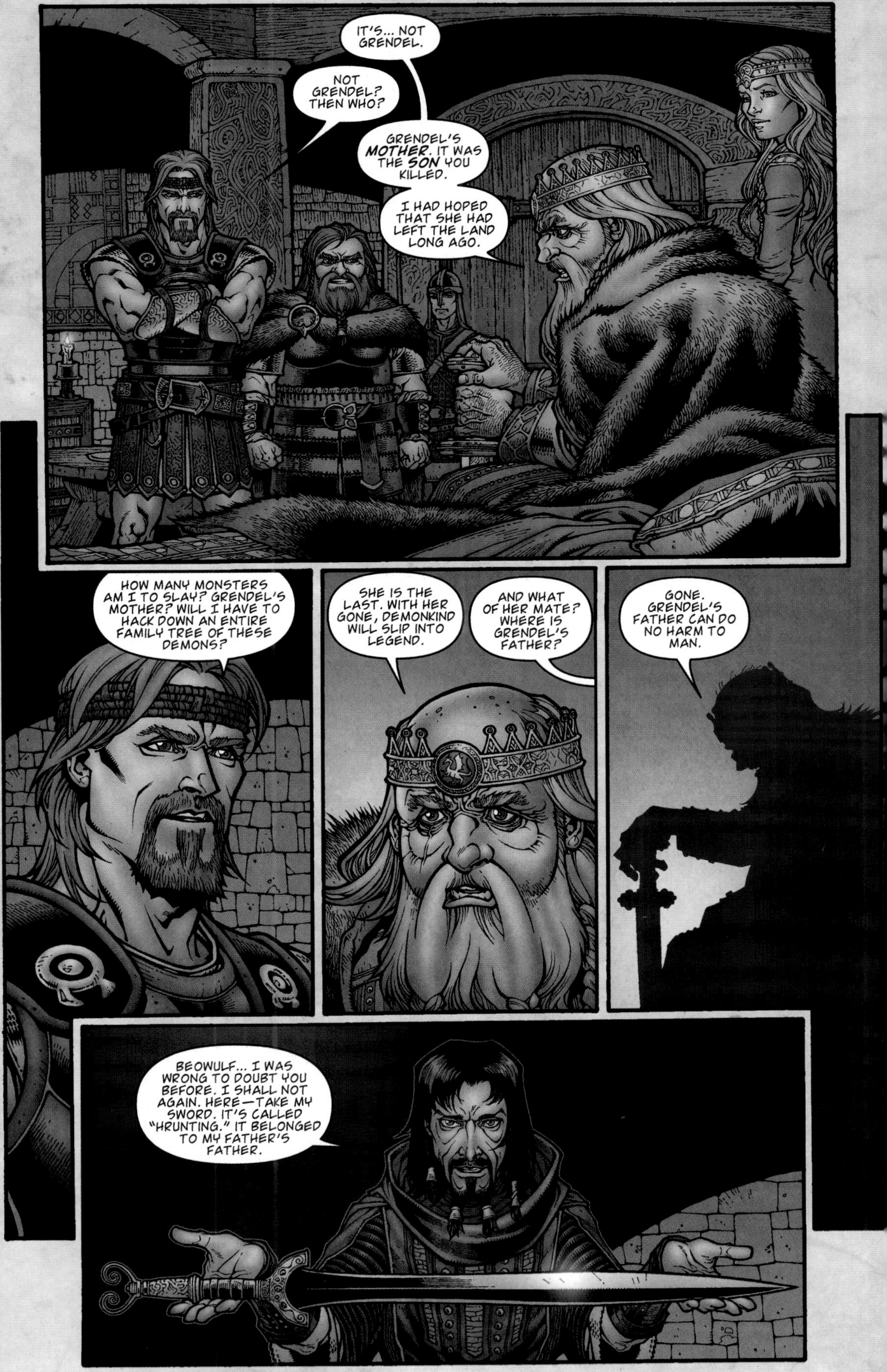

IT'S... NOT GRENDEL.
NOT GRENDEL? THEN WHO?
GRENDEL'S **MOTHER**. IT WAS THE **SON** YOU KILLED.
I HAD HOPED THAT SHE HAD LEFT THE LAND LONG AGO.
HOW MANY MONSTERS AM I TO SLAY? GRENDEL'S MOTHER? WILL I HAVE TO HACK DOWN AN ENTIRE FAMILY TREE OF THESE DEMONS?
SHE IS THE LAST. WITH HER GONE, DEMONKIND WILL SLIP INTO LEGEND.
AND WHAT OF HER MATE? WHERE IS GRENDEL'S FATHER?
GONE. GRENDEL'S FATHER CAN DO NO HARM TO MAN.
BEOWULF... I WAS WRONG TO DOUBT YOU BEFORE. I SHALL NOT AGAIN. HERE—TAKE MY SWORD. IT'S CALLED "HRUNTING." IT BELONGED TO MY FATHER'S FATHER.

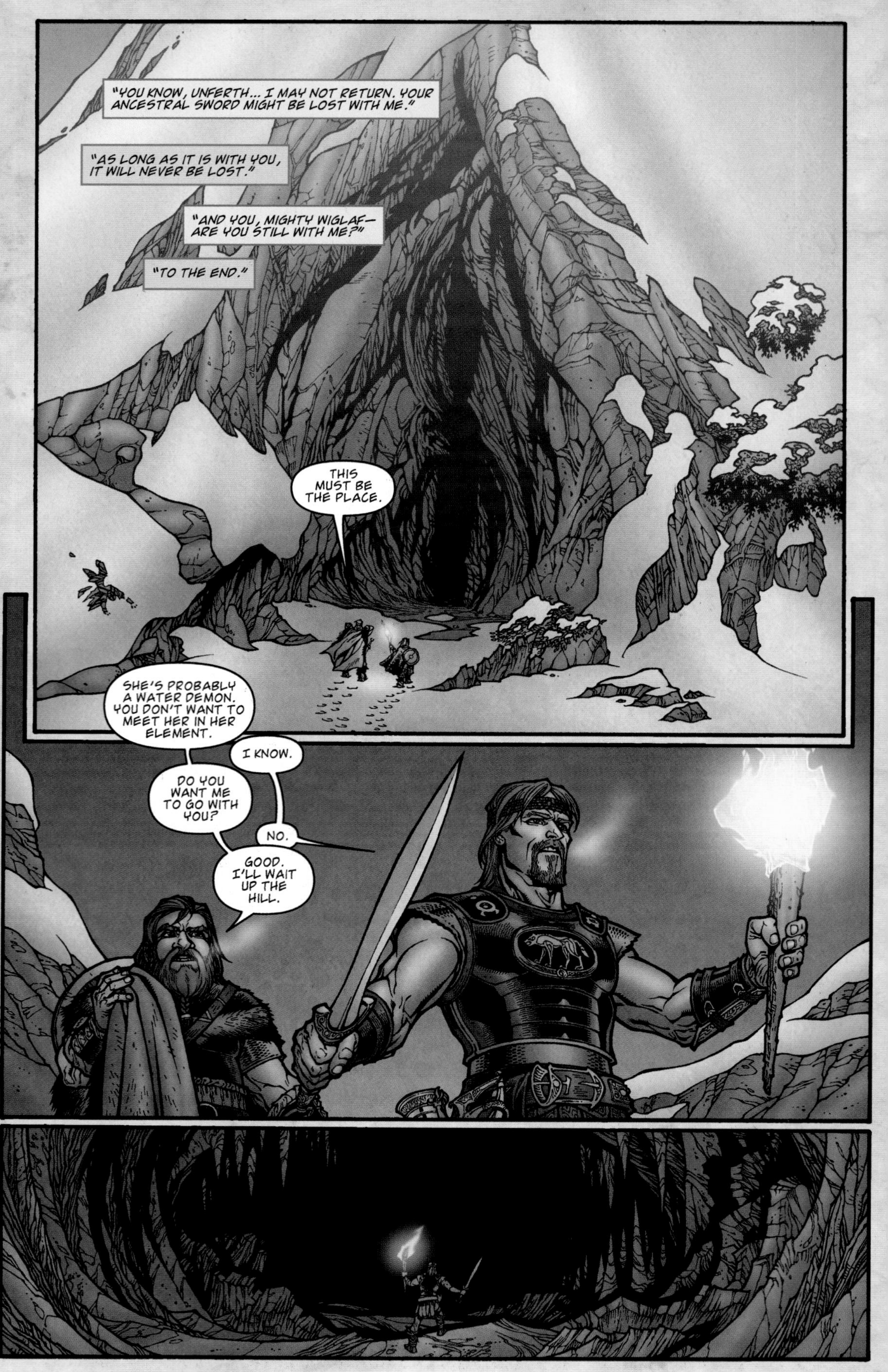

"YOU KNOW, UNFERTH... I MAY NOT RETURN. YOUR ANCESTRAL SWORD MIGHT BE LOST WITH ME."
"AS LONG AS IT IS WITH YOU, IT WILL NEVER BE LOST."
"AND YOU, MIGHTY WIGLAF— ARE YOU STILL WITH ME?"
"TO THE END."
THIS MUST BE THE PLACE.
SHE'S PROBABLY A WATER DEMON. YOU DON'T WANT TO MEET HER IN HER ELEMENT.
I KNOW.
DO YOU WANT ME TO GO WITH YOU?
NO.
GOOD. I'LL WAIT UP THE HILL.

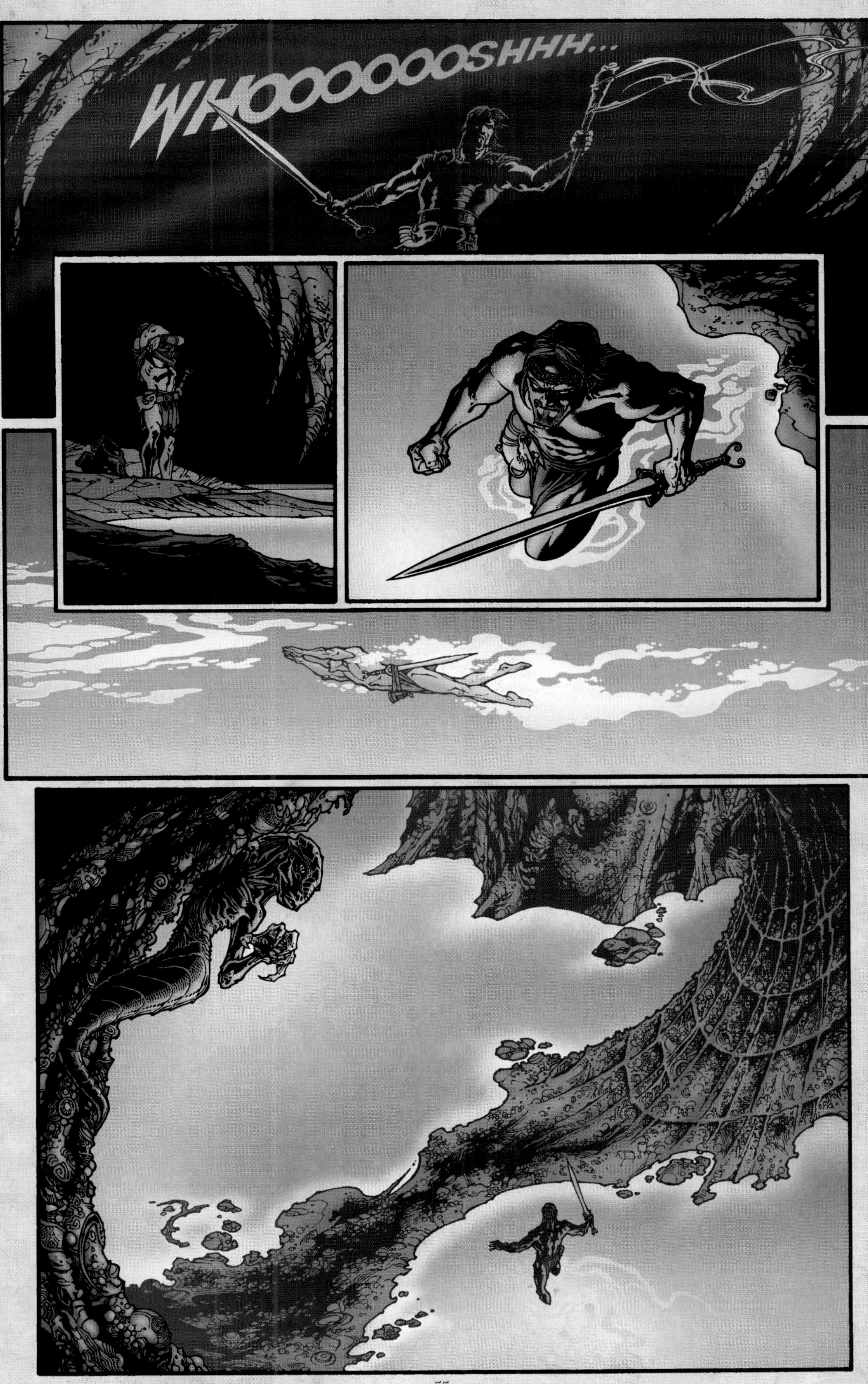
WHOOOOOOOSHHH...

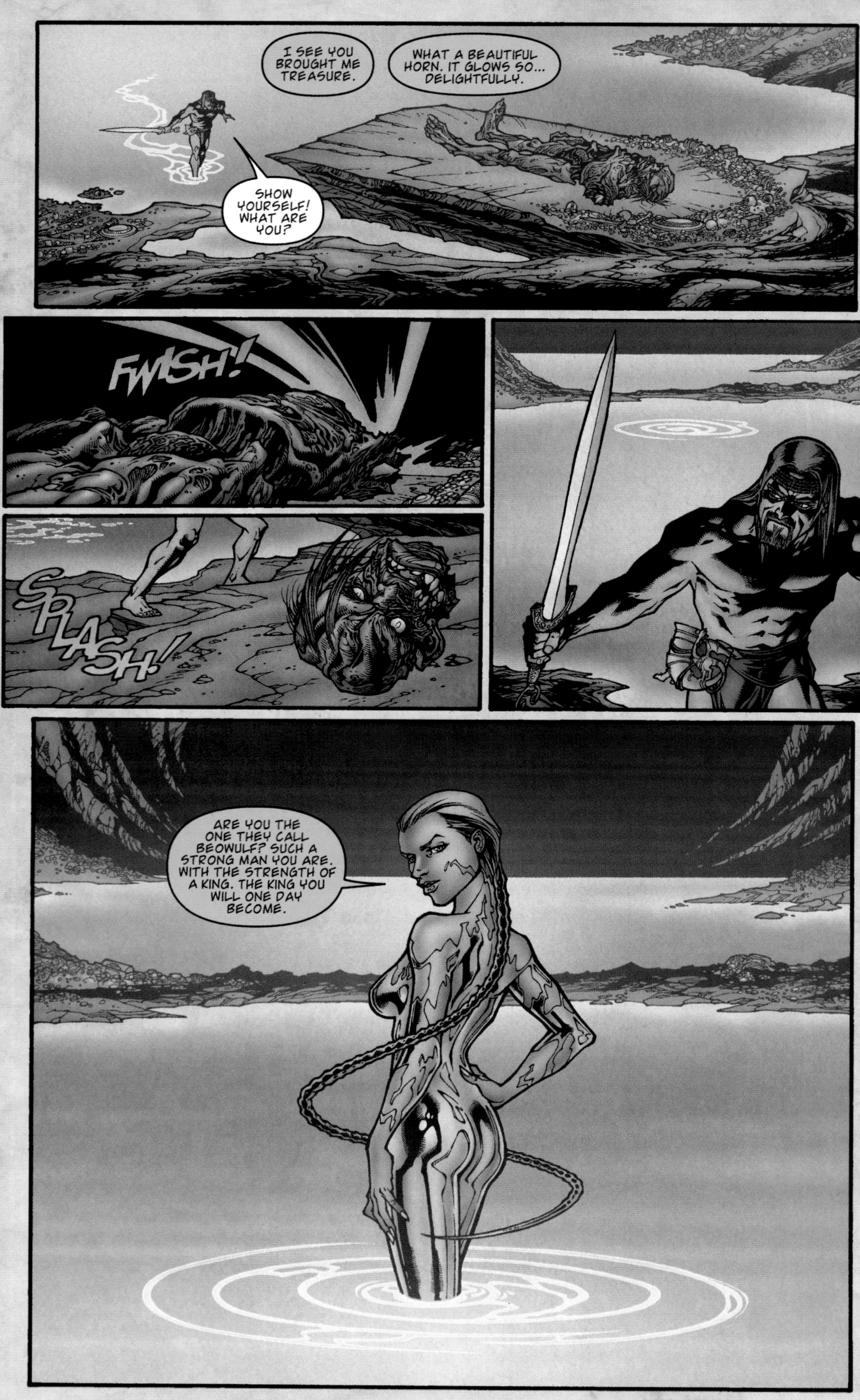
I SEE YOU BROUGHT ME TREASURE.
WHAT A BEAUTIFUL HORN. IT GLOWS SO... DELIGHTFULLY.
SHOW YOURSELF! WHAT ARE YOU?
FWISH!
SPLASH!
ARE YOU THE ONE THEY CALL BEOWULF? SUCH A STRONG MAN YOU ARE. WITH THE STRENGTH OF A KING. THE KING YOU WILL ONE DAY BECOME.

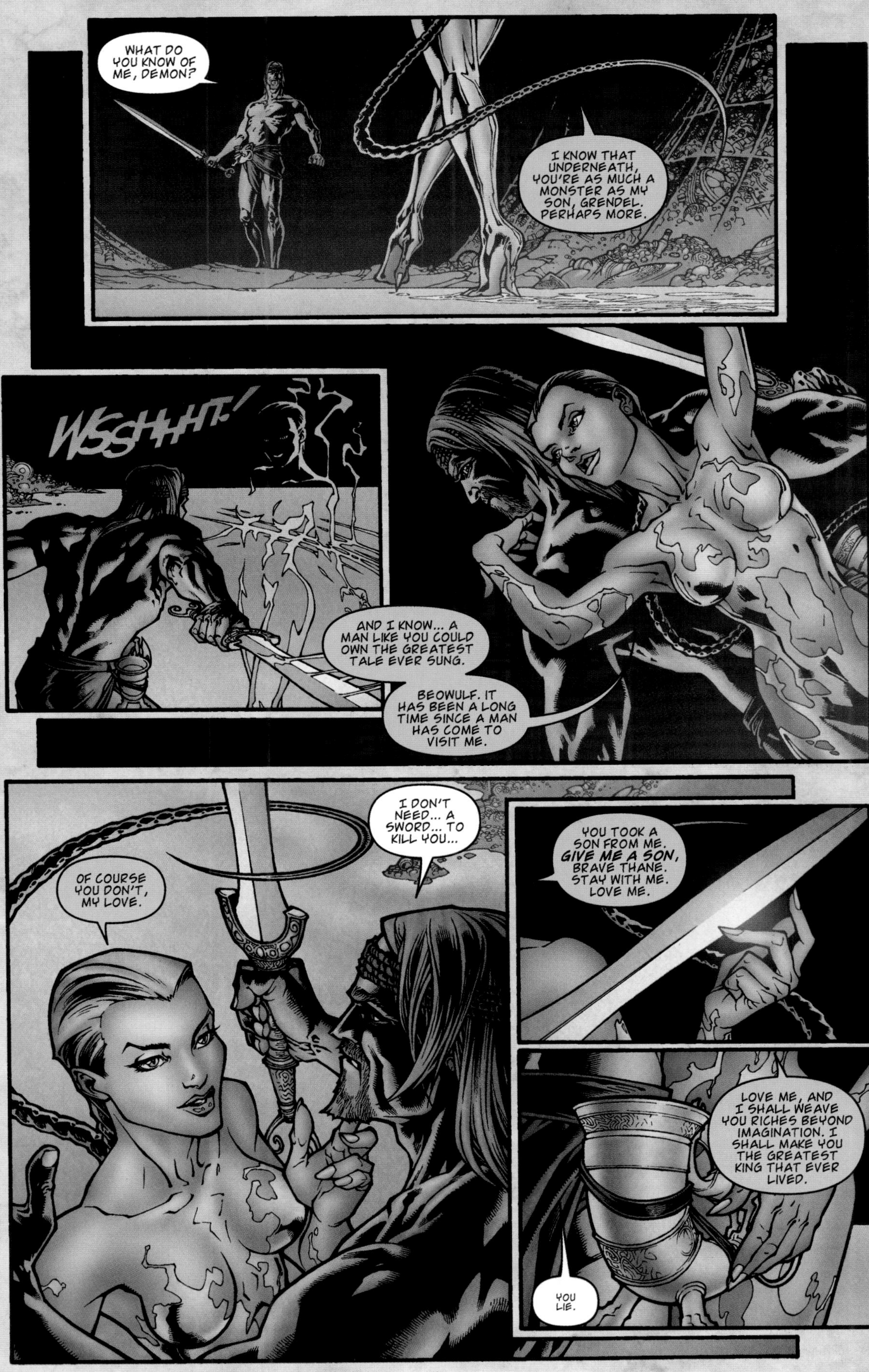
WHAT DO YOU KNOW OF ME, DEMON?
I KNOW THAT UNDERNEATH, YOU'RE AS MUCH A MONSTER AS MY SON, GRENDEL. PERHAPS MORE.
WSSHHHT!
AND I KNOW... A MAN LIKE YOU COULD OWN THE GREATEST TALE EVER SUNG.
BEOWULF. IT HAS BEEN A LONG TIME SINCE A MAN HAS COME TO VISIT ME.
I DON'T NEED... A SWORD... TO KILL YOU...
OF COURSE YOU DON'T, MY LOVE.
YOU TOOK A SON FROM ME. GIVE ME A SON, BRAVE THANE. STAY WITH ME. LOVE ME.
LOVE ME, AND I SHALL WEAVE YOU RICHES BEYOND IMAGINATION. I SHALL MAKE YOU THE GREATEST KING THAT EVER LIVED.
YOU LIE.

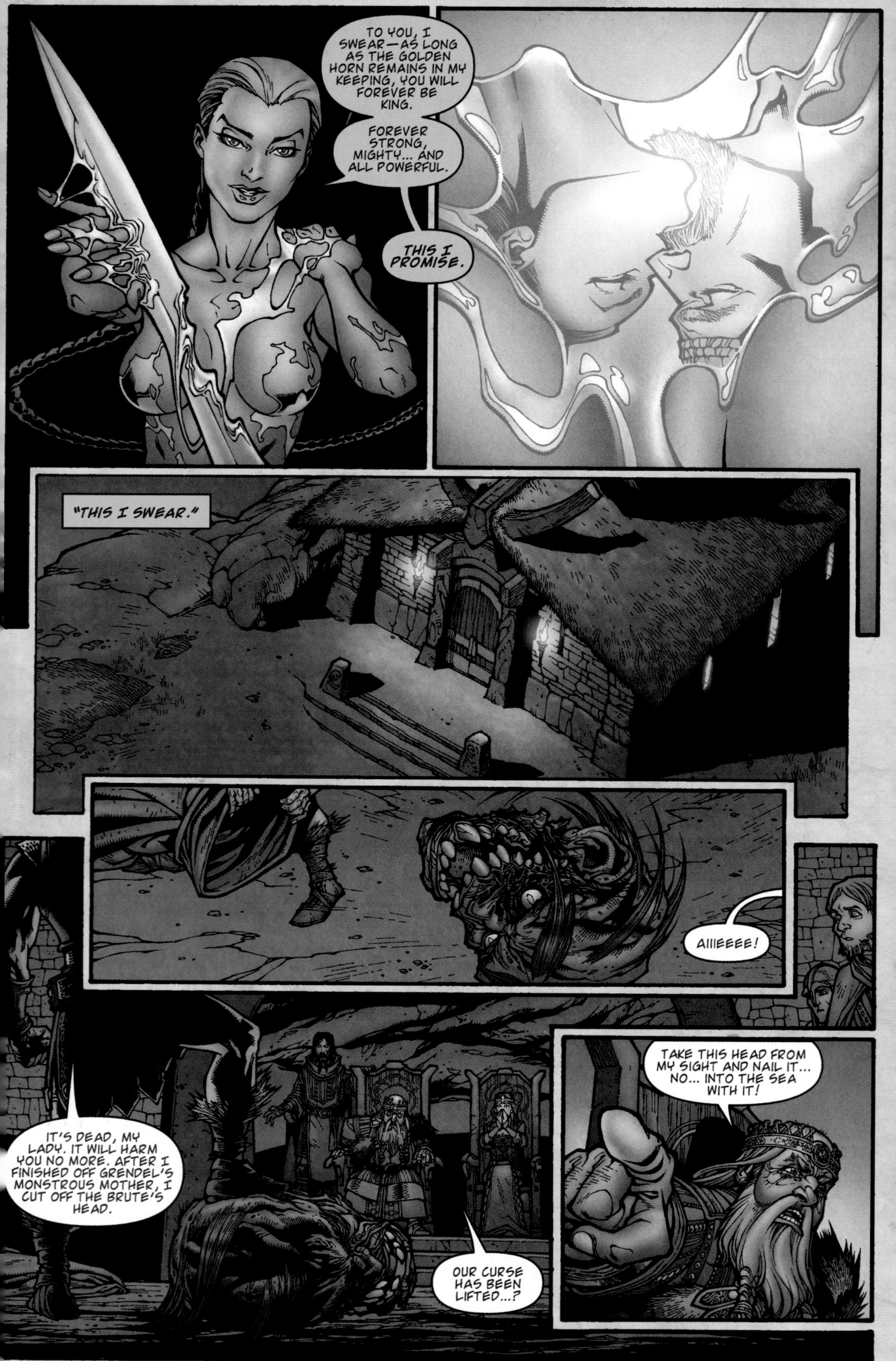
TO YOU, I SWEAR—AS LONG AS THE GOLDEN HORN REMAINS IN MY KEEPING, YOU WILL FOREVER BE KING.
FOREVER STRONG, MIGHTY... AND ALL POWERFUL.
THIS I PROMISE.
"THIS I SWEAR."
AIIIEEEE!
IT'S DEAD, MY LADY. IT WILL HARM YOU NO MORE. AFTER I FINISHED OFF GRENDEL'S MONSTROUS MOTHER, I CUT OFF THE BRUTE'S HEAD.
OUR CURSE HAS BEEN LIFTED...?
TAKE THIS HEAD FROM MY SIGHT AND NAIL IT... NO... INTO THE SEA WITH IT!

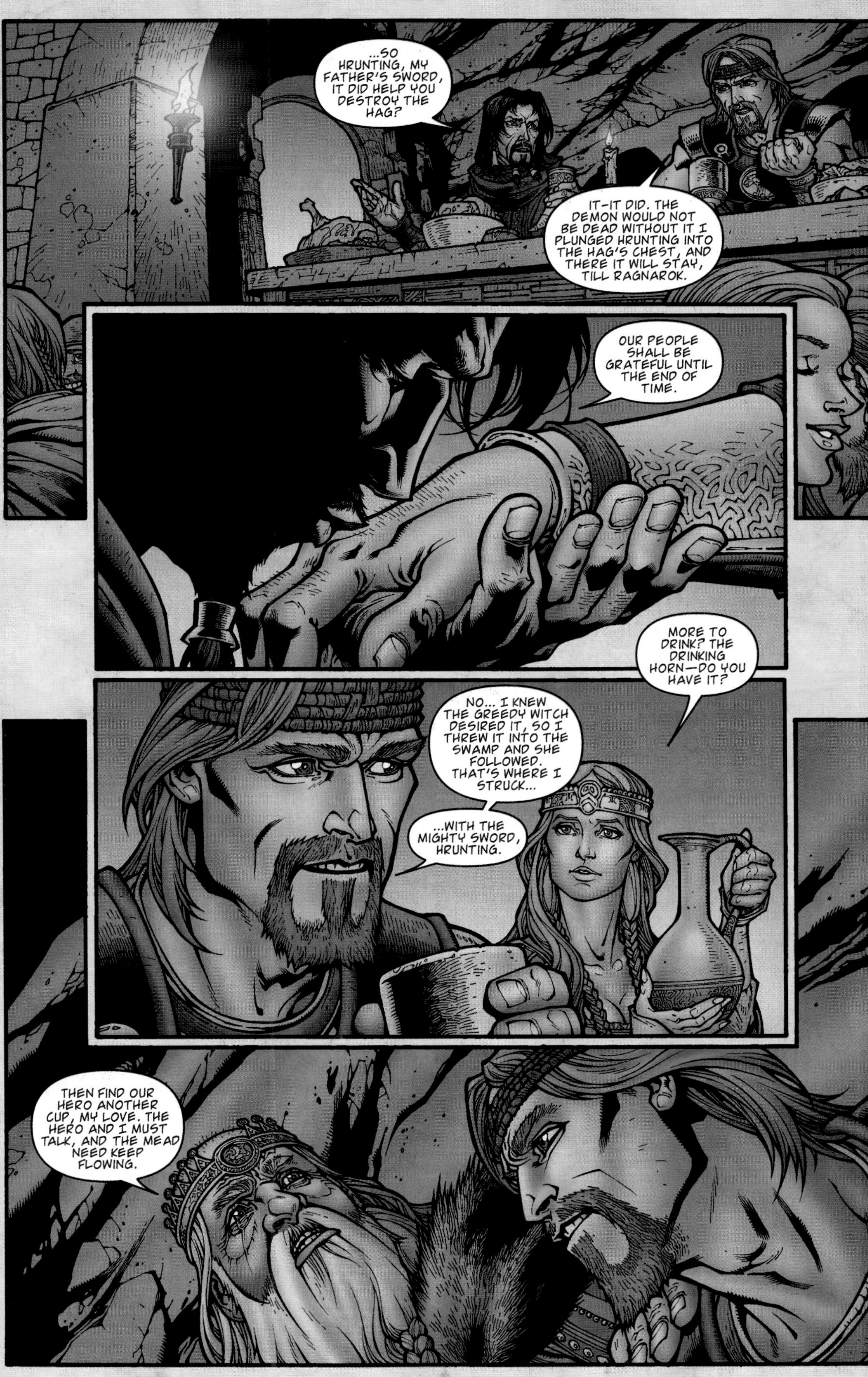
...SO HRUNTING, MY FATHER'S SWORD, IT DID HELP YOU DESTROY THE HAG?
IT-IT DID. THE DEMON WOULD NOT BE DEAD WITHOUT IT I PLUNGED HRUNTING INTO THE HAG'S CHEST, AND THERE IT WILL STAY, TILL RAGNAROK.
OUR PEOPLE SHALL BE GRATEFUL UNTIL THE END OF TIME.
MORE TO DRINK? THE DRINKING HORN—DO YOU HAVE IT?
NO... I KNEW THE GREEDY WITCH DESIRED IT, SO I THREW IT INTO THE SWAMP AND SHE FOLLOWED. THAT'S WHERE I STRUCK...
...WITH THE MIGHTY SWORD, HRUNTING.
THEN FIND OUR HERO ANOTHER CUP, MY LOVE. THE HERO AND I MUST TALK, AND THE MEAD NEED KEEP FLOWING.

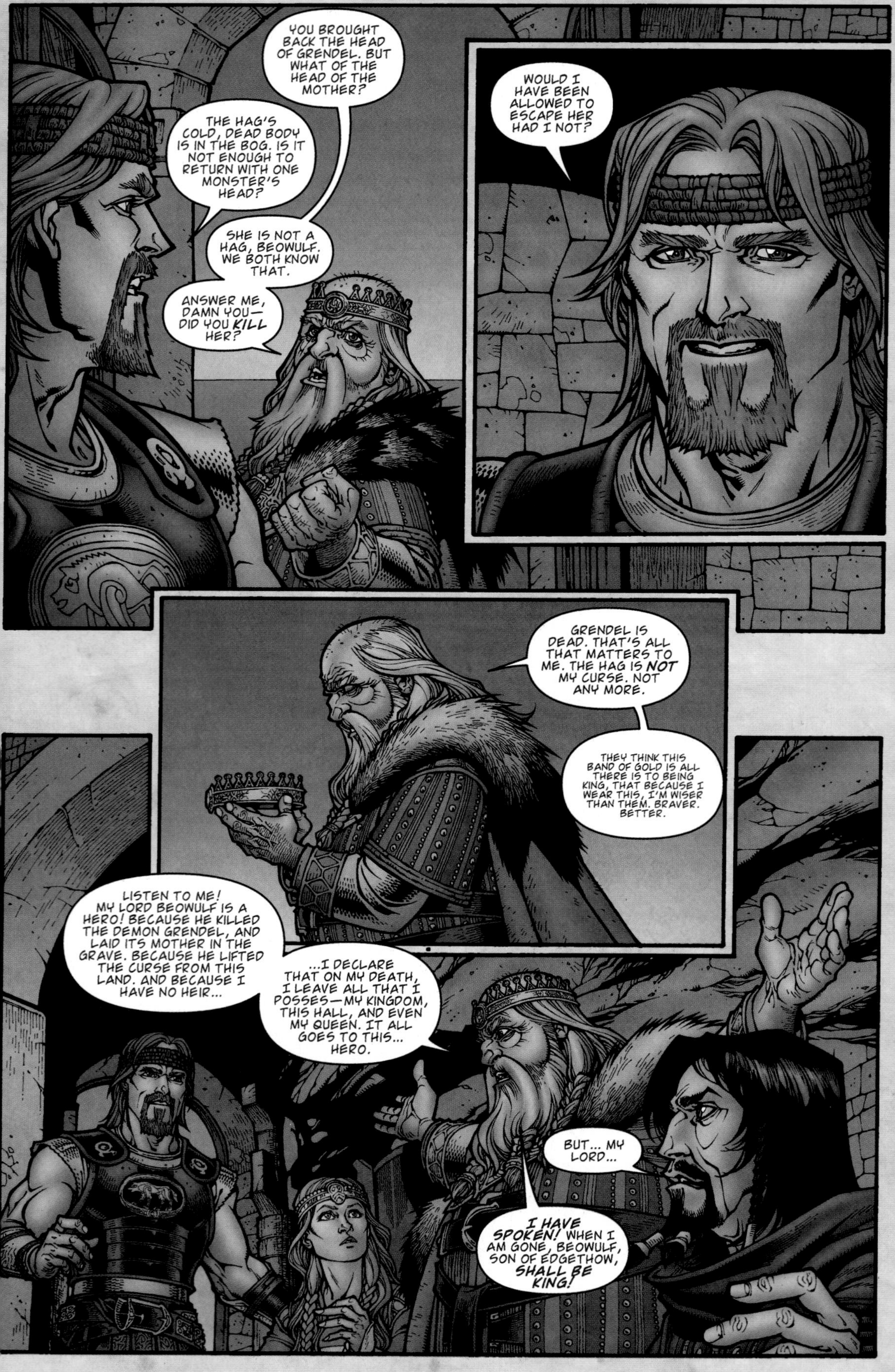
YOU BROUGHT BACK THE HEAD OF GRENDEL. BUT WHAT OF THE HEAD OF THE MOTHER?
THE HAG'S COLD, DEAD BODY IS IN THE BOG. IS IT NOT ENOUGH TO RETURN WITH ONE MONSTER'S HEAD?
SHE IS NOT A HAG, BEOWULF. WE BOTH KNOW THAT.
ANSWER ME, DAMN YOU— DID YOU KILL HER?
WOULD I HAVE BEEN ALLOWED TO ESCAPE HER HAD I NOT?
GRENDEL IS DEAD. THAT'S ALL THAT MATTERS TO ME. THE HAG IS NOT MY CURSE. NOT ANY MORE.
THEY THINK THIS BAND OF GOLD IS ALL THERE IS TO BEING KING, THAT BECAUSE I WEAR THIS, I'M WISER THAN THEM. BRAVER. BETTER.
LISTEN TO ME! MY LORD BEOWULF IS A HERO! BECAUSE HE KILLED THE DEMON GRENDEL, AND LAID ITS MOTHER IN THE GRAVE. BECAUSE HE LIFTED THE CURSE FROM THIS LAND. AND BECAUSE I HAVE NO HEIR...
...I DECLARE THAT ON MY DEATH, I LEAVE ALL THAT I POSSES—MY KINGDOM, THIS HALL, AND EVEN MY QUEEN. IT ALL GOES TO THIS... HERO.
BUT... MY LORD...
I HAVE SPOKEN! WHEN I AM GONE, BEOWULF, SON OF EDGETHOW, SHALL BE KING!

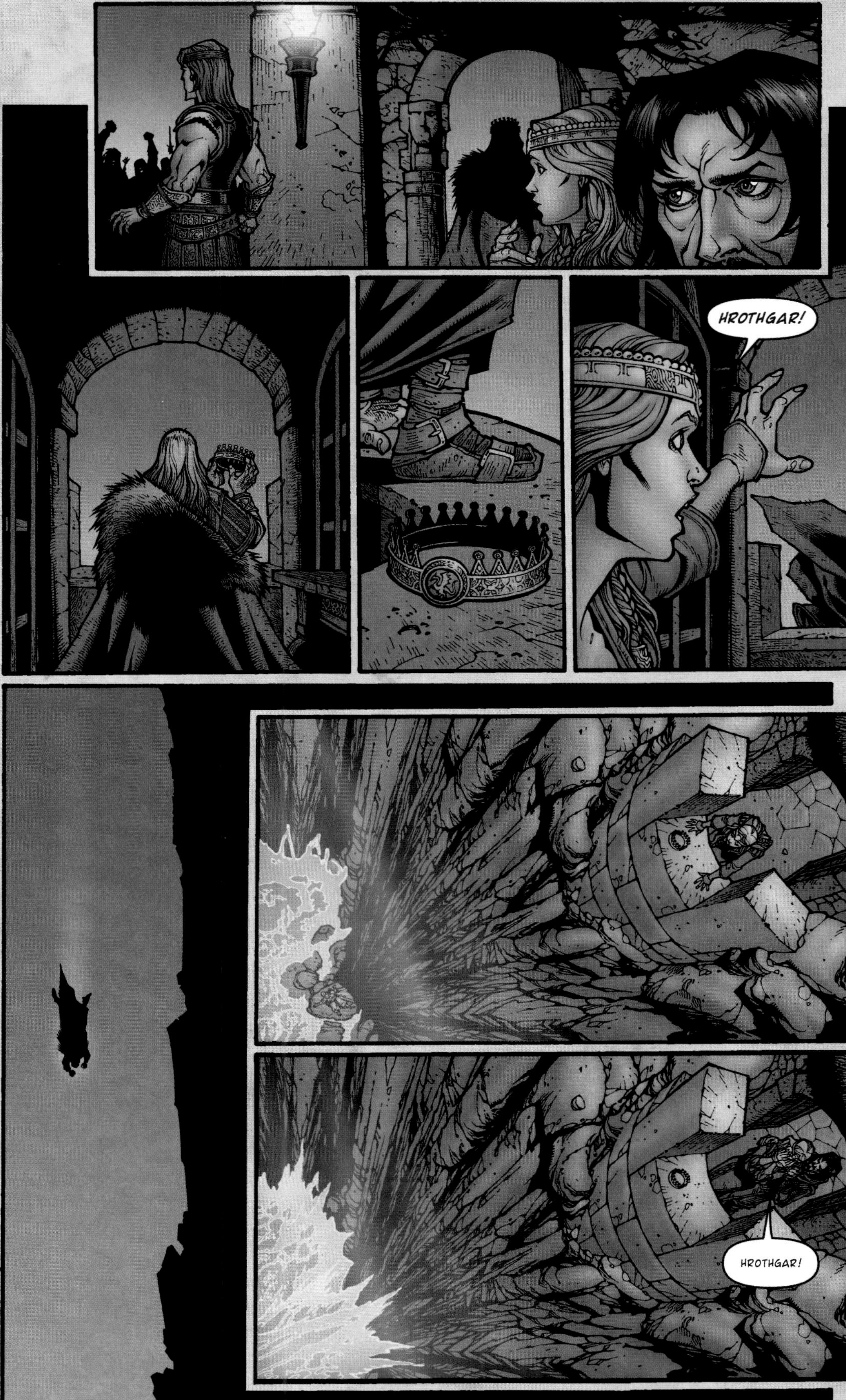
HROTHGAR!
HROTHGAR!

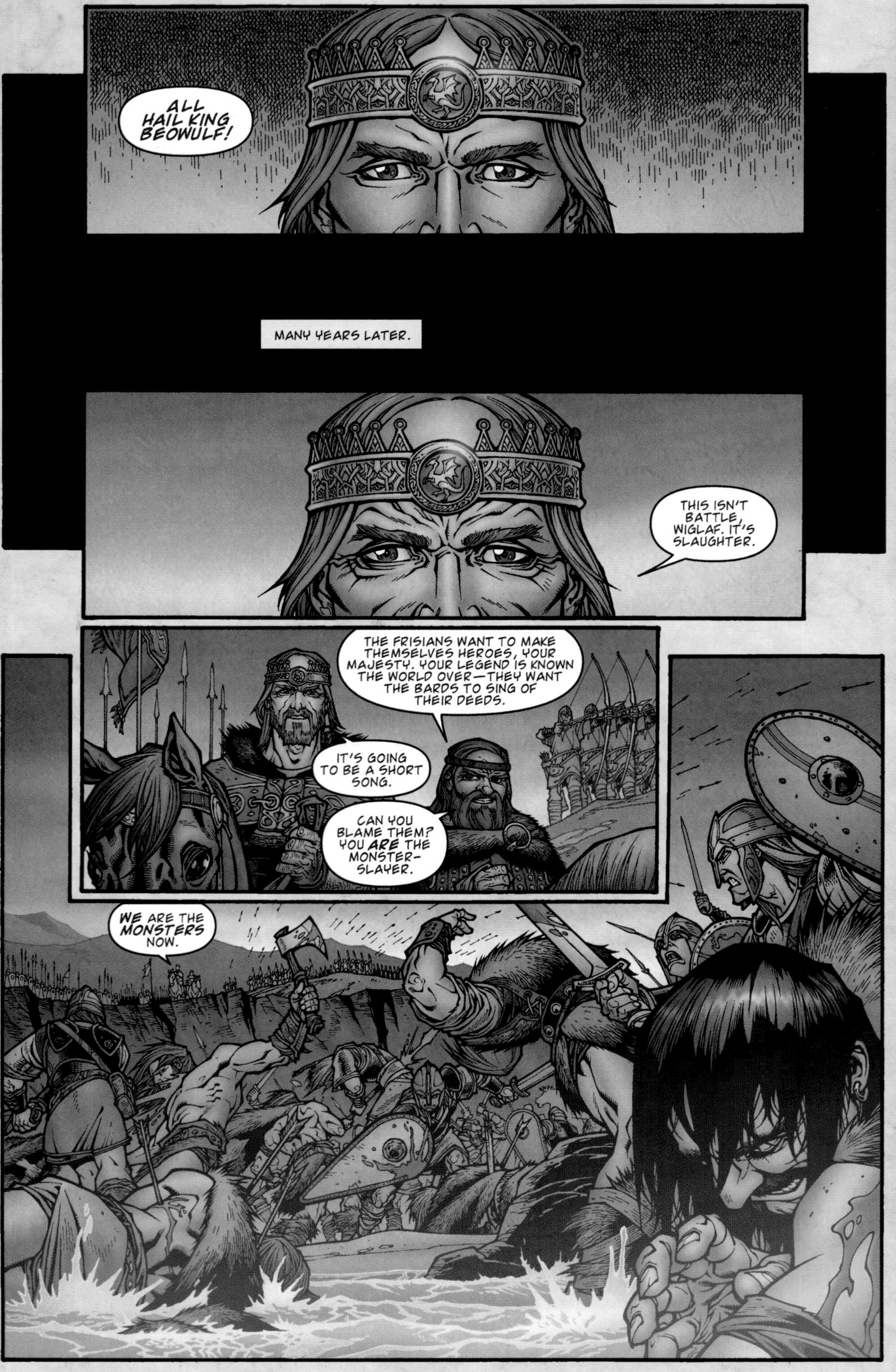
ALL HAIL KING BEOWULF!
MANY YEARS LATER.
THIS ISN'T BATTLE, WIGLAF. IT'S SLAUGHTER.
THE FRISIANS WANT TO MAKE THEMSELVES HEROES, YOUR MAJESTY. YOUR LEGEND IS KNOWN THE WORLD OVER—THEY WANT THE BARDS TO SING OF THEIR DEEDS.
IT'S GOING TO BE A SHORT SONG.
CAN YOU BLAME THEM? YOU ARE THE MONSTER-SLAYER.
WE ARE THE MONSTERS NOW.

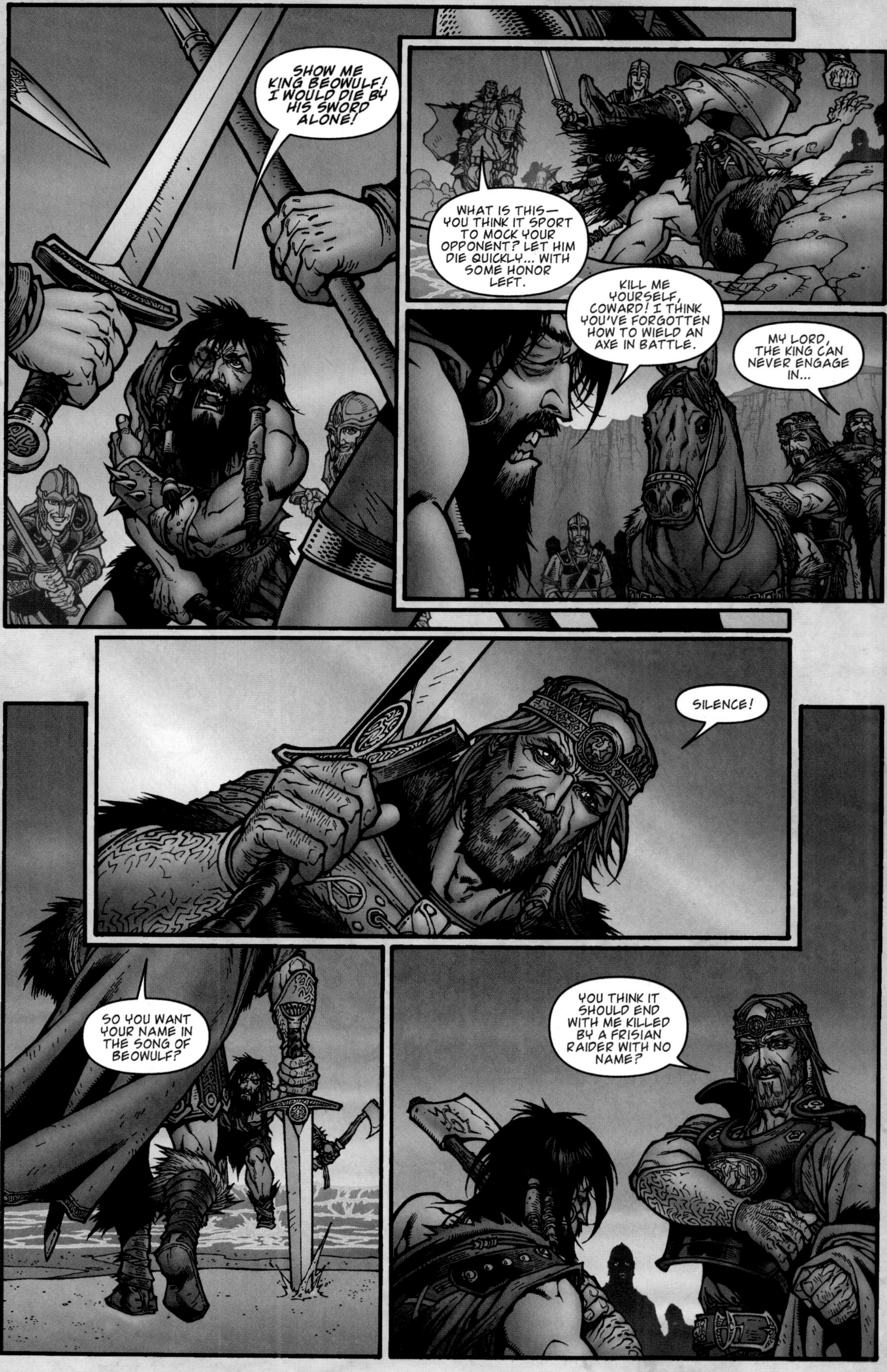
SHOW ME KING BEOWULF! I WOULD DIE BY HIS SWORD ALONE!
WHAT IS THIS— YOU THINK IT SPORT TO MOCK YOUR OPPONENT? LET HIM DIE QUICKLY... WITH SOME HONOR LEFT.
KILL ME YOURSELF, COWARD! I THINK YOU'VE FORGOTTEN HOW TO WIELD AN AXE IN BATTLE.
MY LORD, THE KING CAN NEVER ENGAGE IN...
SILENCE!
SO YOU WANT YOUR NAME IN THE SONG OF BEOWULF?
YOU THINK IT SHOULD END WITH ME KILLED BY A FRISIAN RAIDER WITH NO NAME?

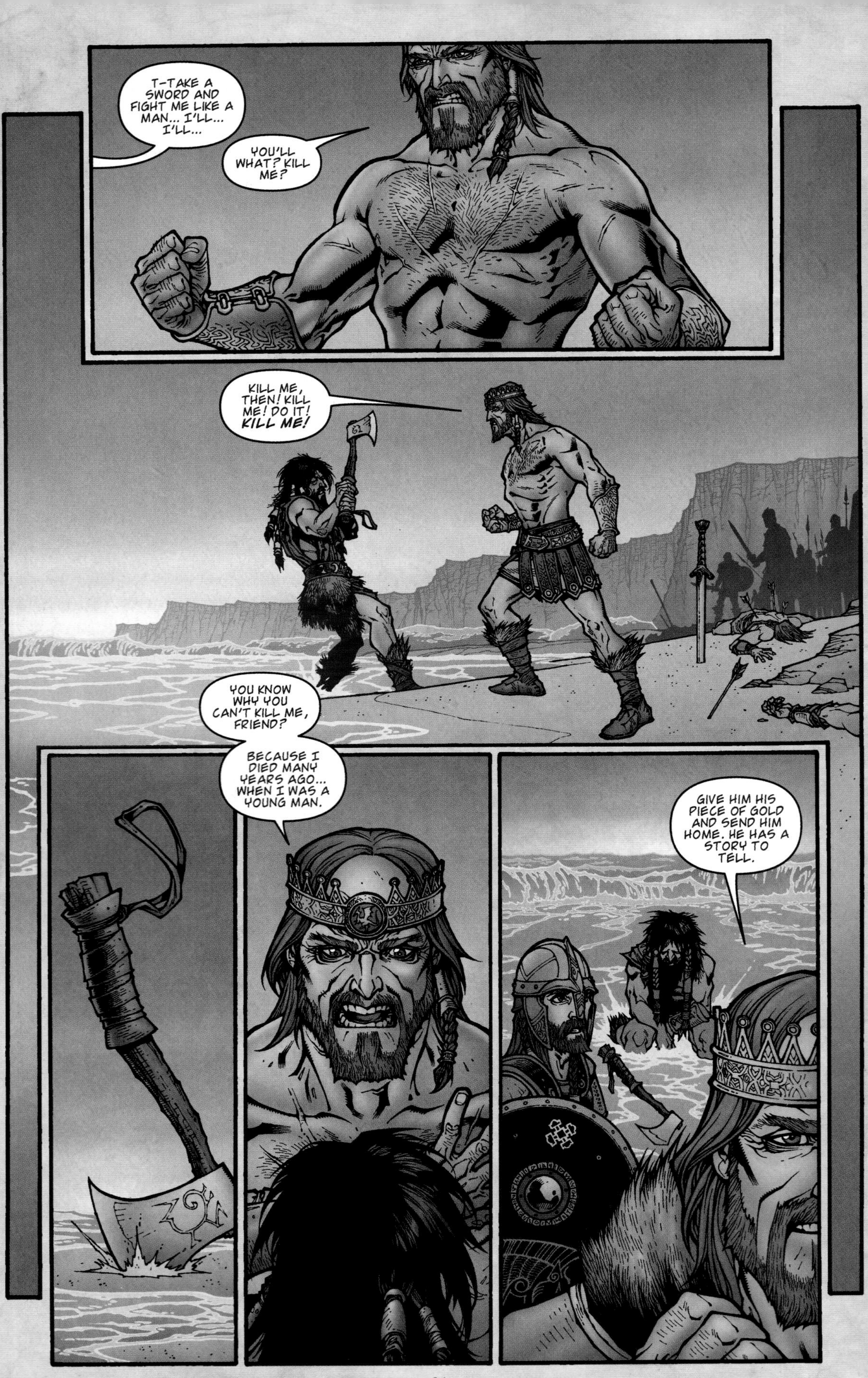
T-TAKE A SWORD AND FIGHT ME LIKE A MAN... I'LL... I'LL...
YOU'LL WHAT? KILL ME?
KILL ME, THEN! KILL ME! DO IT! KILL ME!
YOU KNOW WHY YOU CAN'T KILL ME, FRIEND?
BECAUSE I DIED MANY YEARS AGO... WHEN I WAS A YOUNG MAN.
GIVE HIM HIS PIECE OF GOLD AND SEND HIM HOME. HE HAS A STORY TO TELL.

CASTLE HEROT.

YOUR MAJESTY? ARE YOU HURT?

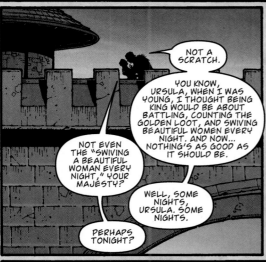

NOT A SCRATCH.

YOU KNOW, URSULA, WHEN I WAS YOUNG, I THOUGHT BEING KING WOULD BE ABOUT BATTLING, COUNTING THE GOLDEN LOOT, AND SWIVING BEAUTIFUL WOMEN EVERY NIGHT. AND NOW... NOTHING'S AS GOOD AS IT SHOULD BE.

NOT EVEN THE "SWIVING A BEAUTIFUL WOMAN EVERY NIGHT," YOUR MAJESTY?

WELL, SOME NIGHTS, URSULA. SOME NIGHTS.

PERHAPS TONIGHT?

NO... I FEEL MY AGE UPON ME. TOMORROW, AFTER THE CELEBRATION. WE CAN'T FORGET WHAT TOMORROW IS, CAN WE NOW?

YOUR DAY. WHEN THE SAGA OF BEOWULF IS TOLD.

I SEE YOU'VE SURVIVED.

ALAS, MY QUEEN. THE FRISIAN INVADERS HAVE BEEN PUSHED INTO THE SEA. YOU ARE NOT A WIDOW... YET.

HOW COMFORTING, MY HUSBAND.

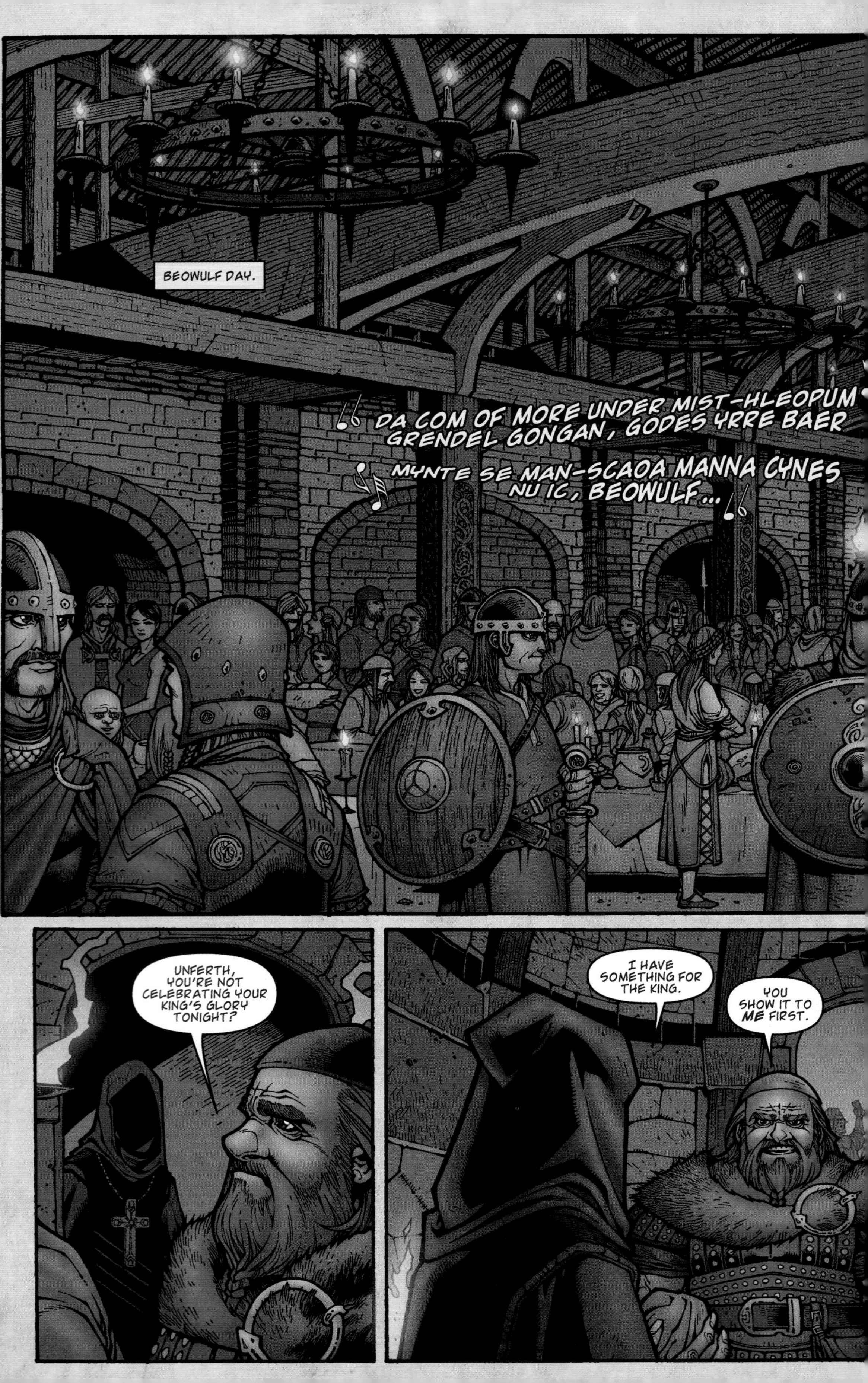
BEOWULF DAY.
DA COM OF MORE UNDER MIST-HLEOPUM GRENDEL GONGAN, GODES YRRE BAER
MYNTE SE MAN-SCAOA MANNA CYNES NU IC, BEOWULF...
UNFERTH, YOU'RE NOT CELEBRATING YOUR KING'S GLORY TONIGHT?
I HAVE SOMETHING FOR THE KING.
YOU SHOW IT TO ME FIRST.

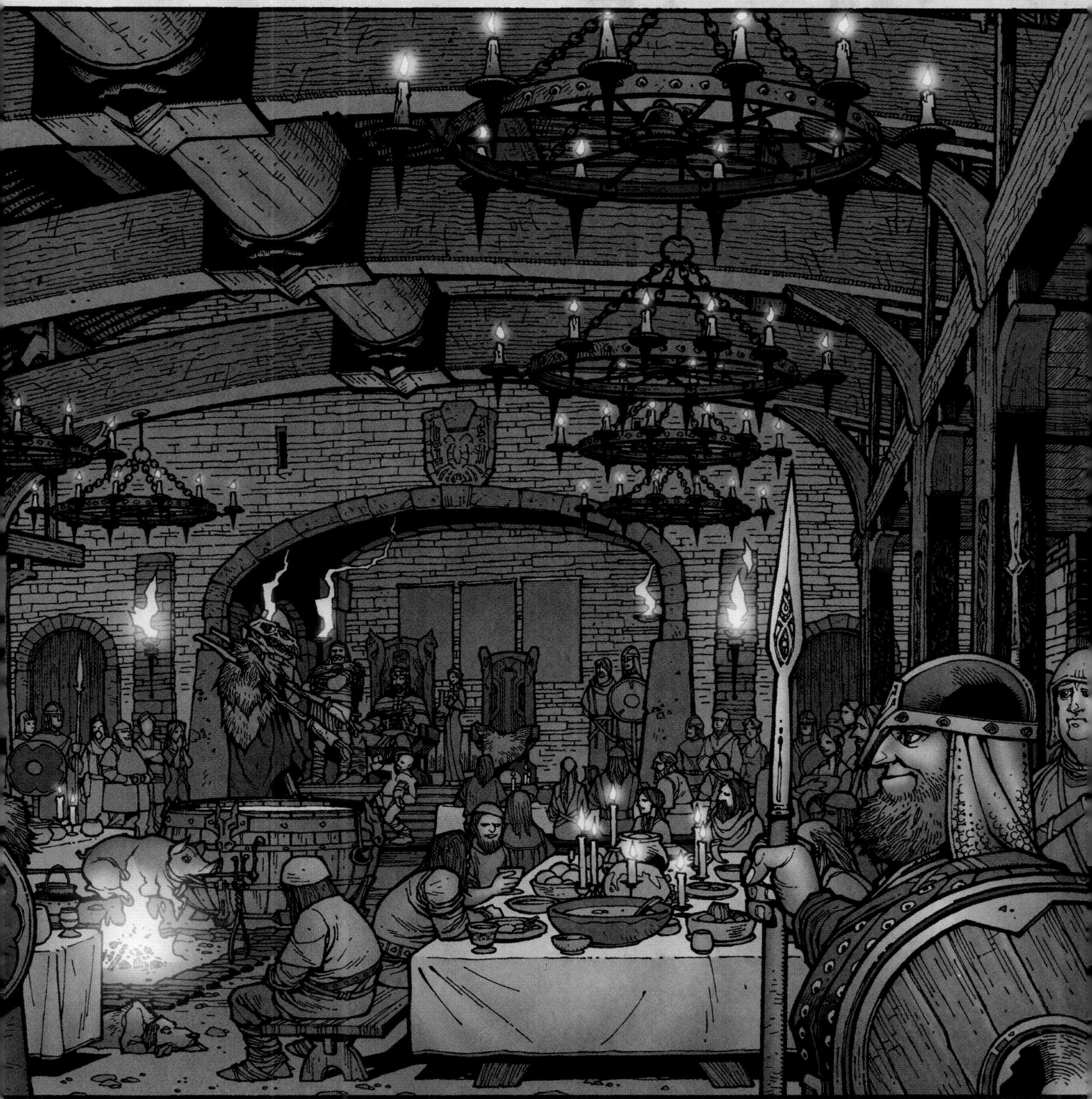

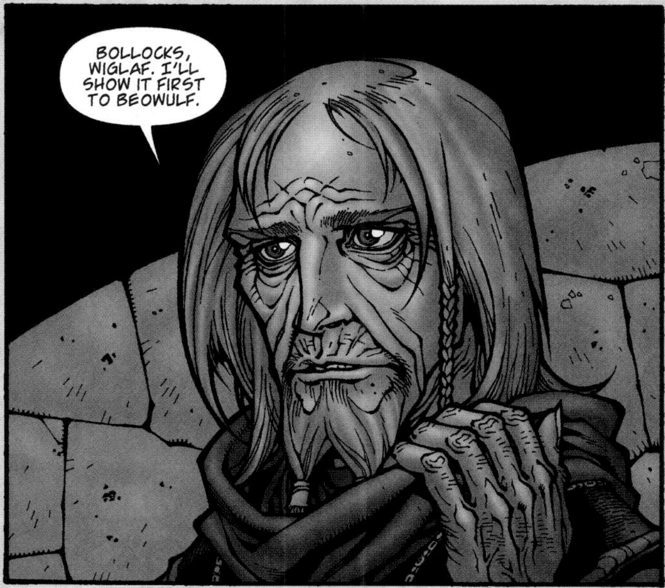
BOLLOCKS, WIGLAF. I'LL SHOW IT FIRST TO BEOWULF.

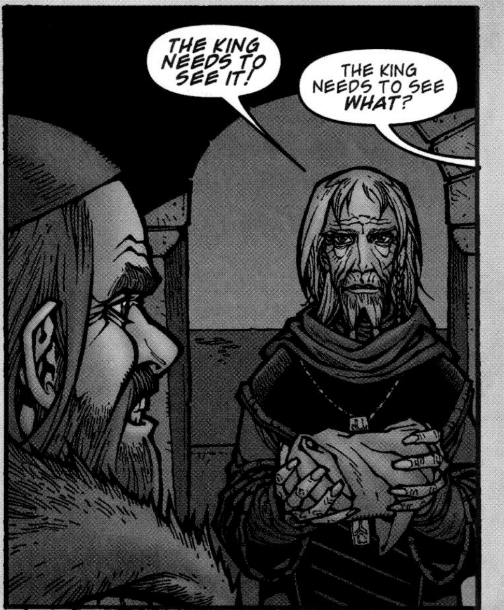
THE KING NEEDS TO SEE IT!
THE KING NEEDS TO SEE WHAT?

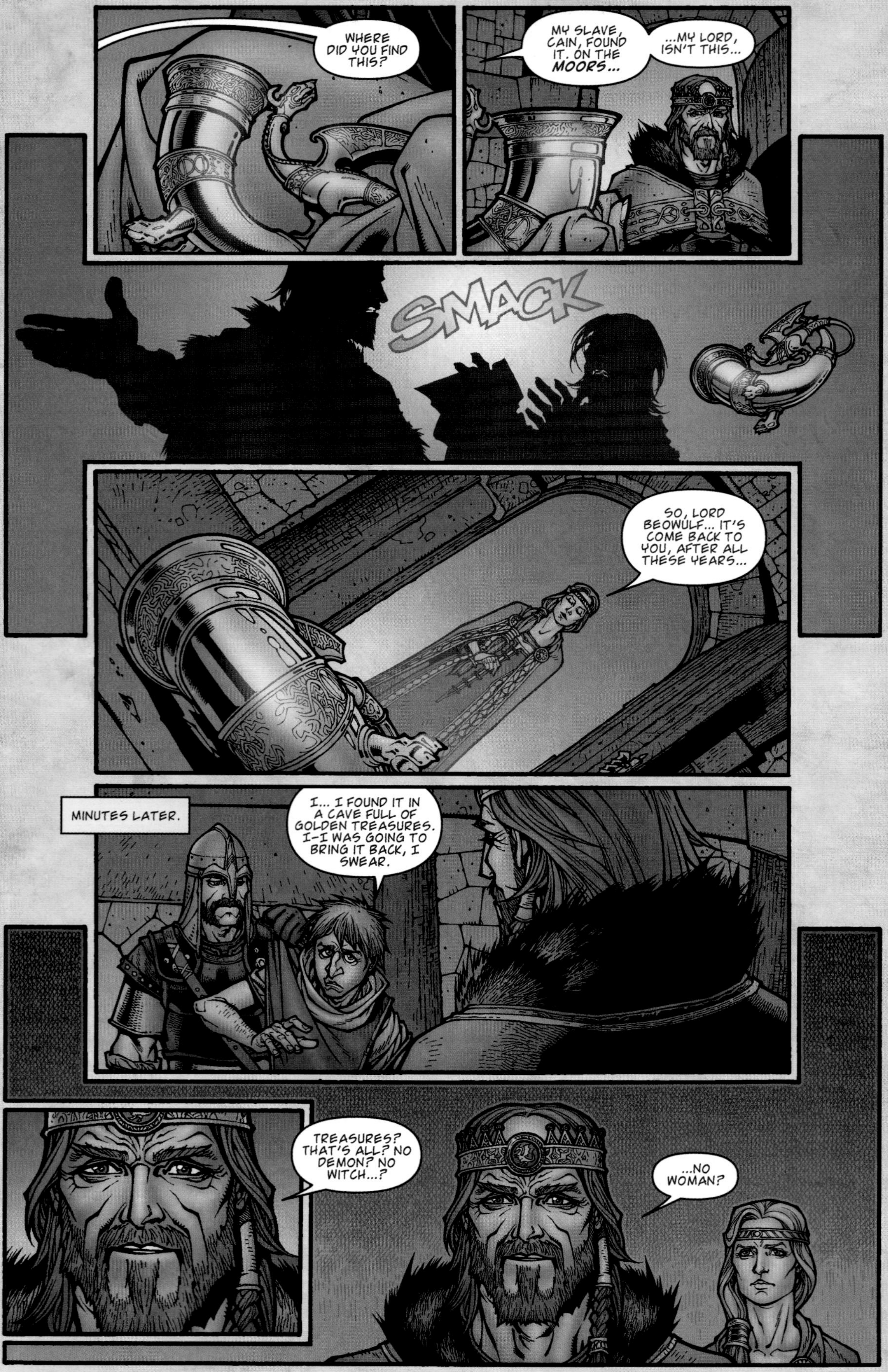
WHERE DID YOU FIND THIS?
MY SLAVE, CAIN, FOUND IT. ON THE MOORS...
...MY LORD, ISN'T THIS...
SMACK
SO, LORD BEOWULF... IT'S COME BACK TO YOU, AFTER ALL THESE YEARS...
MINUTES LATER.
I... I FOUND IT IN A CAVE FULL OF GOLDEN TREASURES. I-I WAS GOING TO BRING IT BACK, I SWEAR.
TREASURES? THAT'S ALL? NO DEMON? NO WITCH...?
...NO WOMAN?

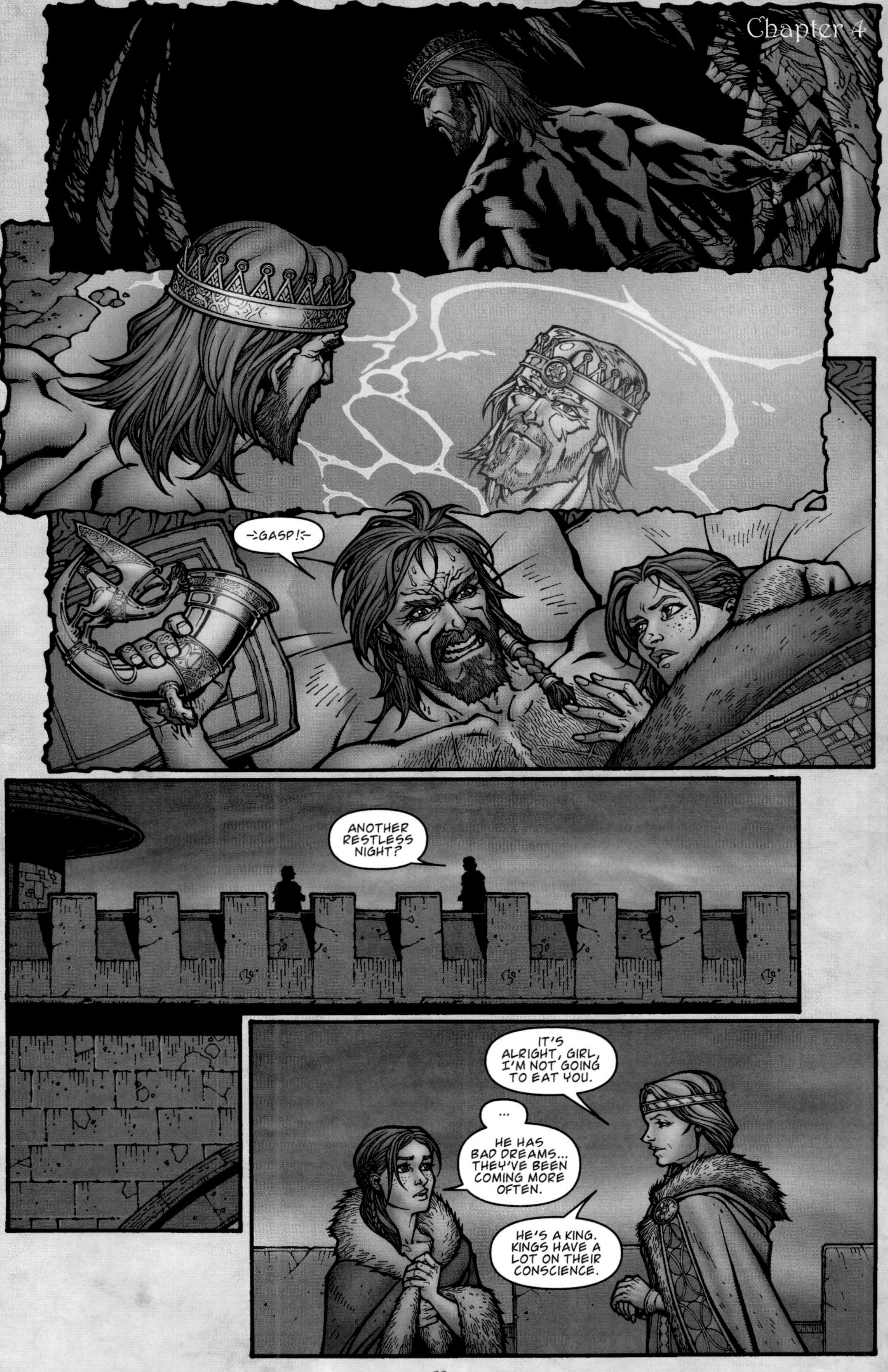
Chapter 4
-GASP!-
ANOTHER RESTLESS NIGHT?
IT'S ALRIGHT, GIRL, I'M NOT GOING TO EAT YOU.
...
HE HAS BAD DREAMS... THEY'VE BEEN COMING MORE OFTEN.
HE'S A KING. KINGS HAVE A LOT ON THEIR CONSCIENCE.

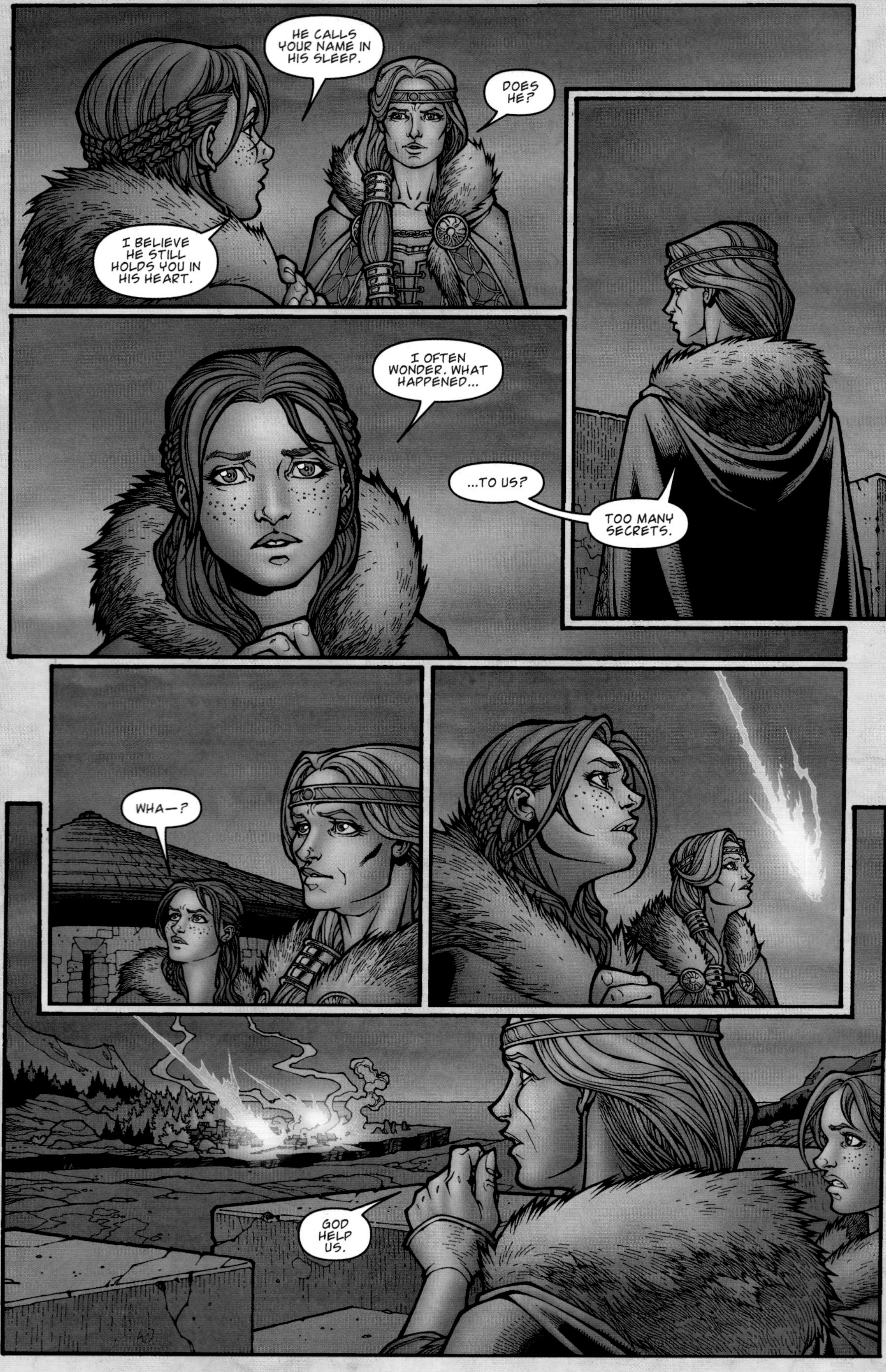
HE CALLS YOUR NAME IN HIS SLEEP.
DOES HE?
I BELIEVE HE STILL HOLDS YOU IN HIS HEART.
I OFTEN WONDER. WHAT HAPPENED...
...TO US?
TOO MANY SECRETS.
WHA—?
GOD HELP US.

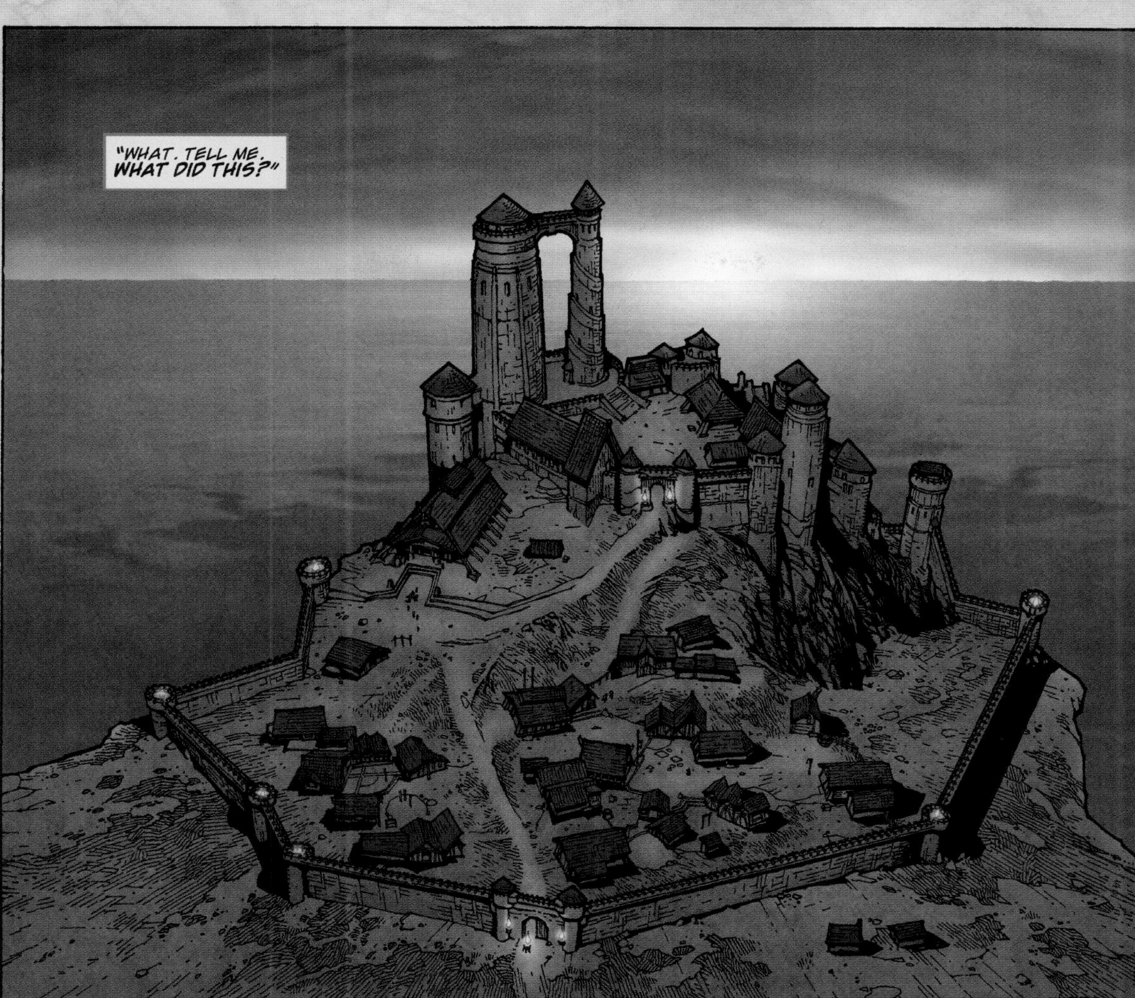
"WHAT. TELL ME. WHAT DID THIS?"

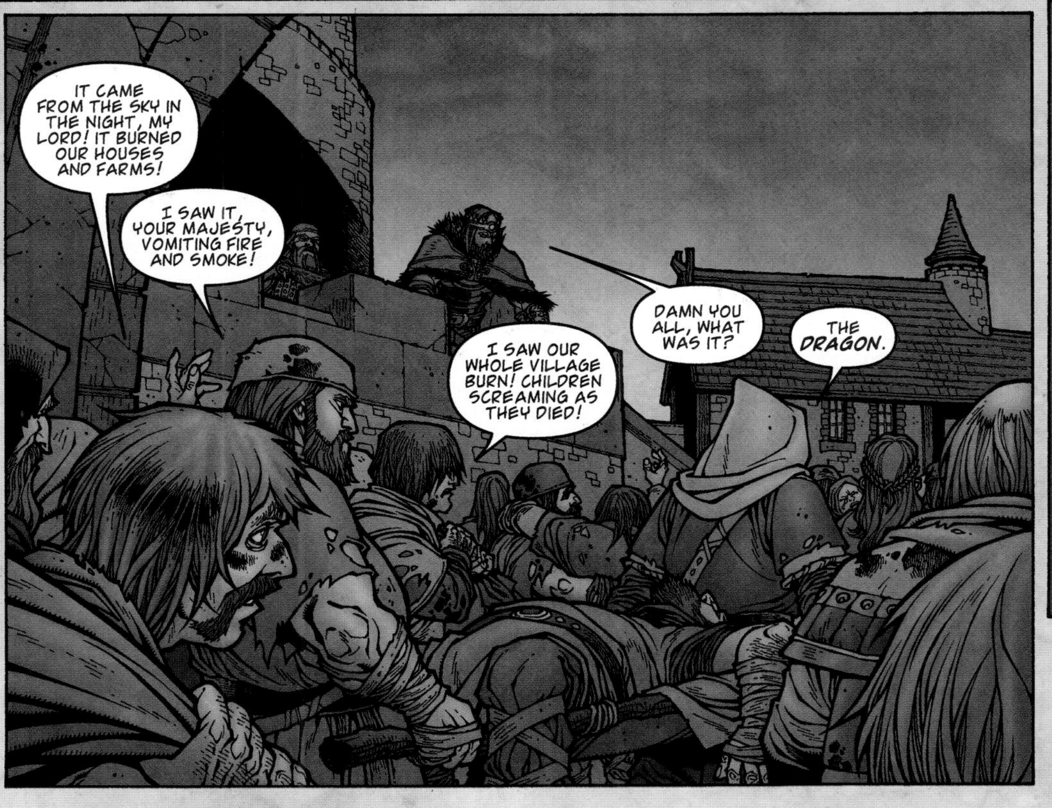
IT CAME FROM THE SKY IN THE NIGHT, MY LORD! IT BURNED OUR HOUSES AND FARMS!
I SAW IT, YOUR MAJESTY, VOMITING FIRE AND SMOKE!
I SAW OUR WHOLE VILLAGE BURN! CHILDREN SCREAMING AS THEY DIED!
DAMN YOU ALL, WHAT WAS IT?
THE DRAGON.

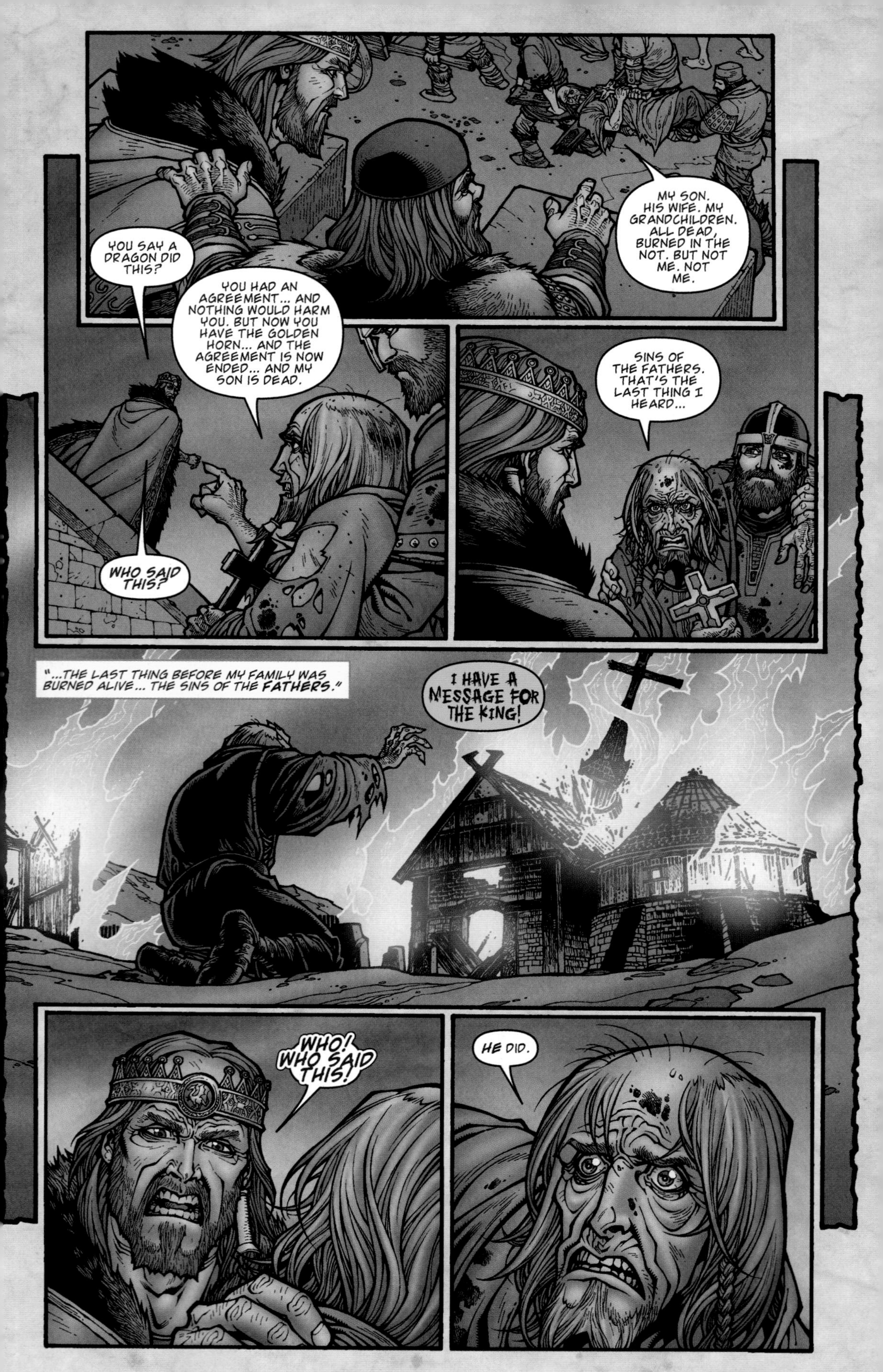
MY SON. HIS WIFE. MY GRANDCHILDREN. ALL DEAD, BURNED IN THE NOT. BUT NOT ME. NOT ME.
YOU SAY A DRAGON DID THIS?
YOU HAD AN AGREEMENT... AND NOTHING WOULD HARM YOU. BUT NOW YOU HAVE THE GOLDEN HORN... AND THE AGREEMENT IS NOW ENDED... AND MY SON IS DEAD.
WHO SAID THIS?
SINS OF THE FATHERS. THAT'S THE LAST THING I HEARD...
"...THE LAST THING BEFORE MY FAMILY WAS BURNED ALIVE... THE SINS OF THE FATHERS."
I HAVE A MESSAGE FOR THE KING!
WHO! WHO SAID THIS!
HE DID.

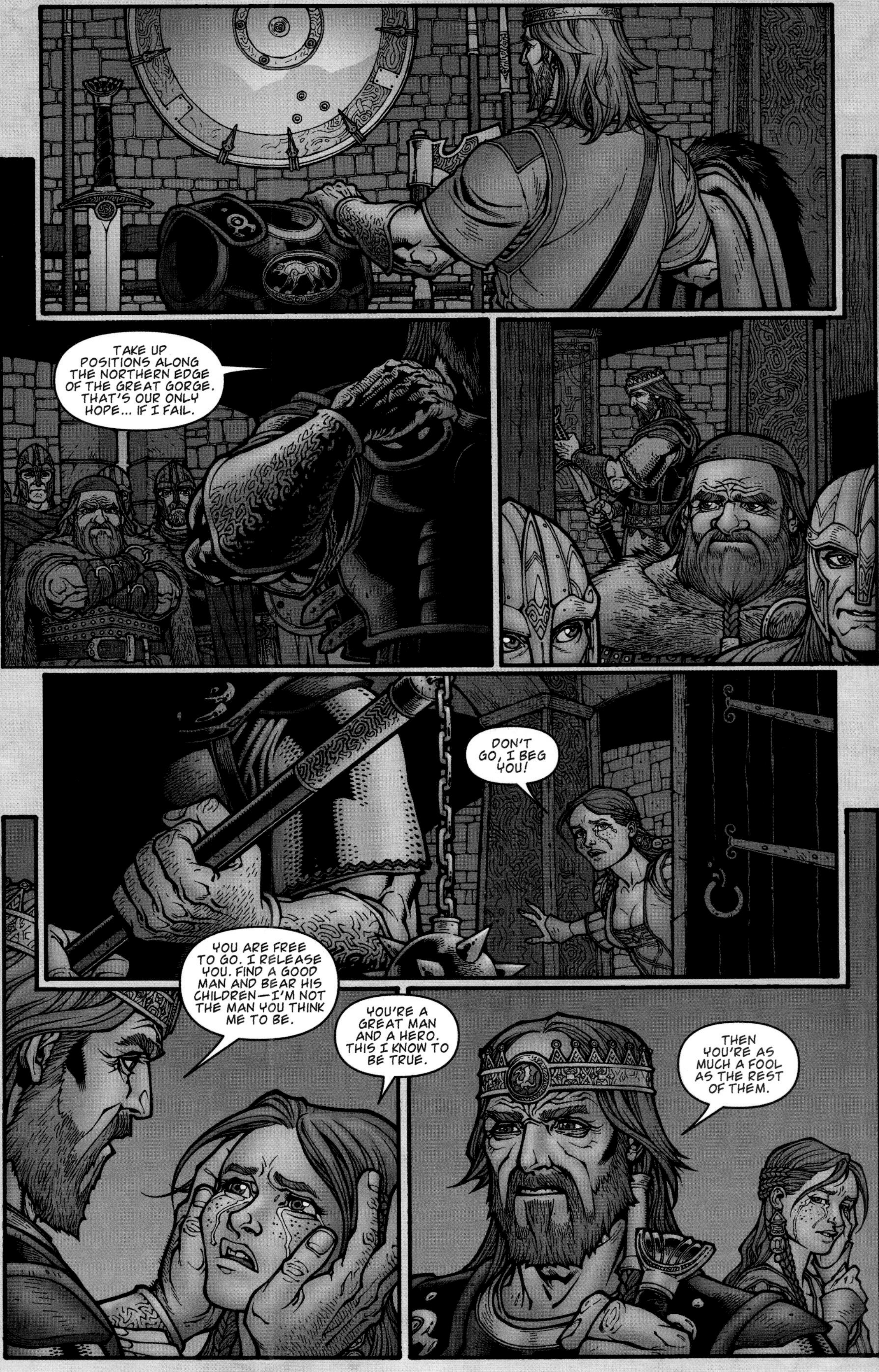
TAKE UP POSITIONS ALONG THE NORTHERN EDGE OF THE GREAT GORGE. THAT'S OUR ONLY HOPE... IF I FAIL.
DON'T GO, I BEG YOU!
YOU ARE FREE TO GO. I RELEASE YOU. FIND A GOOD MAN AND BEAR HIS CHILDREN—I'M NOT THE MAN YOU THINK ME TO BE.
YOU'RE A GREAT MAN AND A HERO. THIS I KNOW TO BE TRUE.
THEN YOU'RE AS MUCH A FOOL AS THE REST OF THEM.

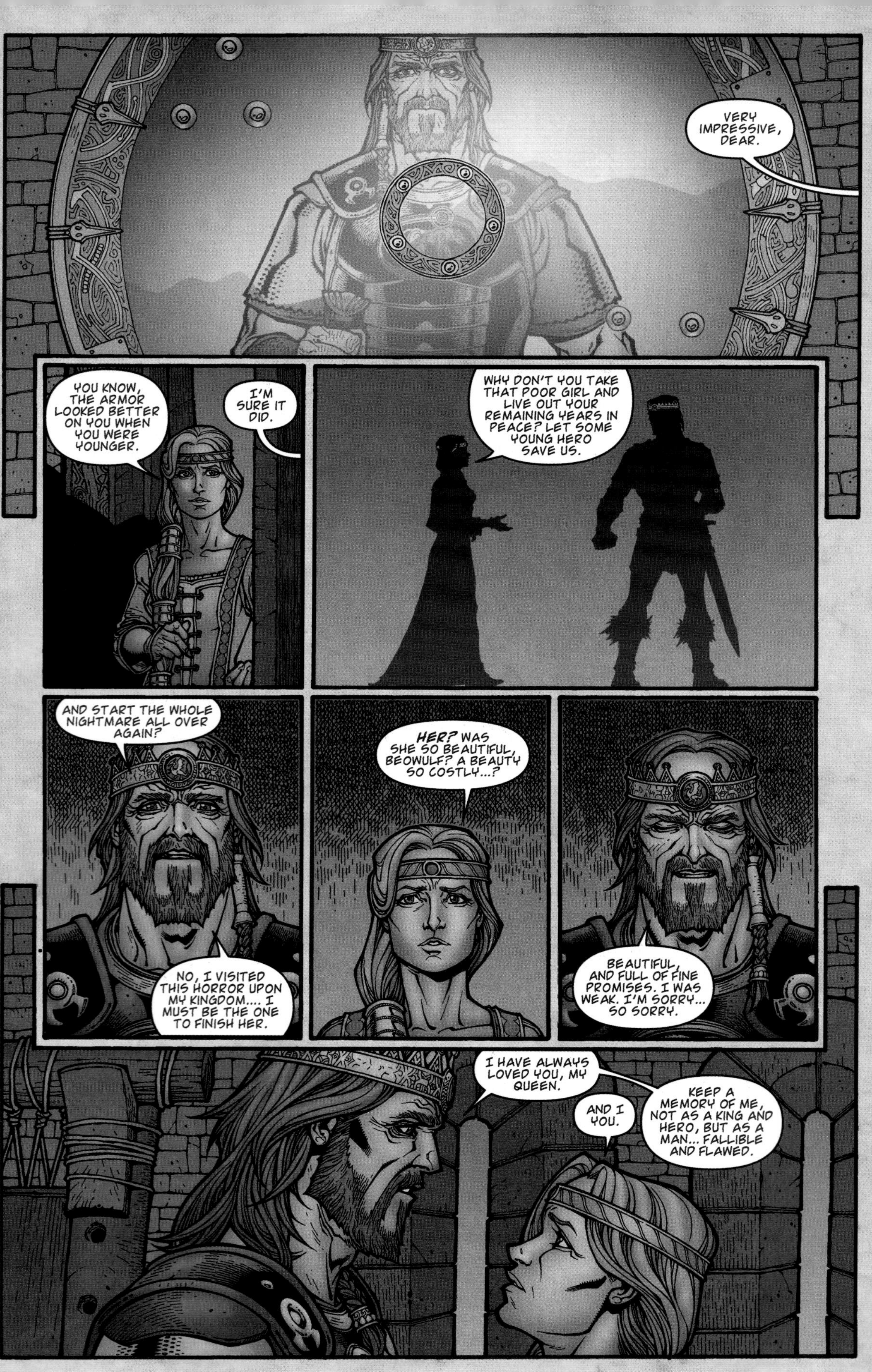

VERY IMPRESSIVE, DEAR.
YOU KNOW, THE ARMOR LOOKED BETTER ON YOU WHEN YOU WERE YOUNGER.
I'M SURE IT DID.
WHY DON'T YOU TAKE THAT POOR GIRL AND LIVE OUT YOUR REMAINING YEARS IN PEACE? LET SOME YOUNG HERO SAVE US.
AND START THE WHOLE NIGHTMARE ALL OVER AGAIN?
NO, I VISITED THIS HORROR UPON MY KINGDOM.... I MUST BE THE ONE TO FINISH HER.
HER? WAS SHE SO BEAUTIFUL, BEOWULF? A BEAUTY SO COSTLY...?
BEAUTIFUL, AND FULL OF FINE PROMISES. I WAS WEAK. I'M SORRY... SO SORRY.
I HAVE ALWAYS LOVED YOU, MY QUEEN.
AND I YOU.
KEEP A MEMORY OF ME, NOT AS A KING AND HERO, BUT AS A MAN... FALLIBLE AND FLAWED.

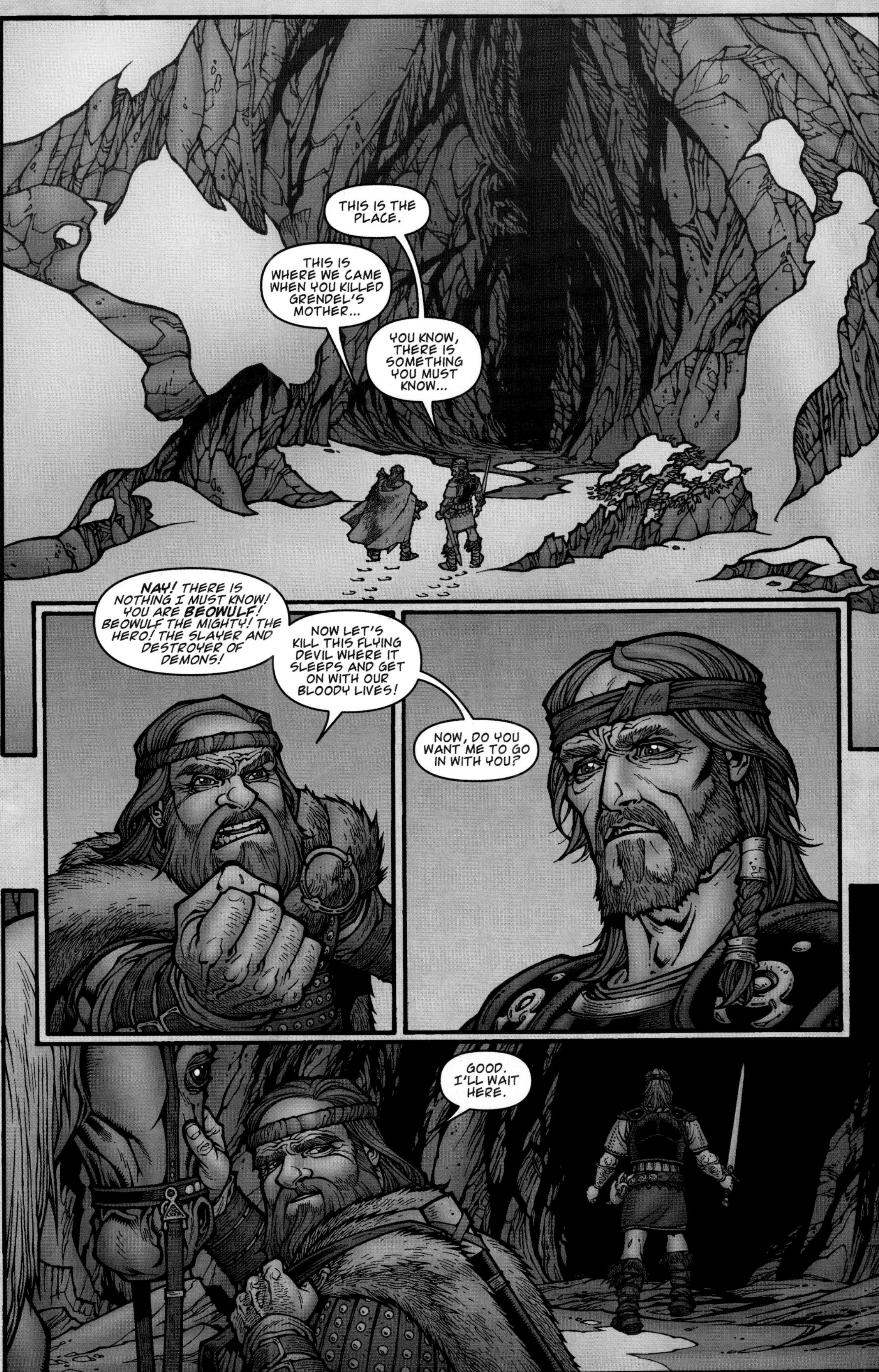
THIS IS THE PLACE.
THIS IS WHERE WE CAME WHEN YOU KILLED GRENDEL'S MOTHER...
YOU KNOW, THERE IS SOMETHING YOU MUST KNOW...
NAY! THERE IS NOTHING I MUST KNOW! YOU ARE BEOWULF! BEOWULF THE MIGHTY! THE HERO! THE SLAYER AND DESTROYER OF DEMONS!
NOW LET'S KILL THIS FLYING DEVIL WHERE IT SLEEPS AND GET ON WITH OUR BLOODY LIVES!
NOW, DO YOU WANT ME TO GO IN WITH YOU?
GOOD. I'LL WAIT HERE.

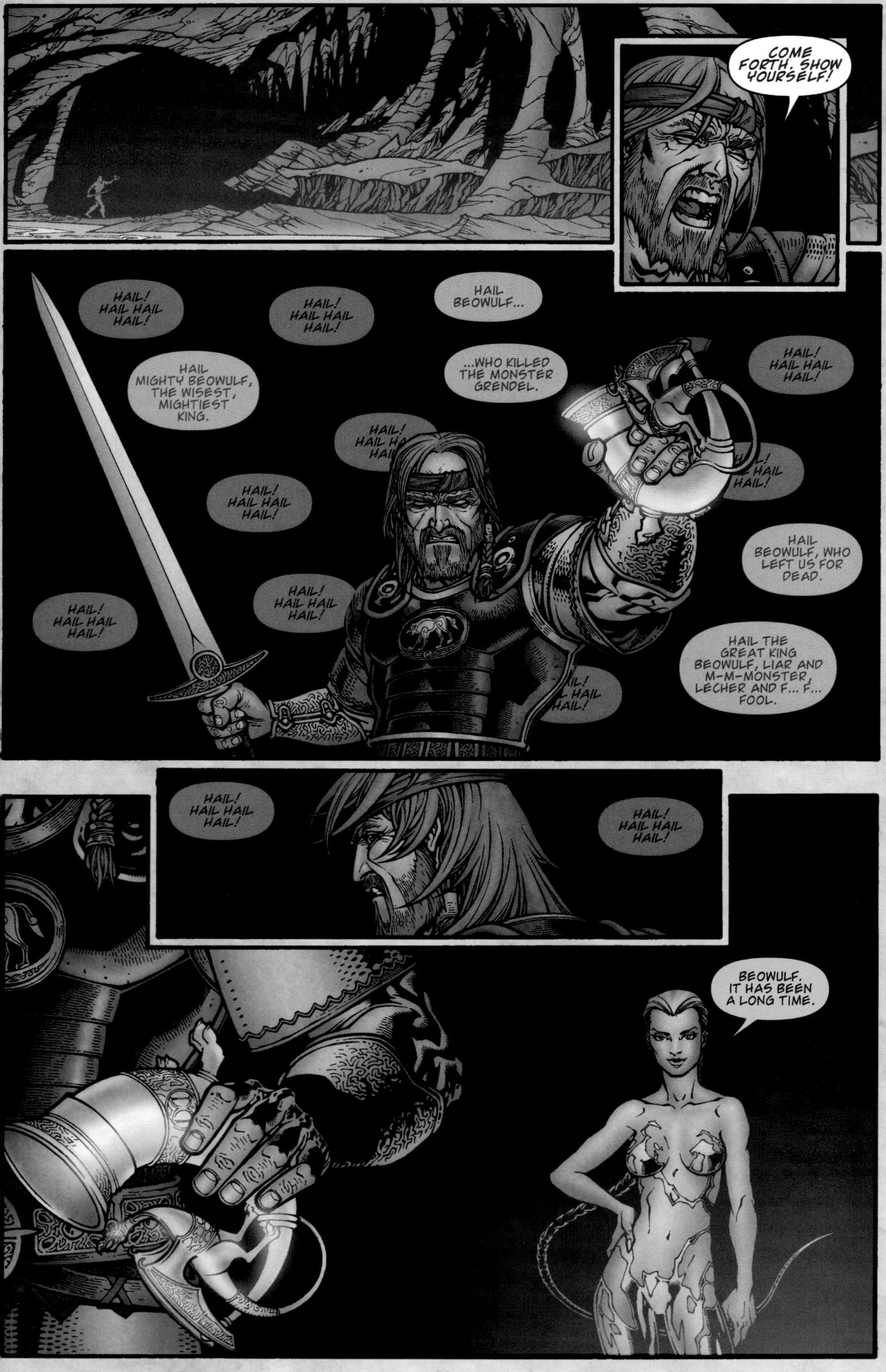
COME FORTH. SHOW YOURSELF!
HAIL! HAIL HAIL HAIL!
HAIL! HAIL HAIL HAIL!
HAIL BEOWULF...
HAIL MIGHTY BEOWULF, THE WISEST, MIGHTIEST KING.
...WHO KILLED THE MONSTER GRENDEL.
HAIL! HAIL HAIL HAIL!
HAIL! HAIL HAIL HAIL!
HAIL BEOWULF, WHO LEFT US FOR DEAD.
HAIL! HAIL HAIL HAIL!
HAIL! HAIL HAIL HAIL!
HAIL THE GREAT KING BEOWULF, LIAR AND M-M-MONSTER, LECHER AND F... F... FOOL.
HAIL! HAIL HAIL HAIL!
HAIL! HAIL HAIL HAIL!
BEOWULF. IT HAS BEEN A LONG TIME.

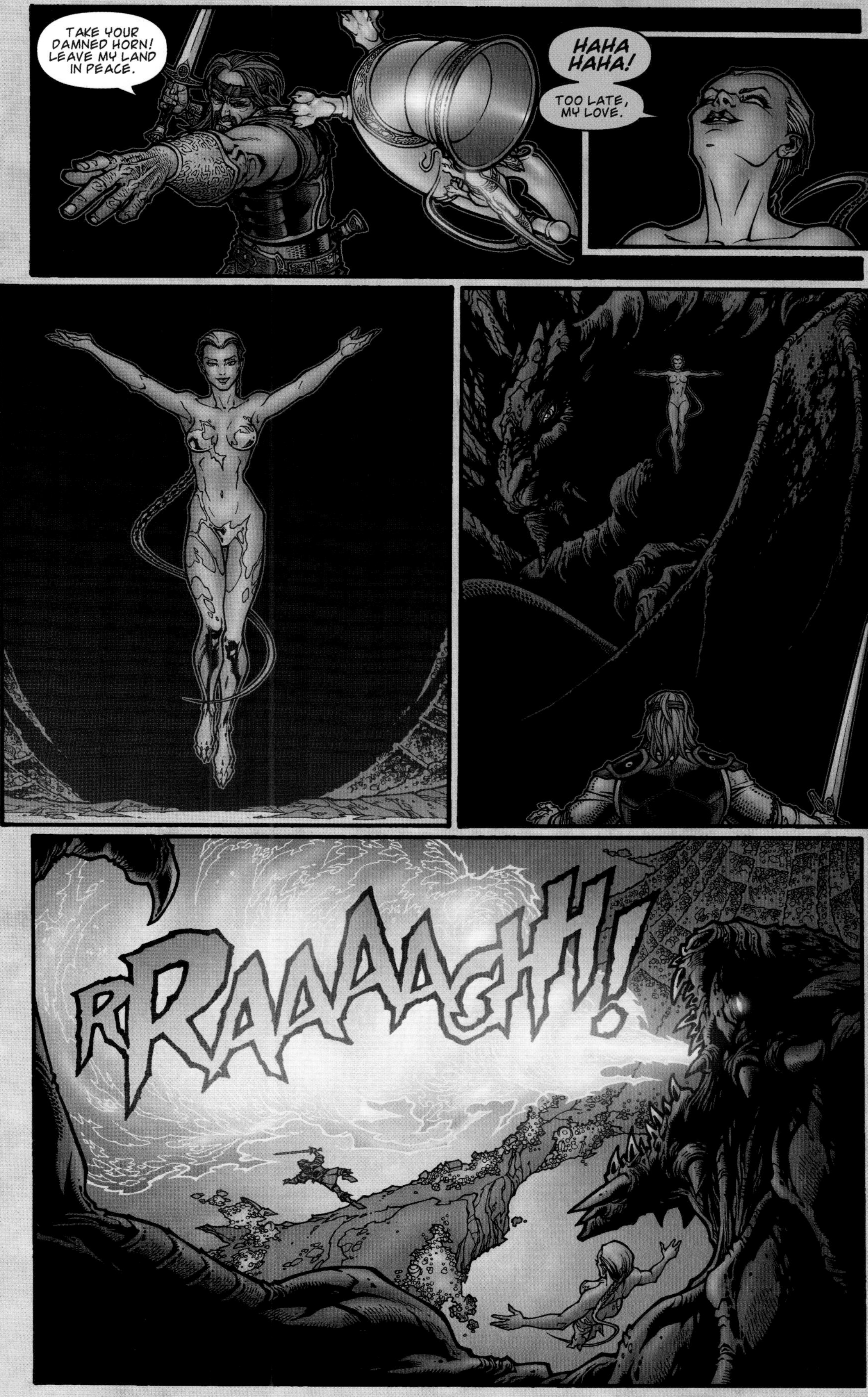
TAKE YOUR DAMNED HORN! LEAVE MY LAND IN PEACE.
HAHA HAHA!
TOO LATE, MY LOVE.
rRAAAACH!

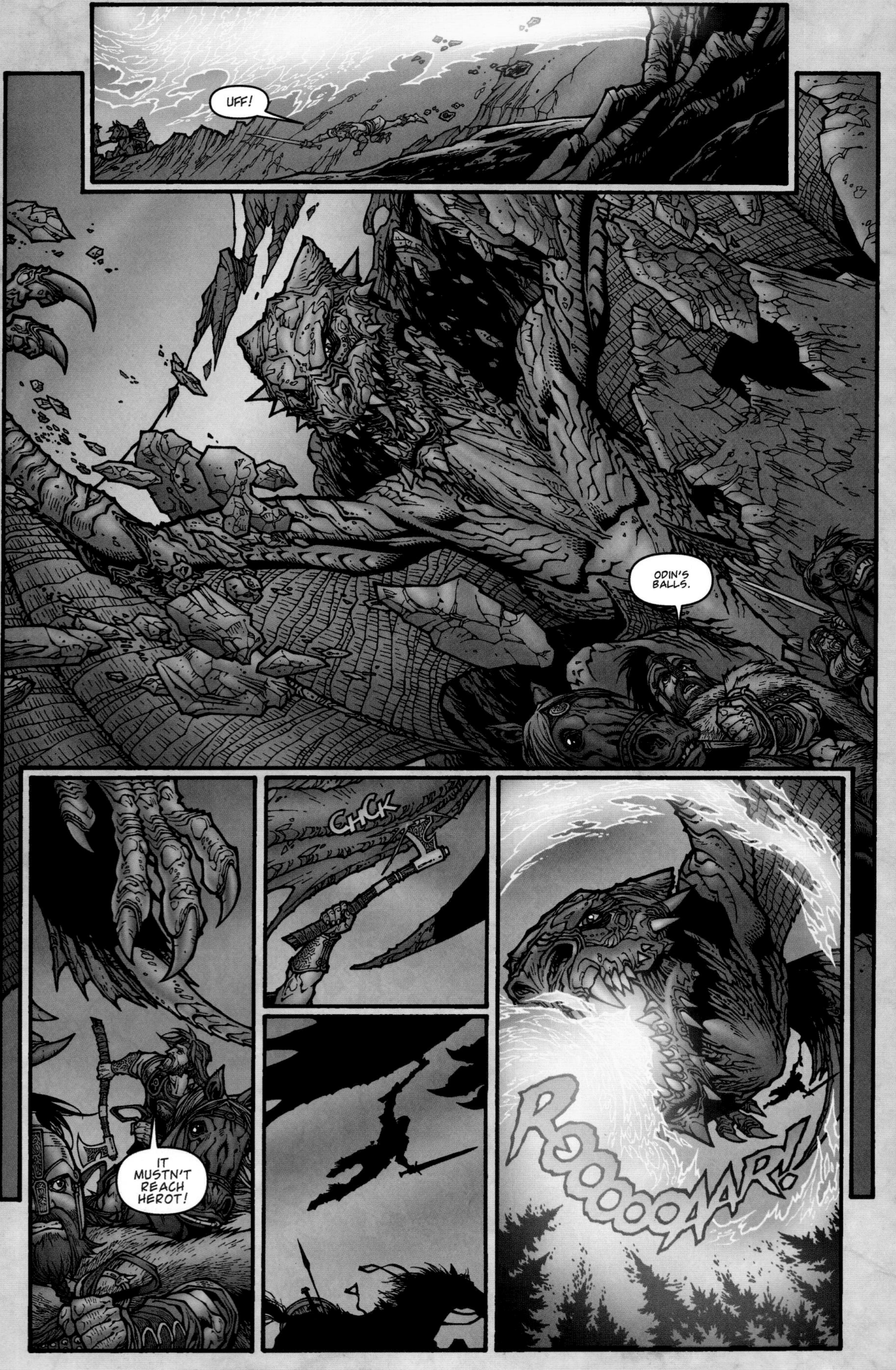
UFF!
ODIN'S BALLS.
IT MUSTN'T REACH HEROT!
CHCK
ROOOOOAAR!

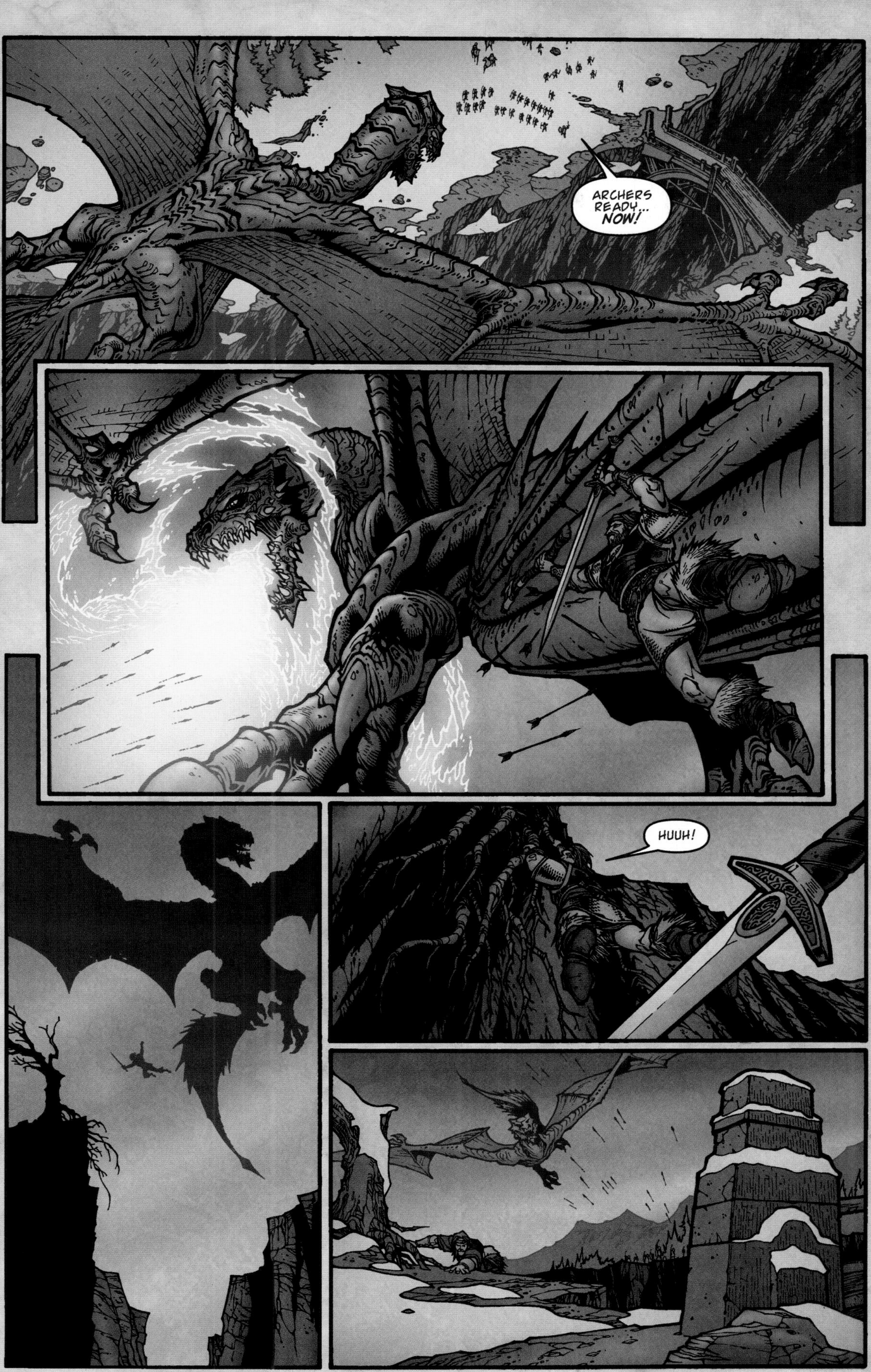
ARCHERS READY... NOW!
HUUH!

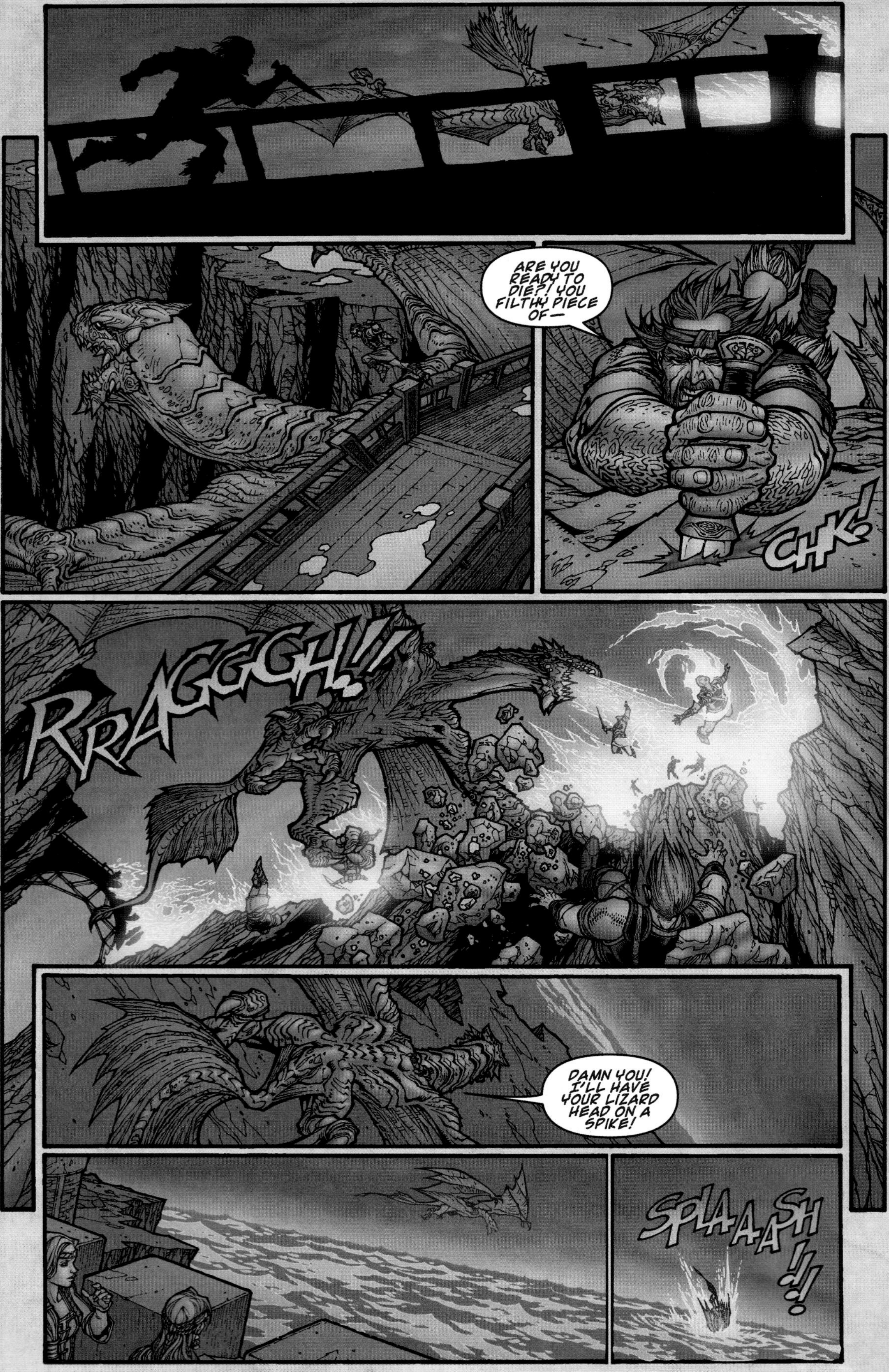
ARE YOU READY TO DIE?! YOU FILTHY PIECE OF—
CHK!
RRAGGGH!!
DAMN YOU! I'LL HAVE YOUR LIZARD HEAD ON A SPIKE!
SPLAAASH!!!

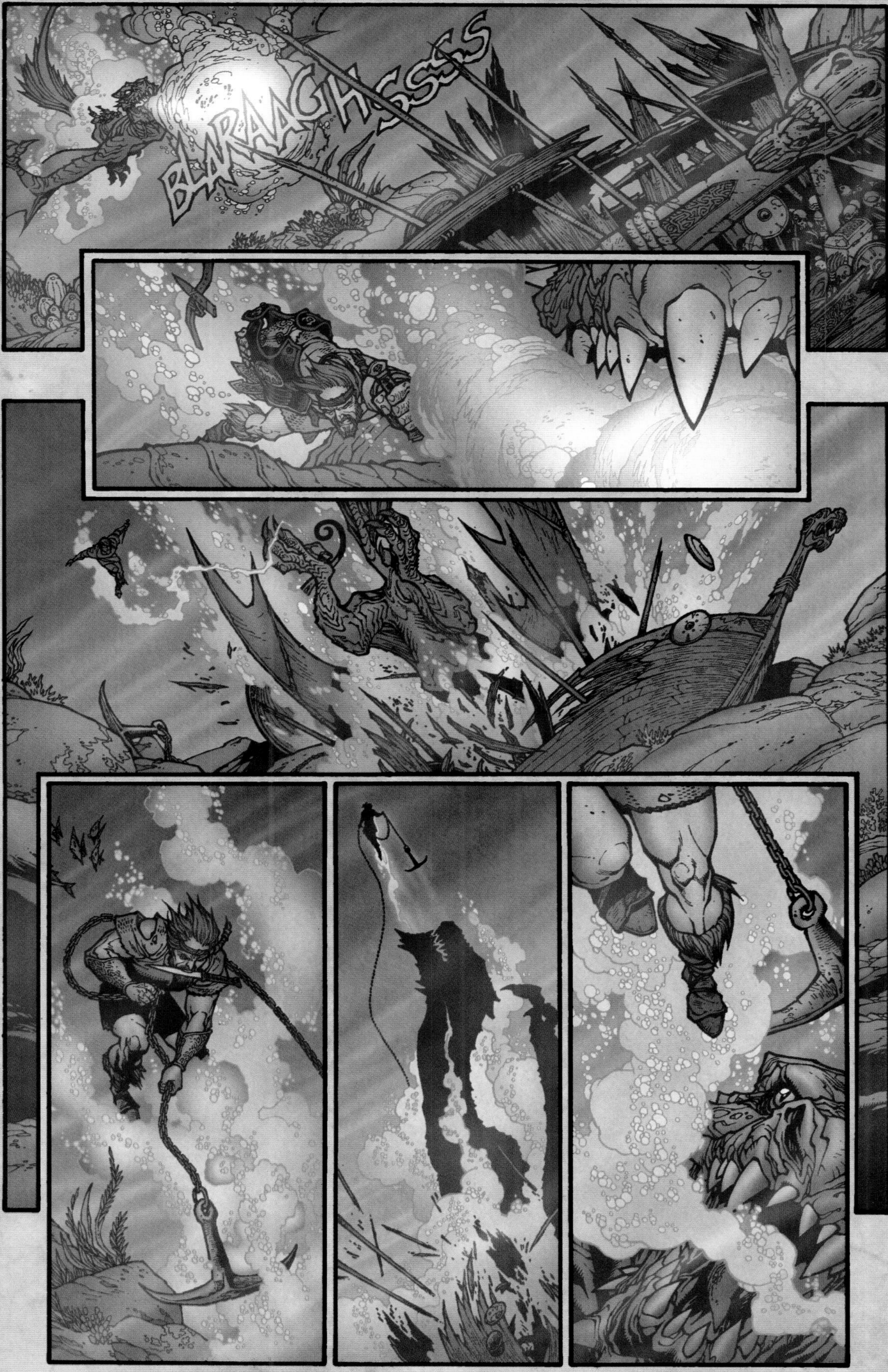
BLARAAGHSSSS

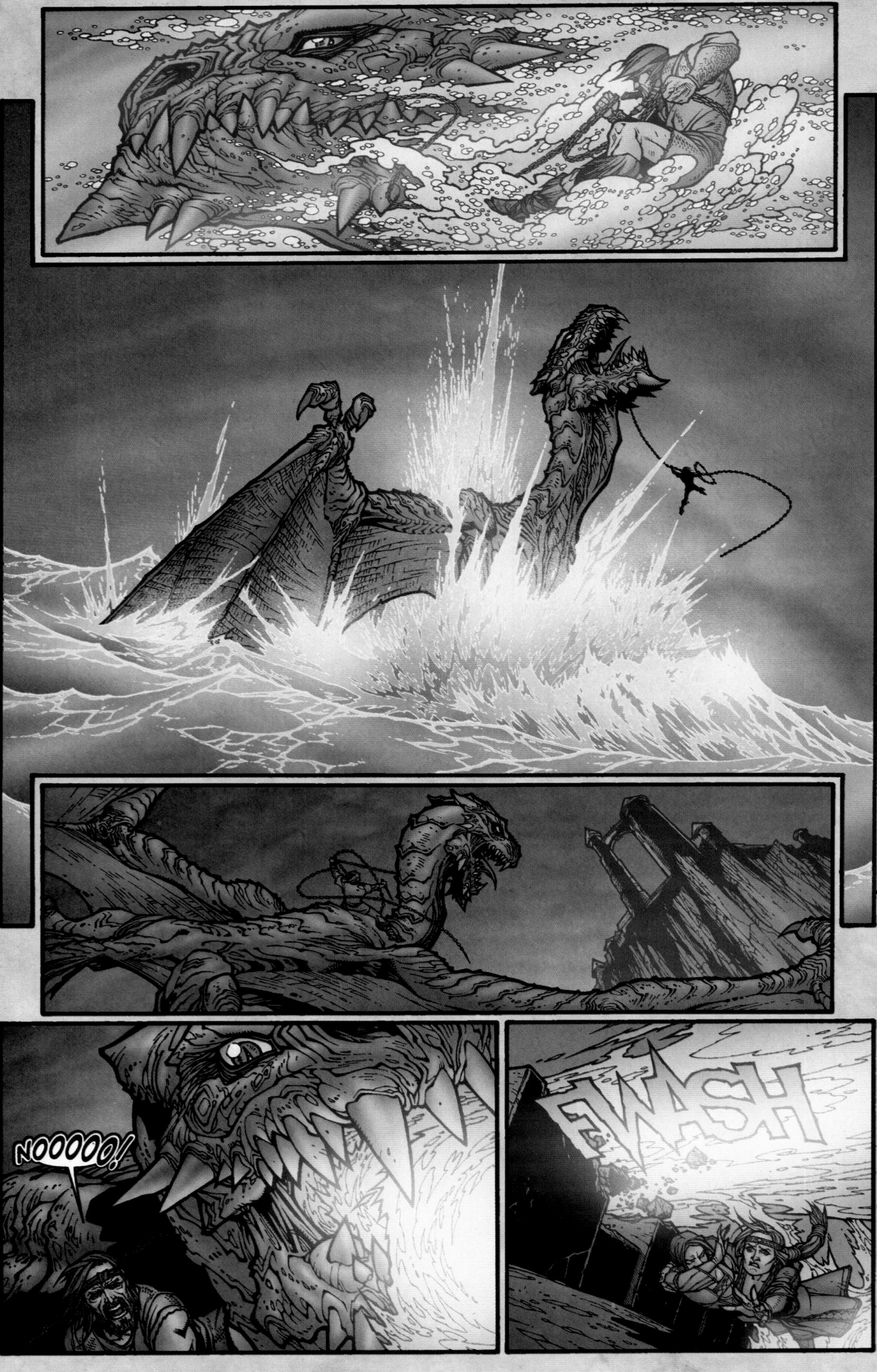
NOOOOO!
FWASH

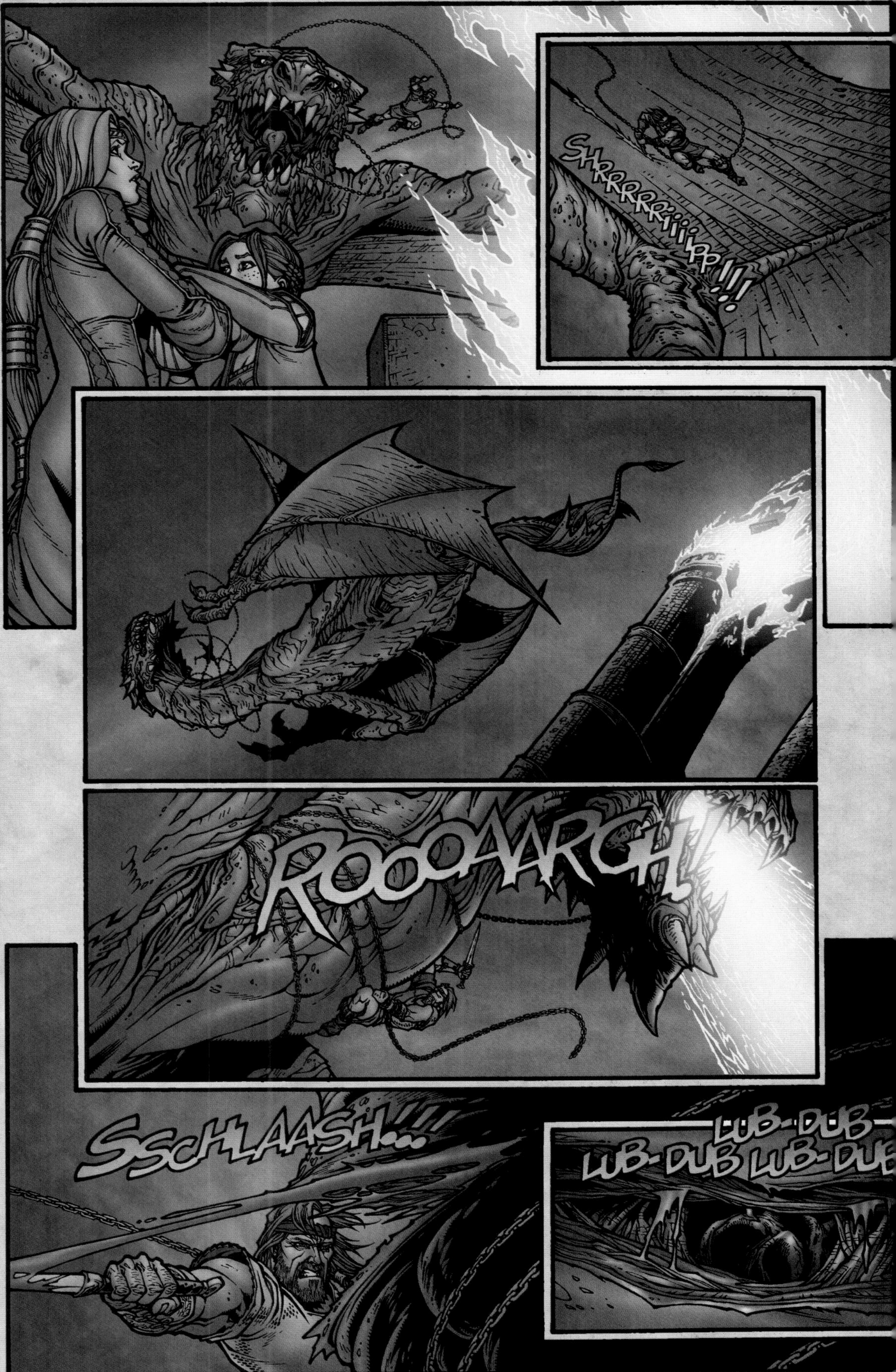
SHRRRRRiiiipp!!!
ROOOAARGH!
SSCHLAASH...!
LUB-DUB-
LUB-DUB LUB-DUB

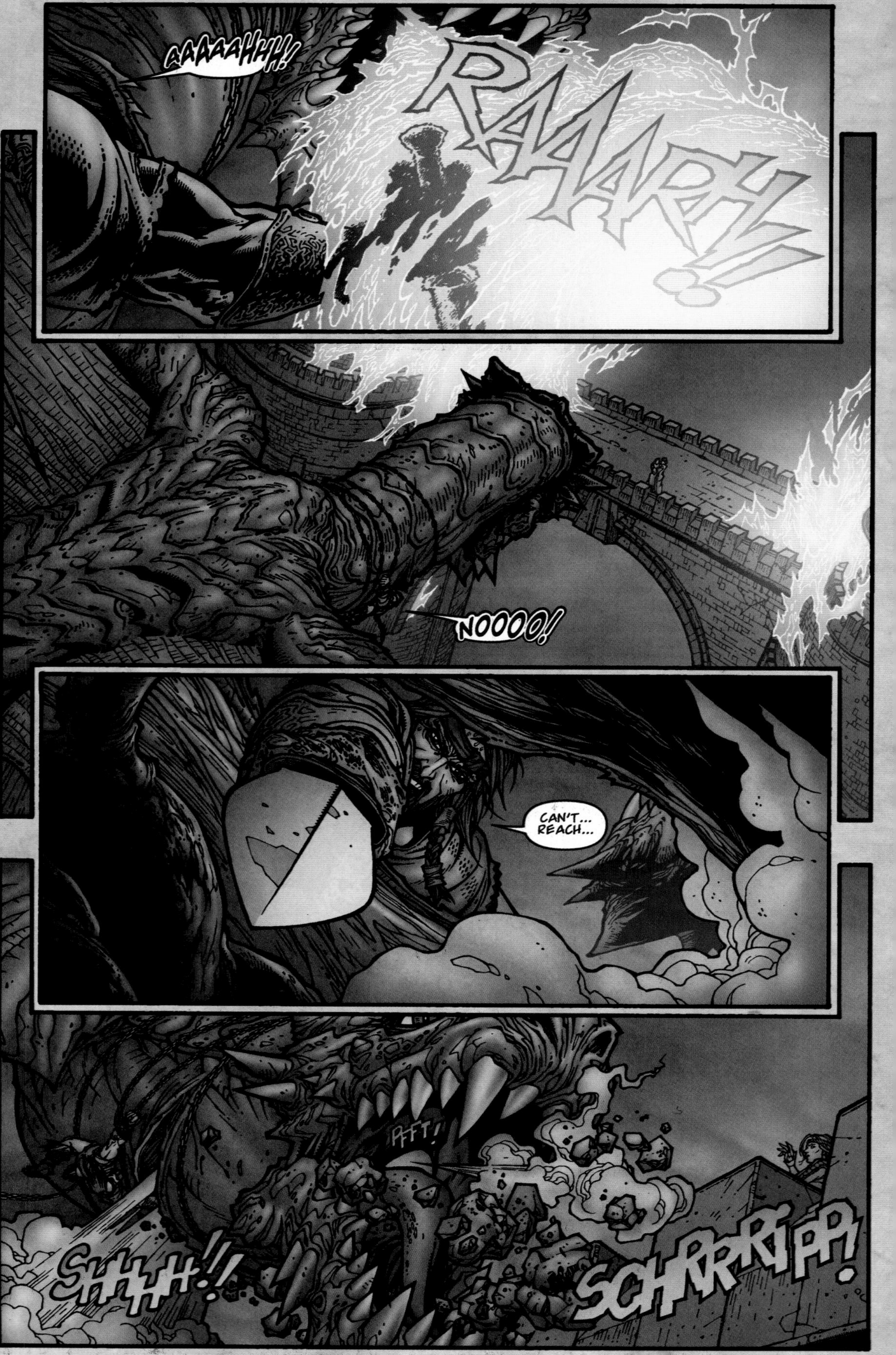
AAAAAHHH!
RAAARH!!
NOOOO!
CAN'T... REACH...
PFFT!
SHHH!!
SCHRRRIPP!

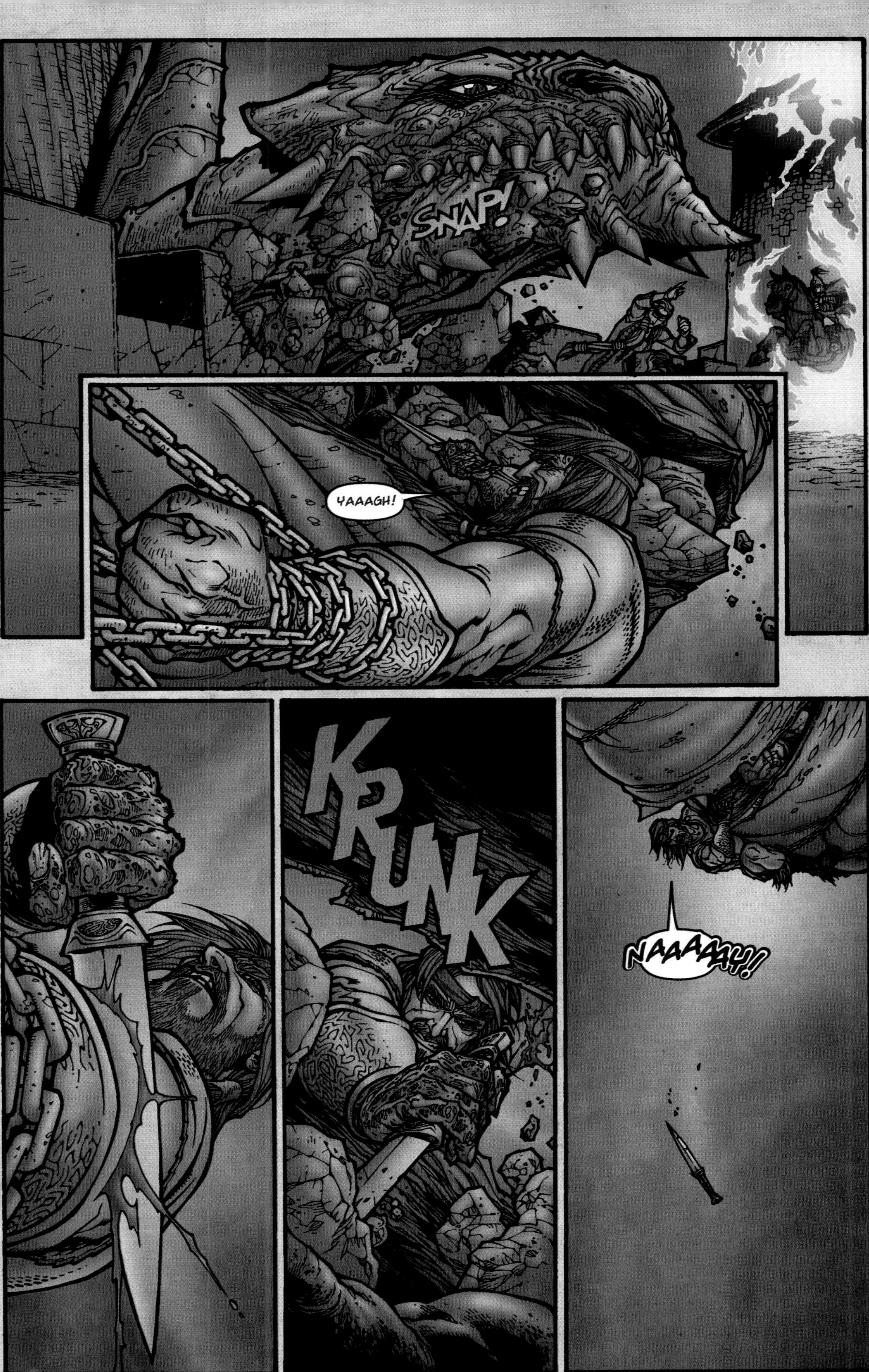
SNAP!
YAAAGH!
KRUNK
NAAAAAY!!

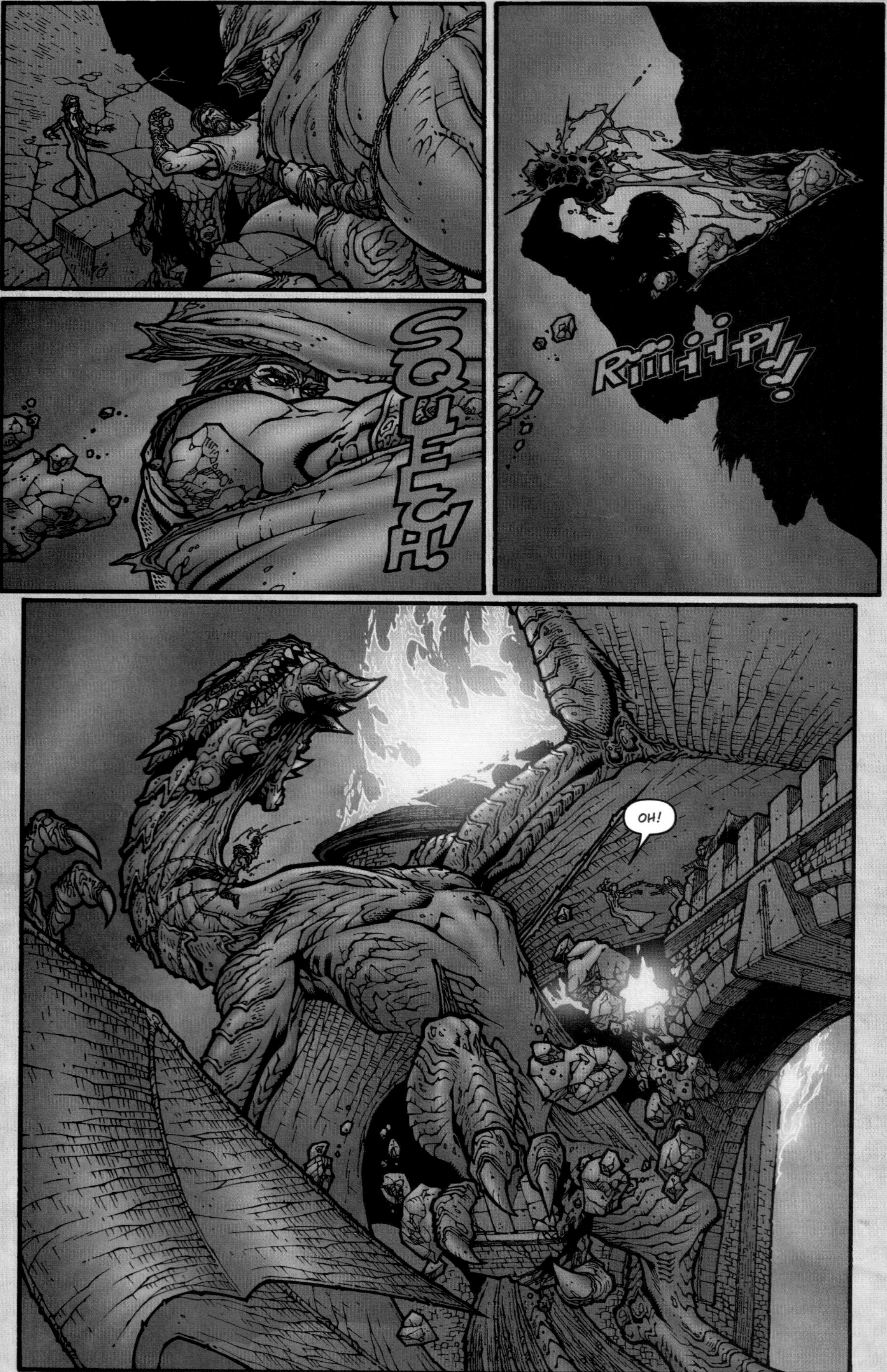
SQUELCH!
RIIIIIP!!
OH!

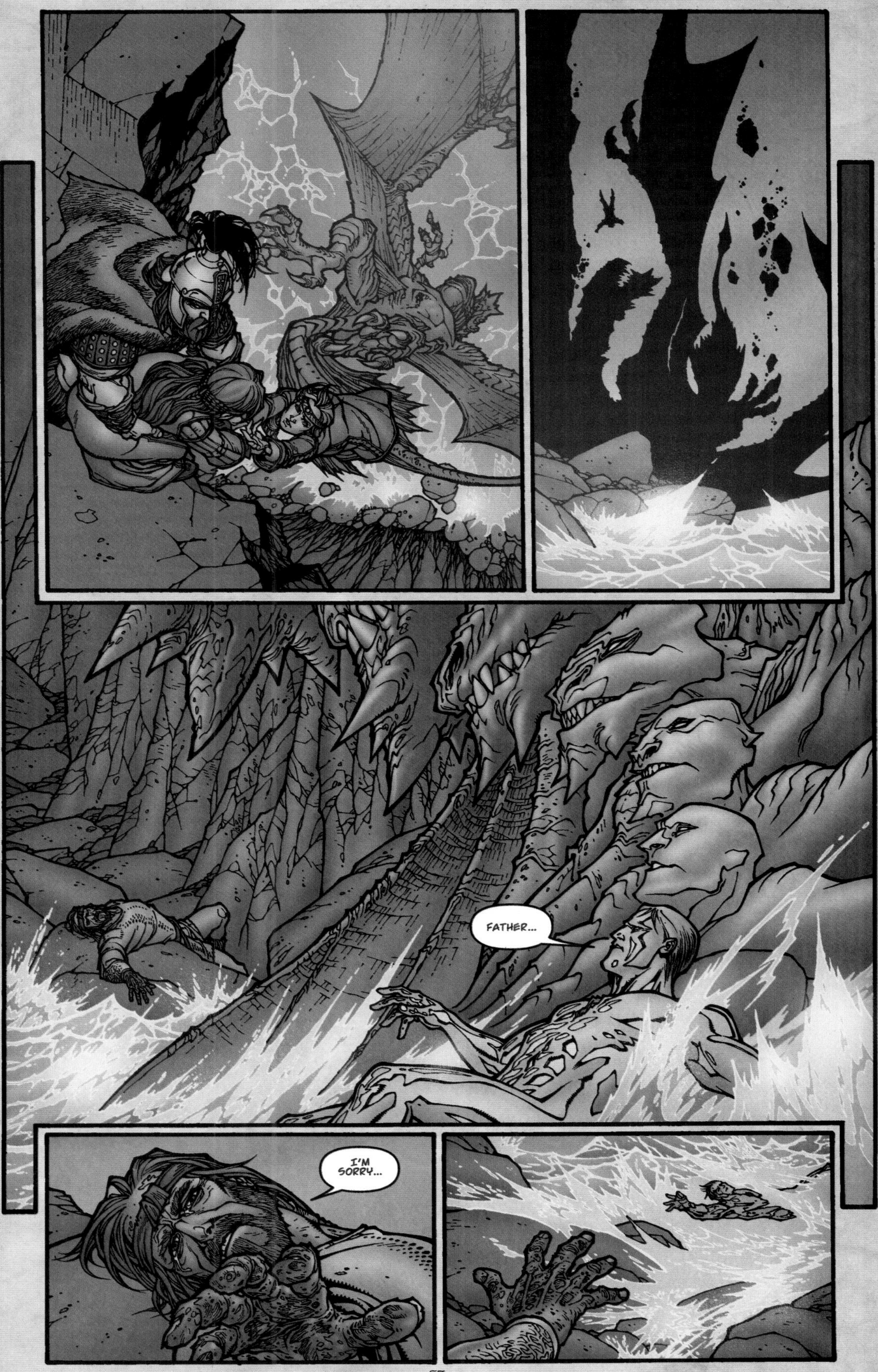
FATHER...
I'M SORRY...

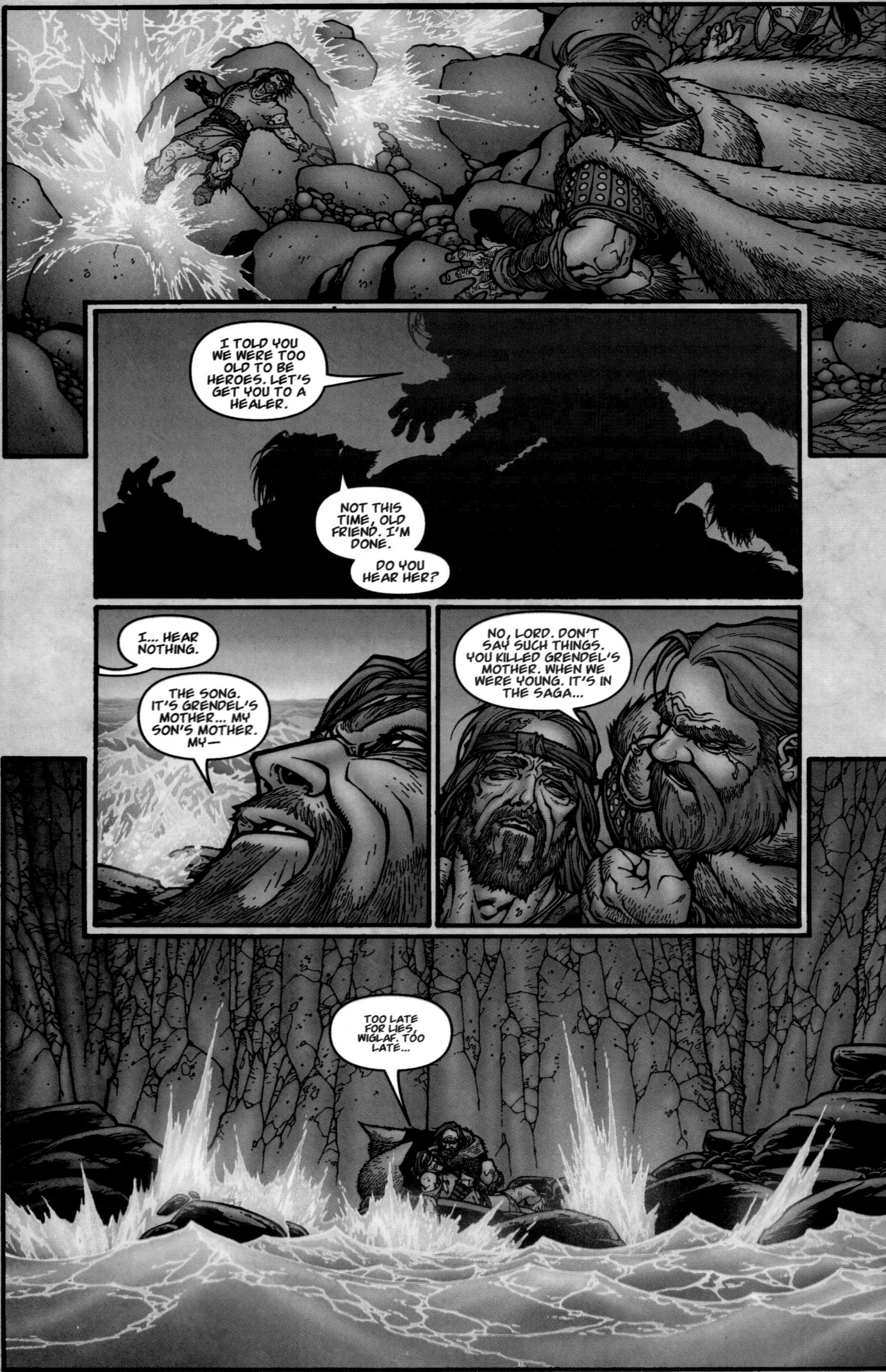
I TOLD YOU WE WERE TOO OLD TO BE HEROES. LET'S GET YOU TO A HEALER.
NOT THIS TIME, OLD FRIEND. I'M DONE.
DO YOU HEAR HER?
I... HEAR NOTHING.
THE SONG. IT'S GRENDEL'S MOTHER... MY SON'S MOTHER. MY—
NO, LORD. DON'T SAY SUCH THINGS. YOU KILLED GRENDEL'S MOTHER. WHEN WE WERE YOUNG. IT'S IN THE SAGA...
TOO LATE FOR LIES, WIGLAF. TOO LATE...

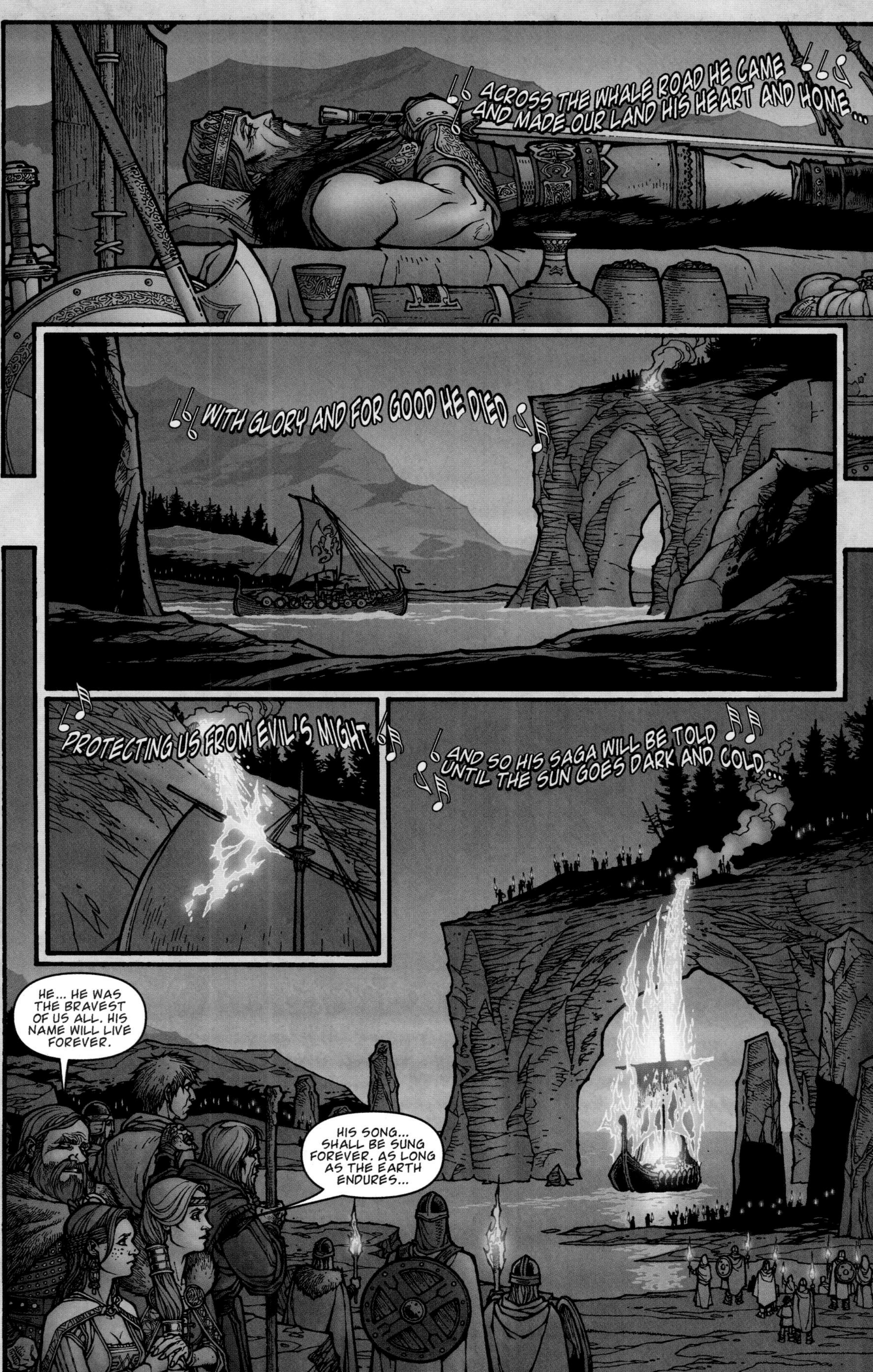
ACROSS THE WHALE ROAD HE CAME AND MADE OUR LAND HIS HEART AND HOME...
WITH GLORY AND FOR GOOD HE DIED
PROTECTING US FROM EVIL'S MIGHT
AND SO HIS SAGA WILL BE TOLD UNTIL THE SUN GOES DARK AND COLD...
HE... HE WAS THE BRAVEST OF US ALL. HIS NAME WILL LIVE FOREVER.
HIS SONG... SHALL BE SUNG FOREVER. AS LONG AS THE EARTH ENDURES...

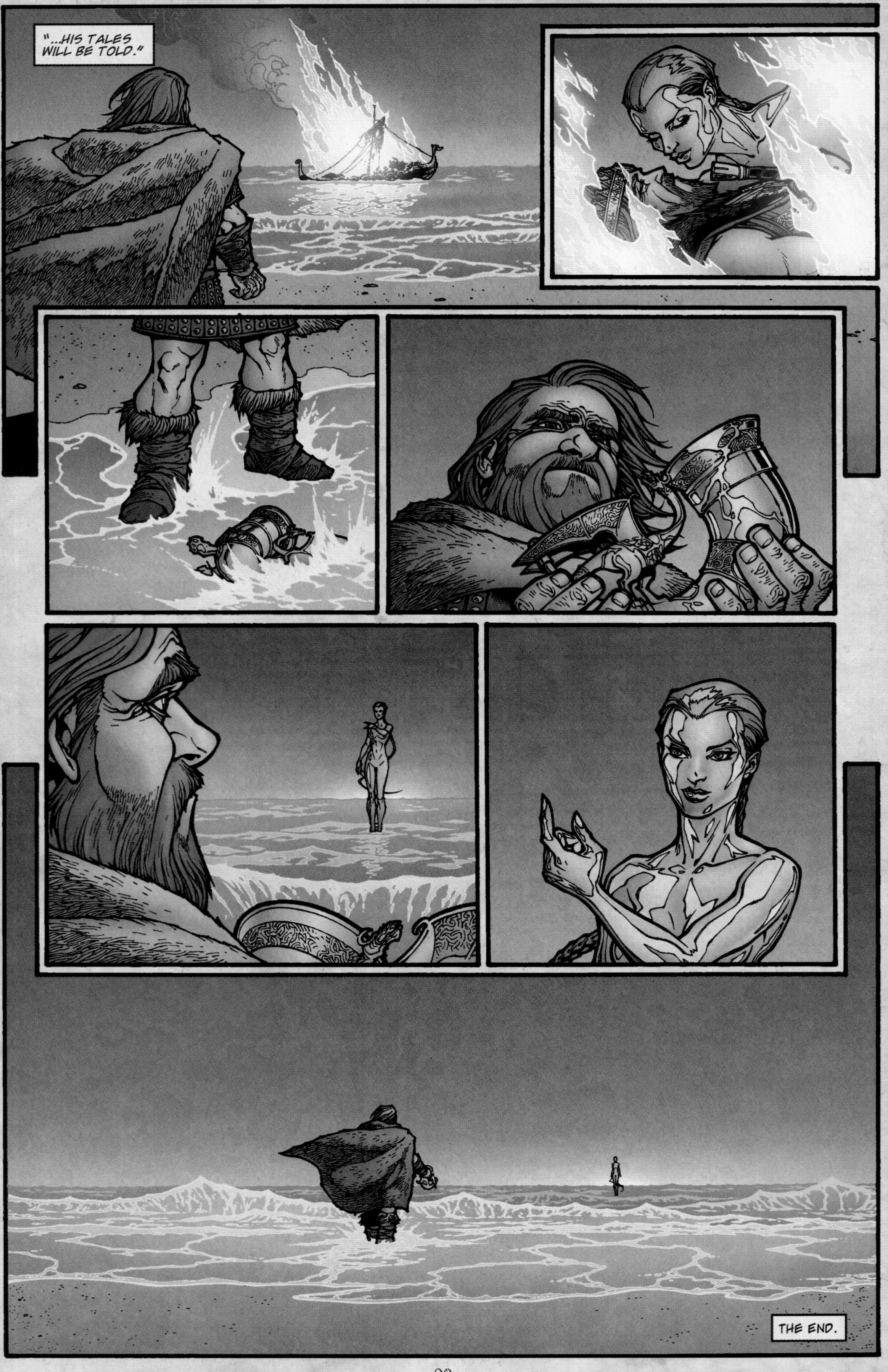
"...HIS TALES
WILL BE TOLD."
THE END.

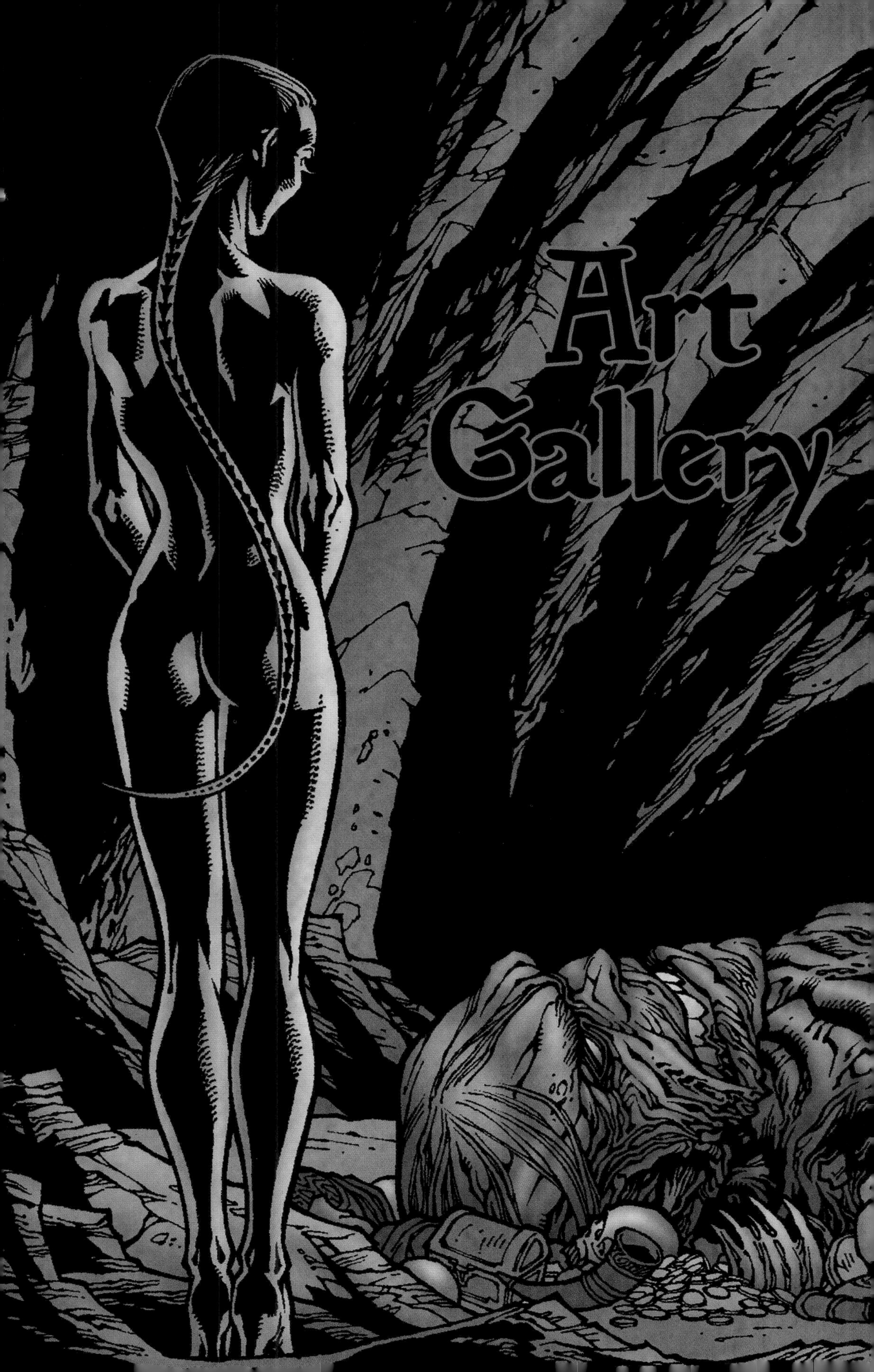
Art Gallery

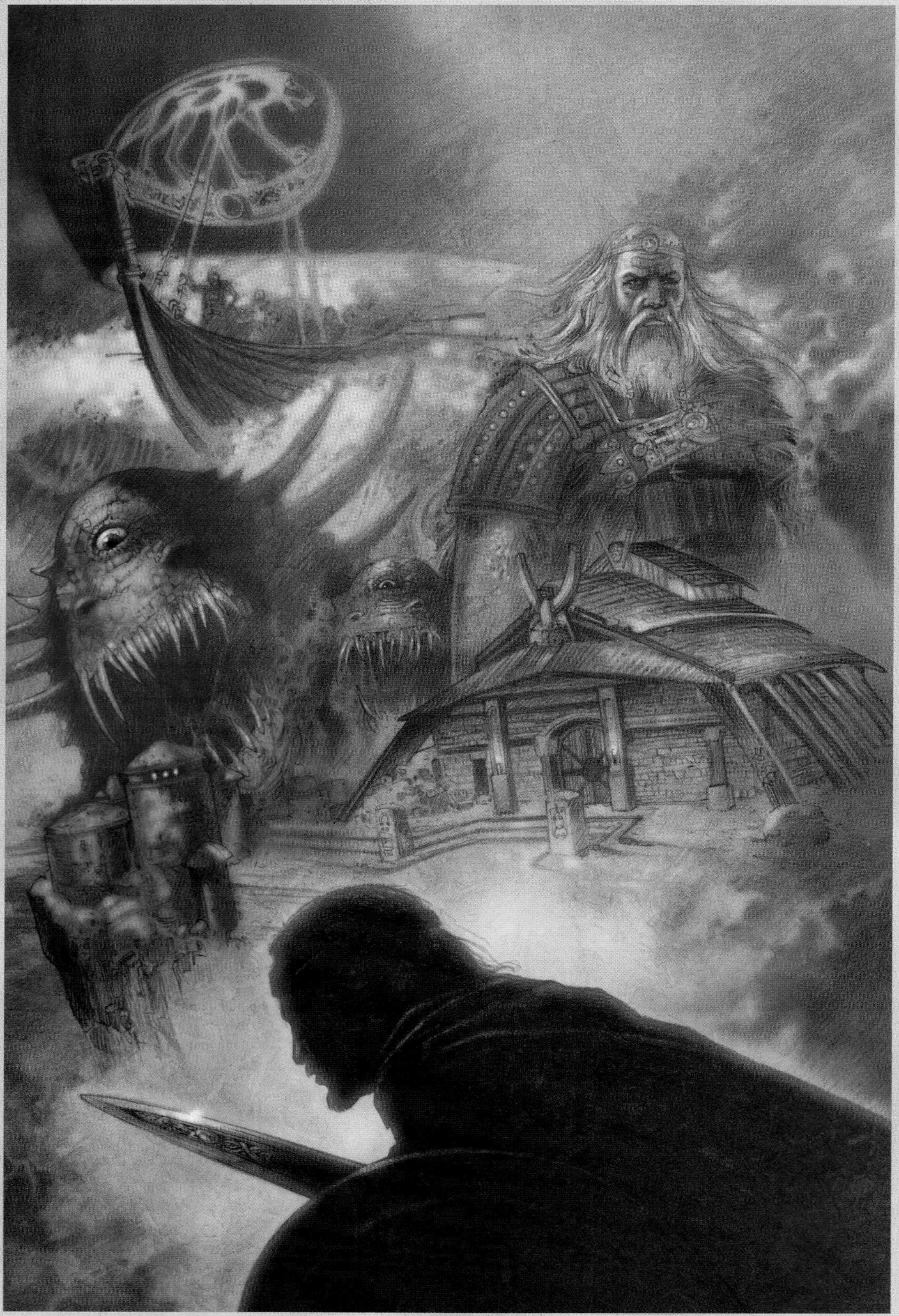

this page: by Mark A. Nelson
facing page: by Mark A. Nelson

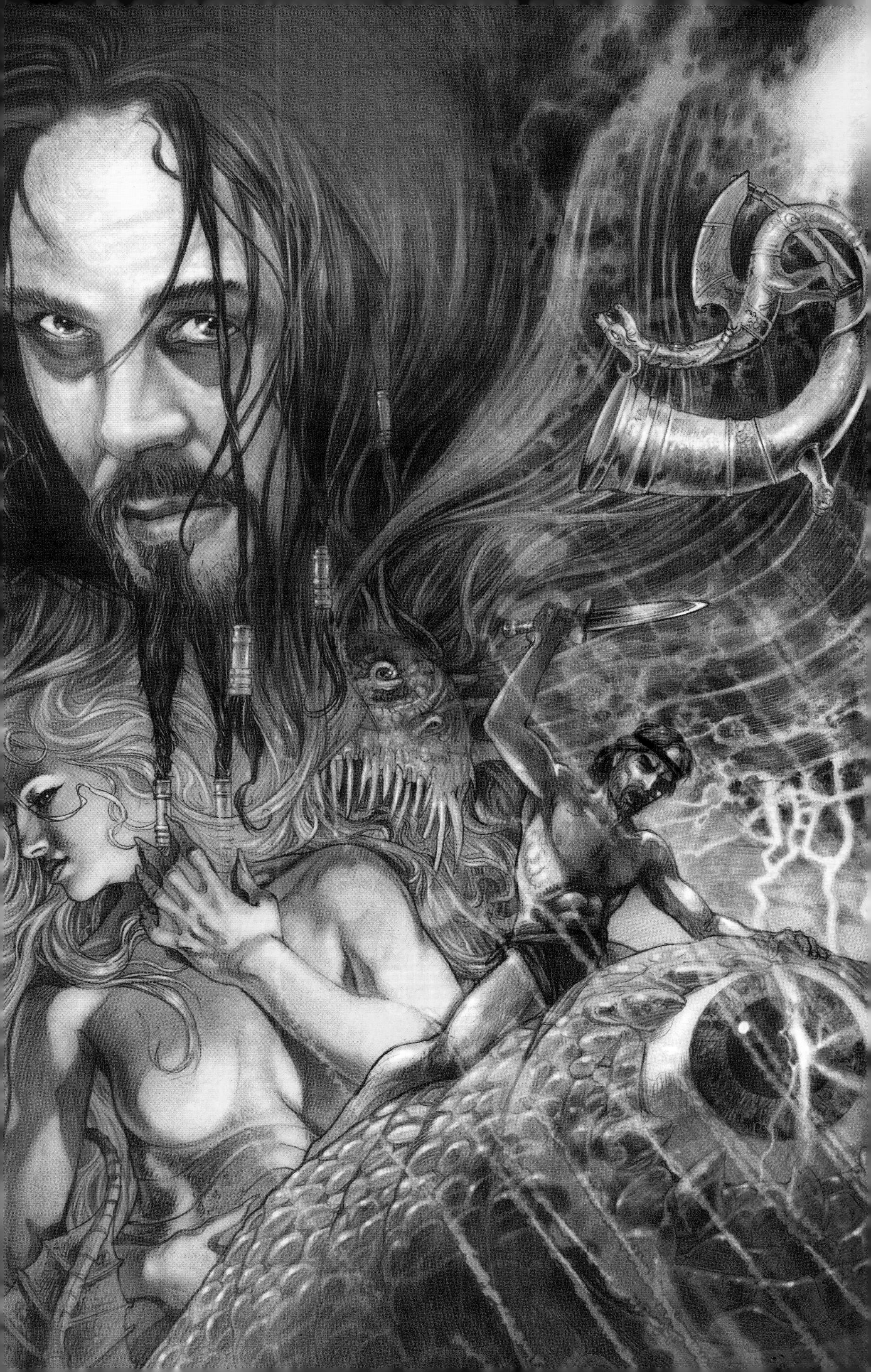

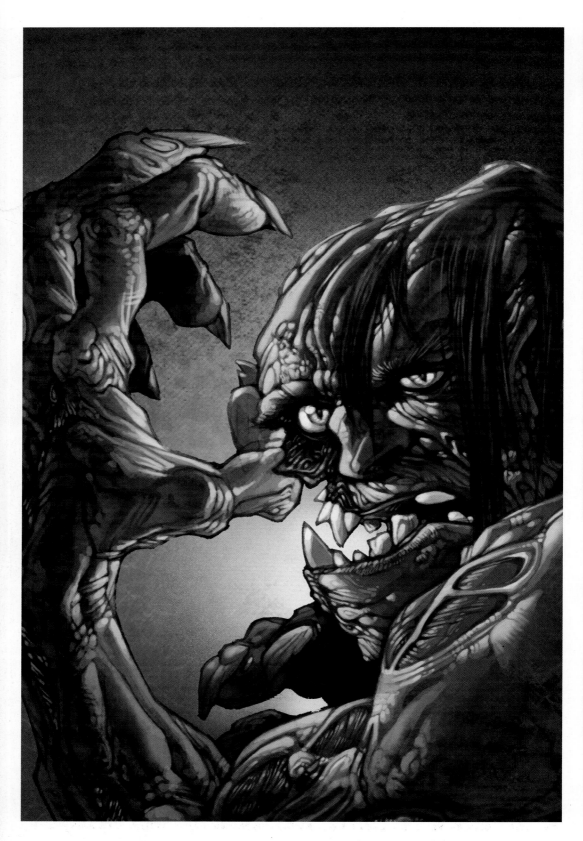

this page: by Gabriel Rodriguez
facing page: by Mark A. Nelson

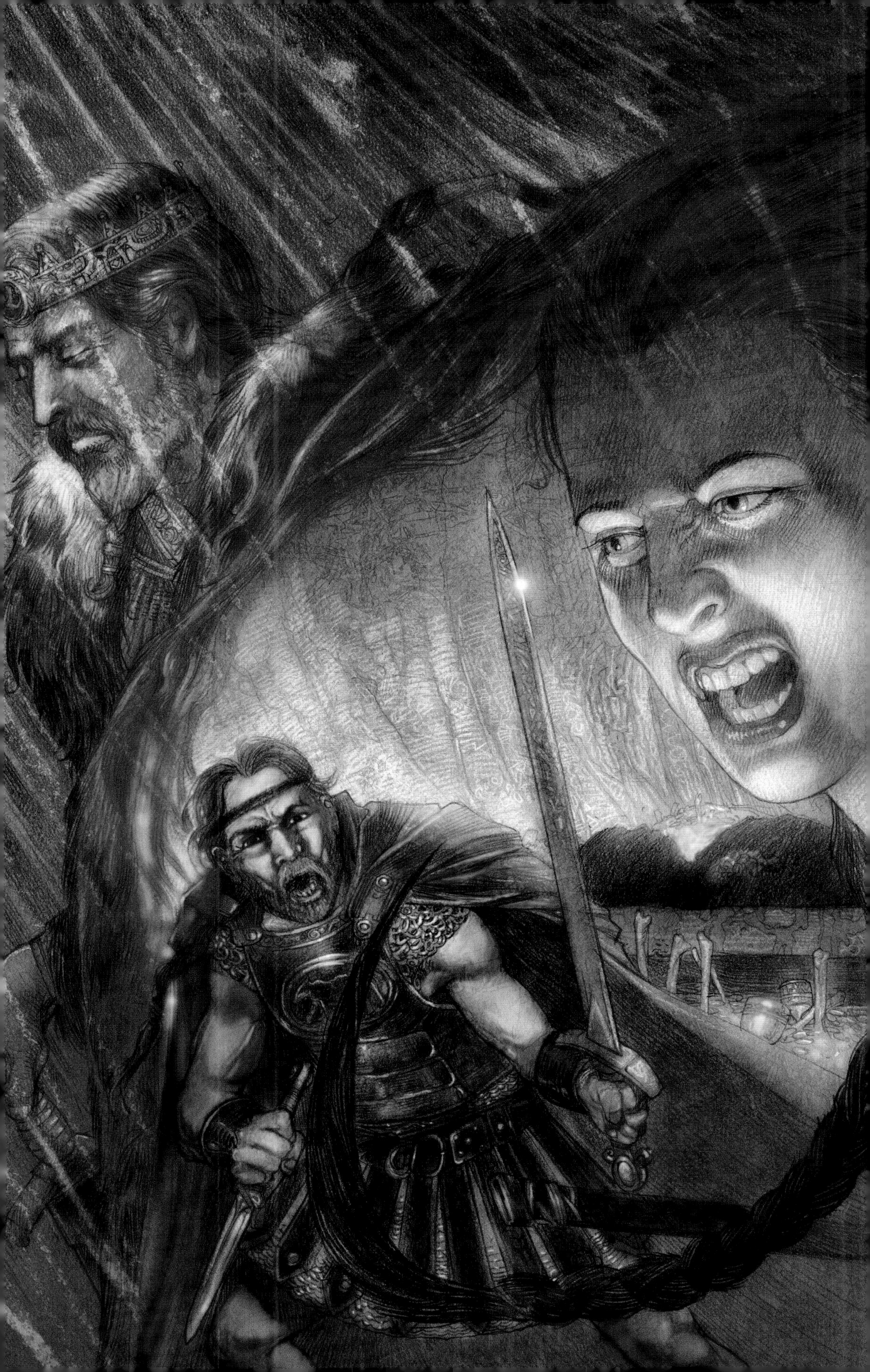

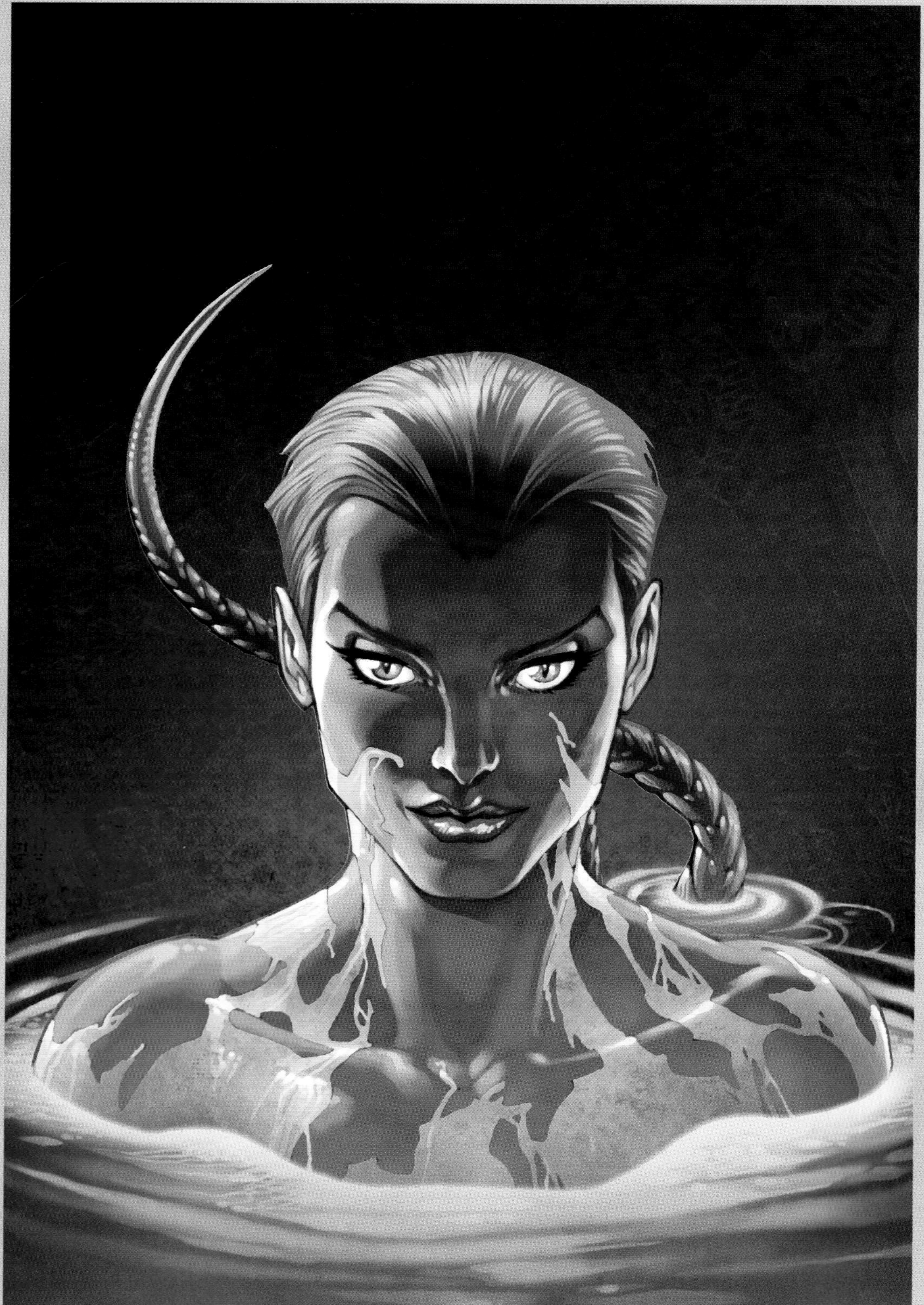

this page: by Gabriel Rodriguez
facing page: by Mark A. Nelson

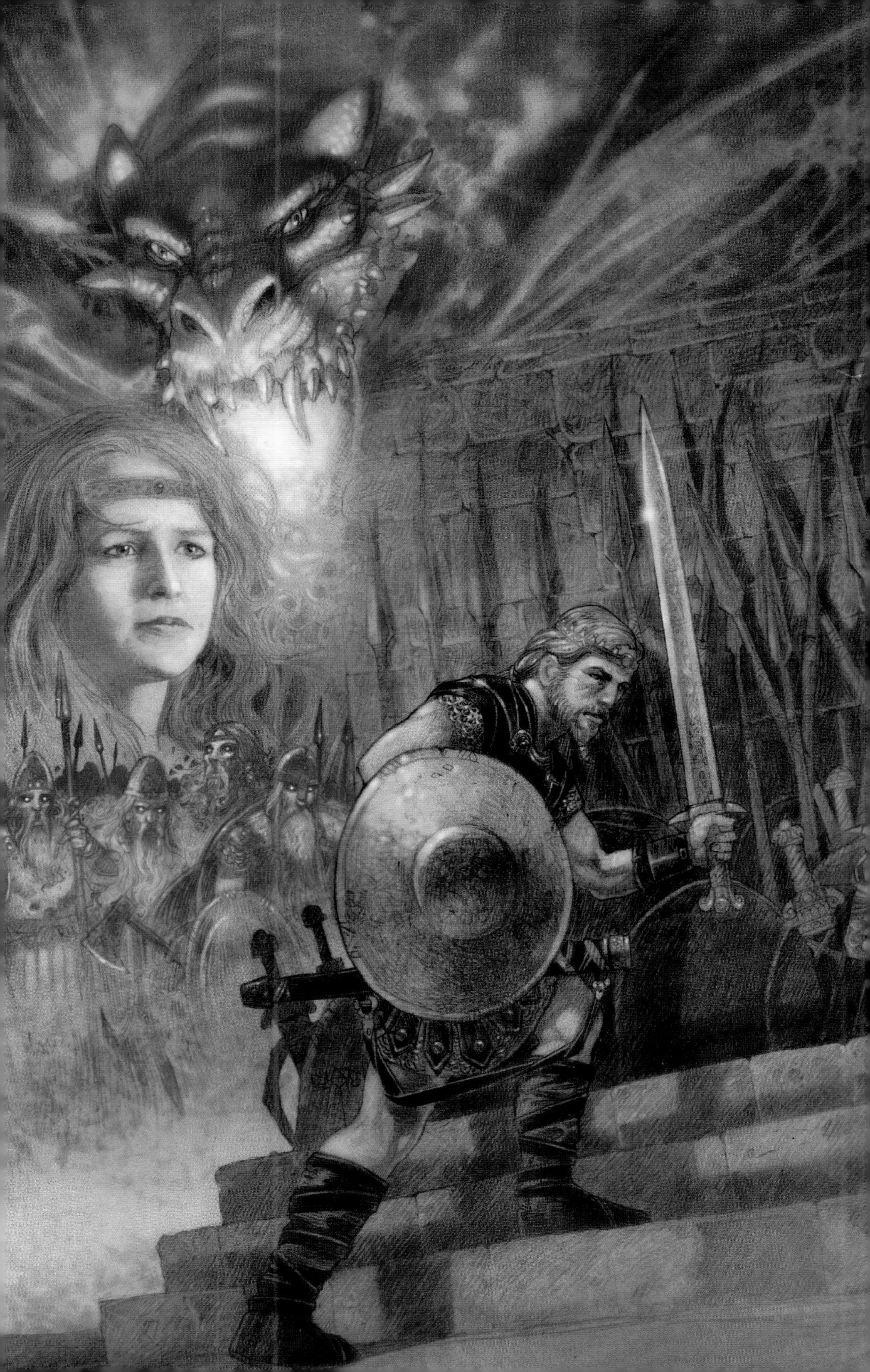

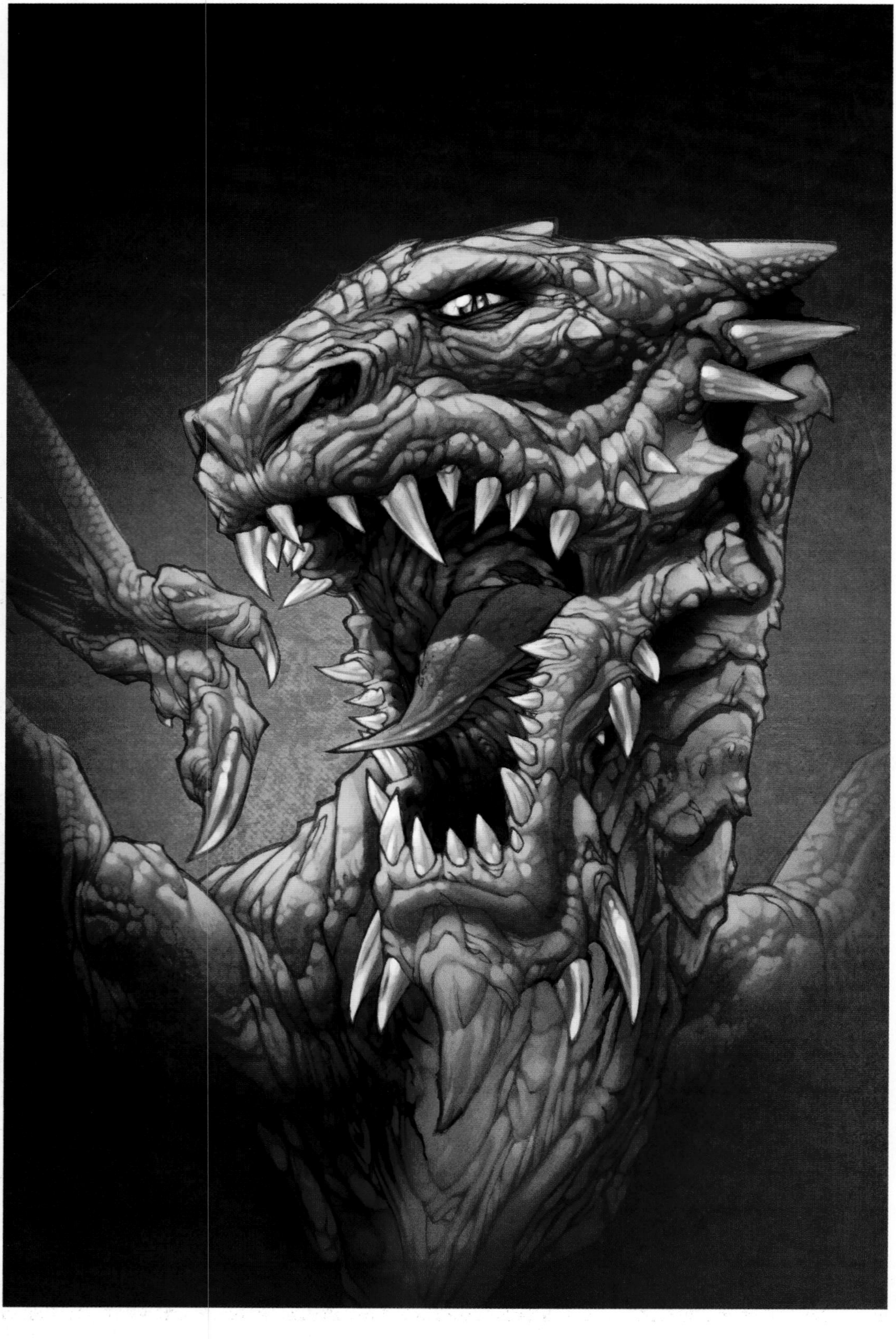

by Gabriel Rodriguez

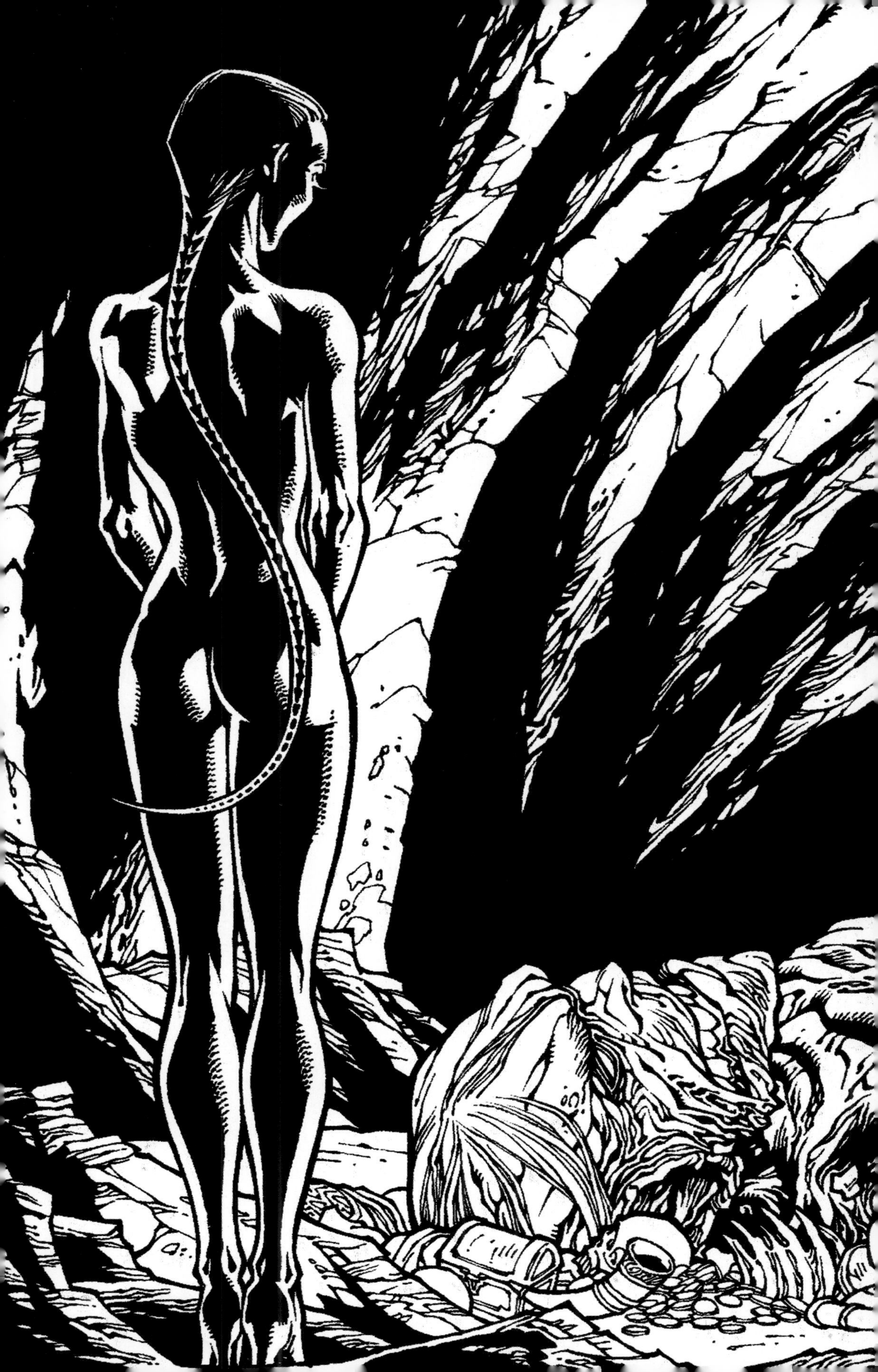

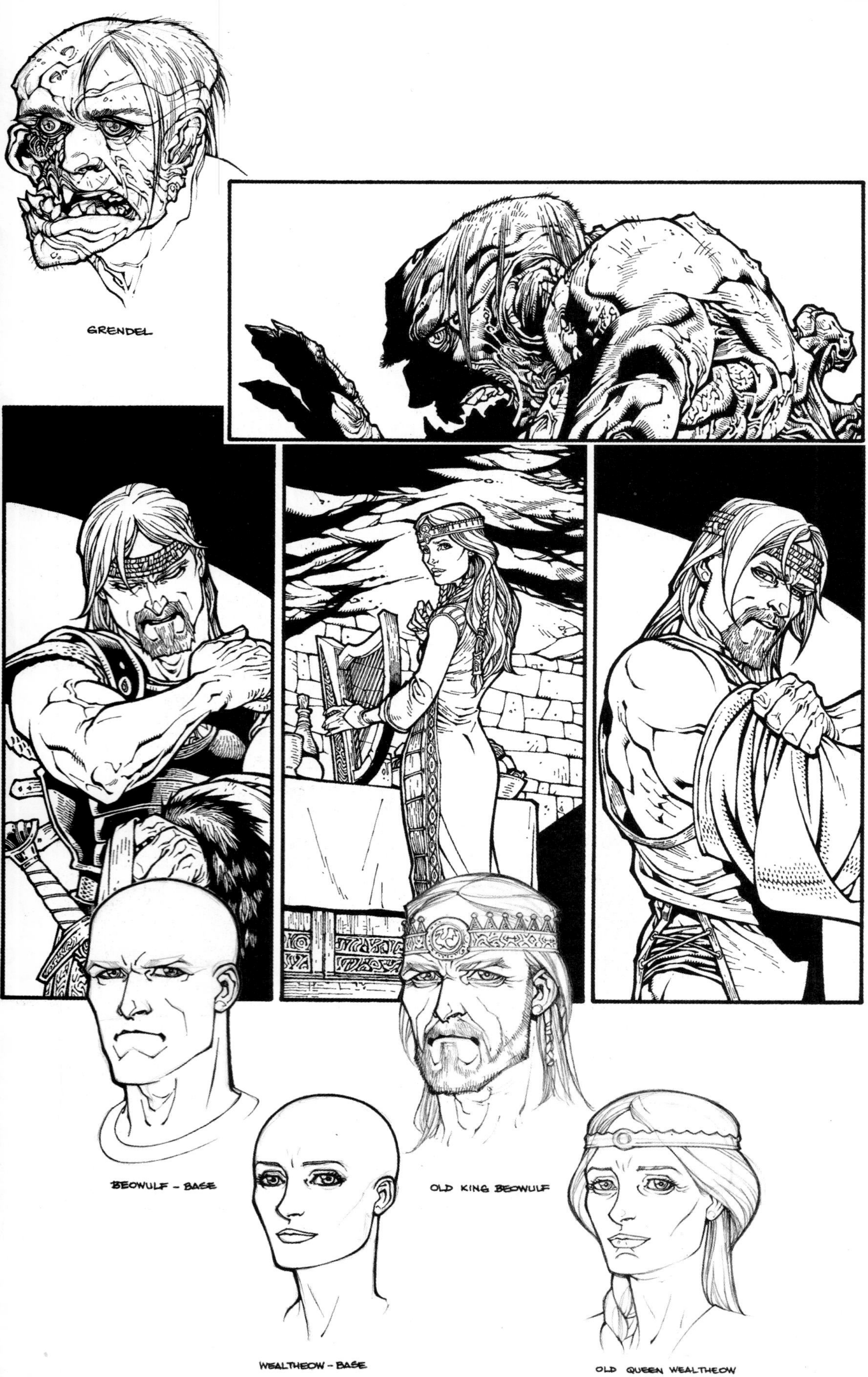
GRENDEL
BEOWULF - BASE
OLD KING BEOWULF
WEALTHEOW - BASE
OLD QUEEN WEALTHEOW

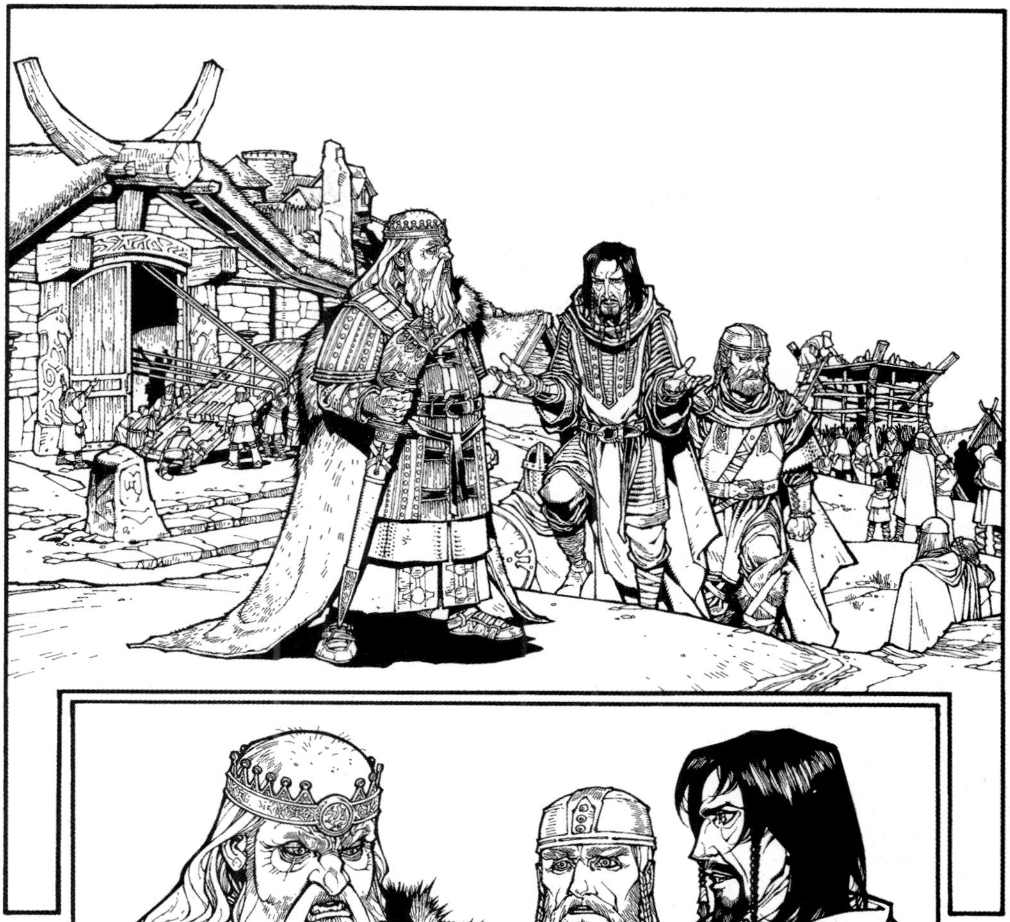

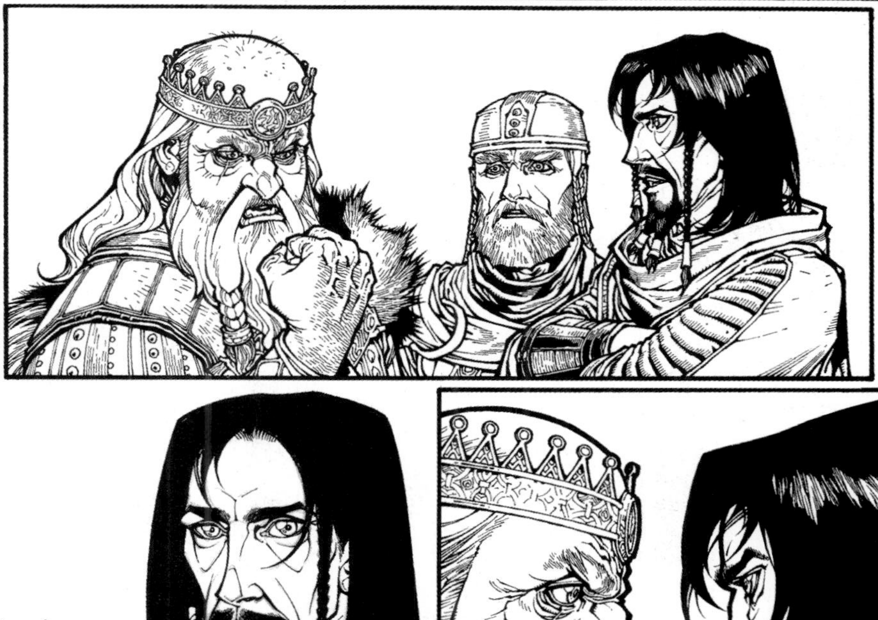

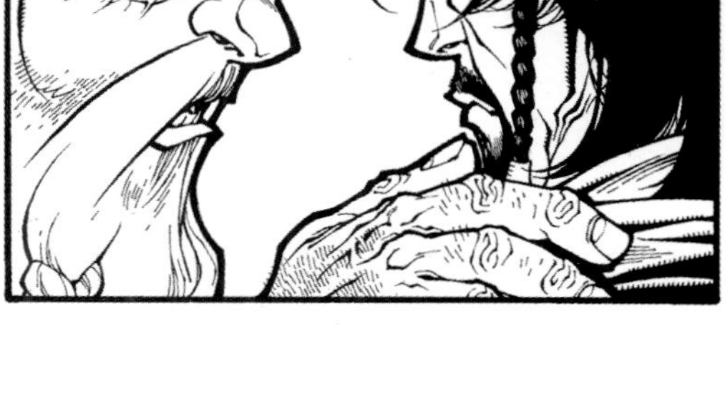

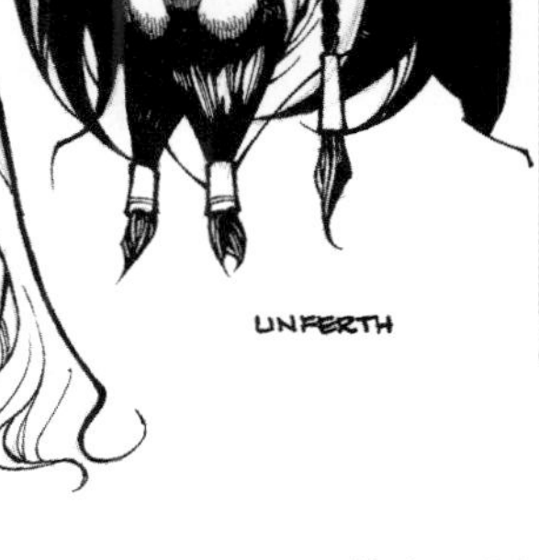
UNFERTH

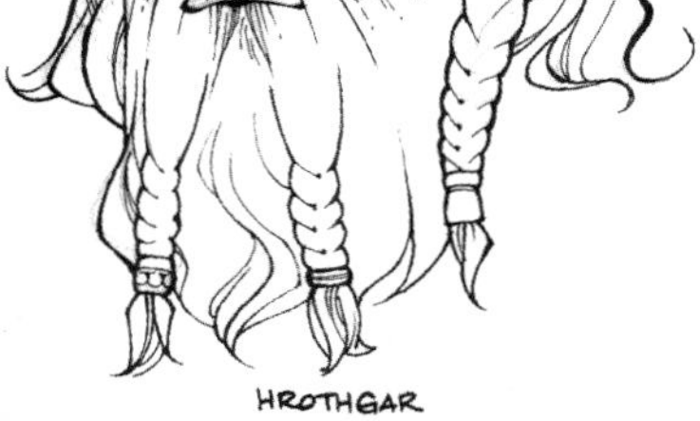
HROTHGAR

Various Ink Illustrations and Concept Sketches by Gabriel Rodriguez

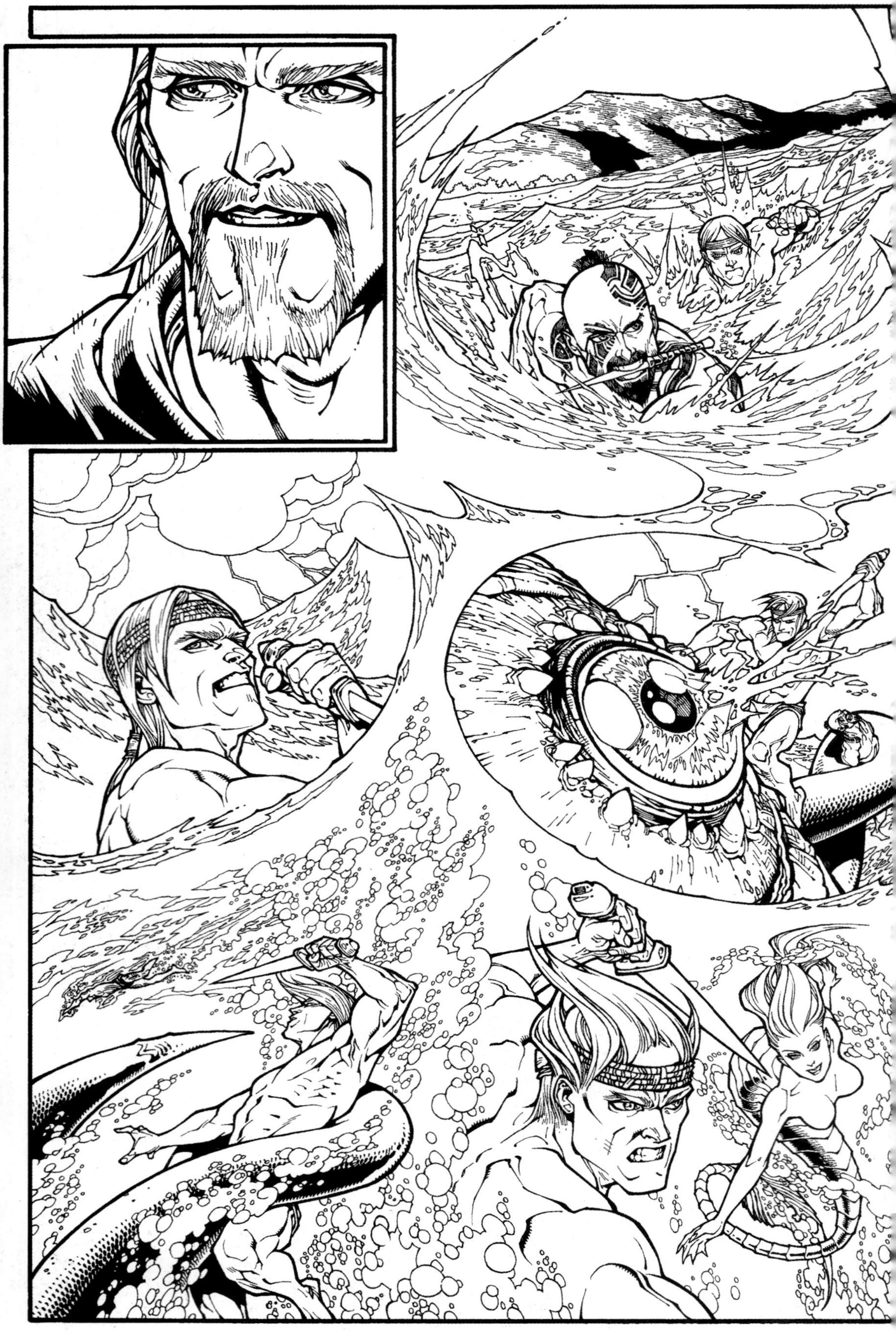

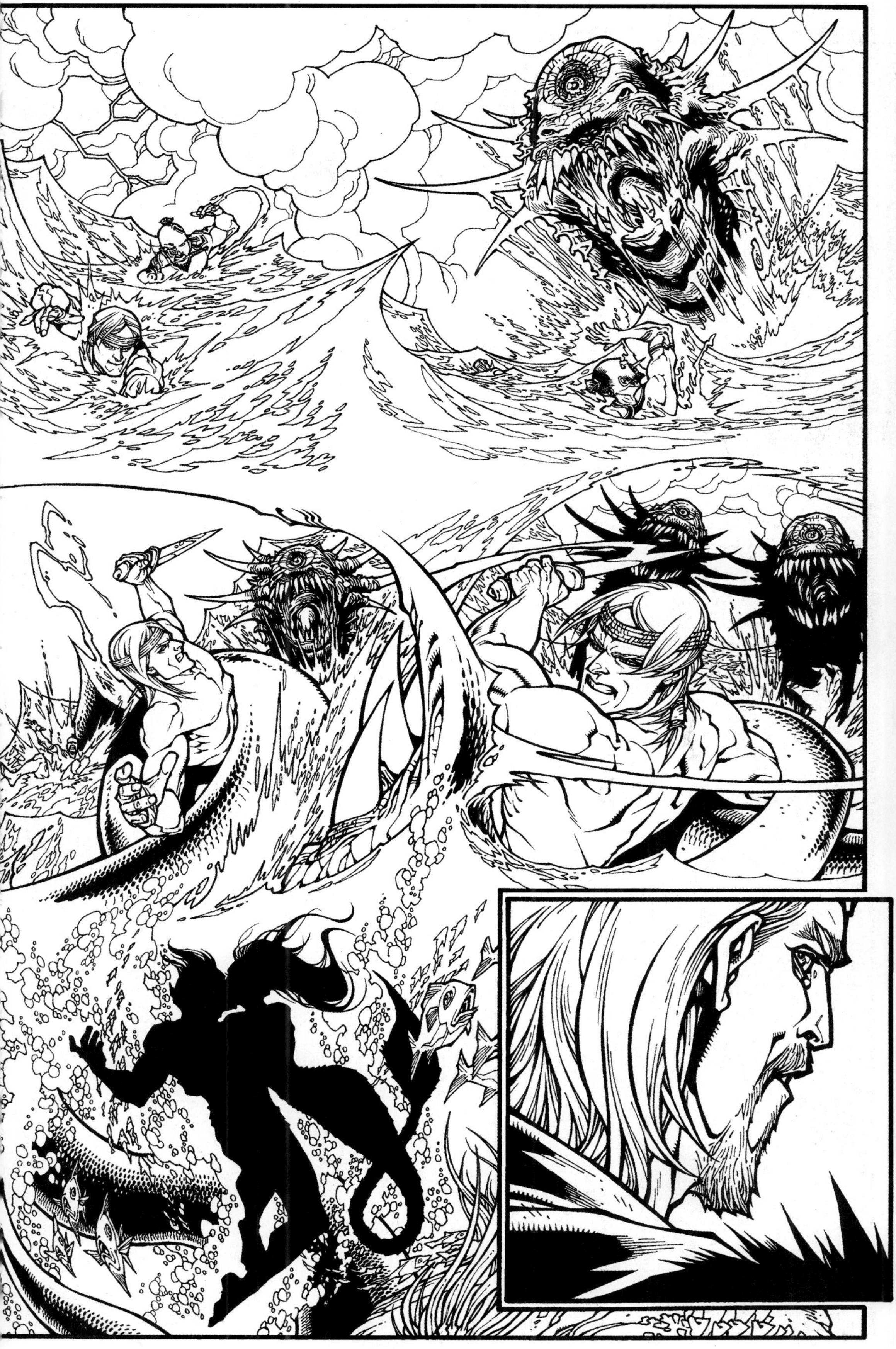

Ink Illustration of pages 26-27 by Gabriel Rodriguez

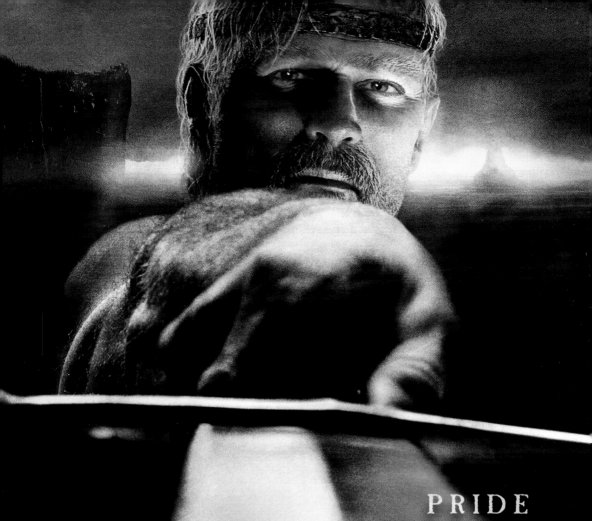

PRIDE
IS THE
CURSE

RAY
WINSTONE
ANTHONY
HOPKINS
JOHN
MALKOVICH
ROBIN
WRIGHT PENN
AND ANGELINA
JOLIE

A ROBERT ZEMECKIS FILM

BEOWULF

PARAMOUNT PICTURES PRESENTS IN ASSOCIATION WITH SHANGRI-LA ENTERTAINMENT AN IMAGEMOVERS PRODUCTION A ROBERT ZEMECKIS FILM 'BEOWULF'
RAY WINSTONE ANTHONY HOPKINS JOHN MALKOVICH ROBIN WRIGHT PENN BRENDAN GLEESON CRISPIN GLOVER ALISON LOHMAN AND ANGELINA JOLIE
CASTING BY RONNA KRESS C.S.A. AND NINA GOLD C.D.G. COSTUMES DESIGNED BY GABRIELLA PESCUCCI MUSIC BY ALAN SILVESTRI ORIGINAL SONGS BY GLEN BALLARD AND ALAN SILVESTRI IMAGERY AND ANIMATION BY SONY PICTURES IMAGEWORKS, INC.
SENIOR VISUAL EFFECTS SUPERVISOR JEROME CHEN CO-PRODUCER STEVEN BOYD FILM EDITOR JEREMIAH O'DRISCOLL PRODUCTION DESIGNER DOUG CHIANG DIRECTOR OF PHOTOGRAPHY ROBERT PRESLEY EXECUTIVE PRODUCERS MARTIN SHAFER ROGER AVARY NEIL GAIMAN
SCREENPLAY BY NEIL GAIMAN & ROGER AVARY PRODUCED BY STEVE STARKEY ROBERT ZEMECKIS JACK RAPKE DIRECTED BY ROBERT ZEMECKIS "THE ART OF BEOWULF" AVAILABLE FROM CHRONICLE BOOKS READ THE NOVEL FROM HARPERCOLLINS

SHANGRI-LA
ENTERTAINMENT
IMAGEMOVERS
IN THEATRES EVERYWHERE AND
IMAX 2D AND DIGITAL 3D
Paramount

IN THEATRES THIS NOVEMBER   BeowulfMovie.com